South Africa and the Bomb

Responsibility and Deterrence

Ronald W. Walters
Howard University

Lexington Books
D.C. Heath and Company/Lexington, Massachusetts/Toronto

Library of Congress Cataloging-in-Publication Data

Walters, Ronald W.
   South Africa and the bomb.

   Bibliography: p.
   Includes index.
   1. Nuclear weapons—South Africa.   2. South
Africa—Military policy.   I. Title.
U264.W35   1987   355.8'25119'0968   86-45738
ISBN 0-669-14197-6 (alk. paper)

Published simultaneously in Canada
Printed in the United States of America
Casebound International Standard Book Number: 0-669-14197-6
Library of Congress Catalog Card Number: 86-45738

The paper used in this publication meets the minimum requirements
of American National Standard for Information Sciences—Permanence
of Paper for Printed Library Materials, ANSI Z39.48-1984.
♾ ™

87   88   89   90   8   7   6   5   4   3   2   1

For the people of Southern Africa

Contents

Tables

Preface and Acknowledgments

I n the course of several years of research on the political and security problems of Southern Africa, I became struck by the almost universal concentration of activists and scholars alike on the guerilla war in the region, including the low-level war waged by the African National Congress of South Africa against the white minority regime, while the Afrikaners appeared to be preparing what has come to be known as "total war." This concern launched a series of articles and at least one monograph on South African nuclear capability.[1] The point of this concern was that whereas in the early 1960s, South Africa was declared a threat to the peace and security of the international system by virtue of global racial tensions, its present possession of nuclear weapons potential has made it a threat to the very survival of peoples and states in the region of Southern Africa and, perhaps, far beyond.

The growing response to the dangers posed by South African nuclear capability began to alert analysts and decision makers to the necessity of including the nation in the priority listing of states where nonproliferation was a major concern, especially after the promulgation of the Nuclear Nonproliferation Act of 1978 by President Carter. Indeed, the literature on nonproliferation routinely began to suggest that South Africa was a problem state (perhaps even an outcast), inferring, therefore, that South Africa might benefit from the various aspects in the nuclear proliferation regime, especially should it be interested in improving its status with allies such as the United States. South Africa, however, has not taken the bait of nonproliferation safeguards where its most troublesome nuclear facilities are concerned, and there are strong indications of its involvement in nuclear testing.

Now, following a policy of "ambiguous proliferation," South Africa straddles the threshold of nuclear capability which divides an ability to make weapons from the naive utilization of nuclear power for civilian electricity. It could very quickly cross this threshold if its raging internal security crisis were to become an external crisis at any time in the near future. In fact, it is the magnitude of the challenge to the regime (a challenge that is sure to become more formidable) that should bring about serious concern, not only with nonproliferation, but with how South Africa might be prevented from employing nuclear weapons in the Southern African theater, some other part of Africa, or the world. Few, thus far, have begun to attempt this sort of agonizing appraisal, perhaps, because the policy prescriptions involved might prove so radically uncomfortable to those who bear prime responsibility for engaging in deterrence by virtue of either their past assistance to the South African nuclear program or their international standing among world powers. This book, written from the perspective of one opposed to the maintenance of apartheid, is dedicated to just such a discussion. I make no case that I have succeeded in treating all the issues adequately. To have raised some appropriate questions for further consideration is the greatest contribution I might claim.

My original research which resulted in a monograph was performed under the auspices of the Social Science Research Center of the Institute for Urban Affairs and Research at Howard University with funding by a grant from the Ford Foundation from 1975 to 1977. I would like to thank Dr. Lawrence Gary, director of the Institute (who gave me the flexibility to perform such research) and Daisy Hannah and Stephanie Honeywood for their assistance. Because of the limited distribution of the original monograph, I would also like to thank for their encouragement: Dr. John Spence of the University of Manchester (England); officials of the United Nations Center against Apartheid such as Ambassador Leslie Harriman and the Center's former director, Mr. Reddy; and those involved in similar work such as Abdul Minty (chairman of the World Campaign on Military and Nuclear Collaboration with South Africa) and Dr. Frank Barnaby of the Stockholm International Peace Research Institute, from whose writings I learned a great deal about the technical aspects of the subject.

I have also appreciated the continued assistance of the staff of the Subcommittee on Africa of the U.S. House of Representatives, dating from the vigorous hearings and investigations of this region conducted by Congressman Charles Diggs, Jr. Chapters 2 and 3 contain material obtained under the Freedom of Information Act respectively by the Lawyers Committee for Civil Rights under Law, Southern Africa Project, and the Washington Office on Africa. I would like to thank Millard Arnold and Dr. Jean Sindab for access to these materials. I would also like to thank my editors at Lexington Books, Susan Cummings and Jaime Welch-Donahue, and my copyeditor, Bruce Sylvester, who helped me to clearly communicate this message.

Finally, my enduring thanks and appreciation to my wife, Patricia, who understandingly encountered the absences and frustrations involved as I conducted research and presented the findings to interested audiences here and abroad.

Note

1. My past articles include "The Nuclear Arming of South Africa," *Black Scholar* 8, no. 1 (September 1976), pp. 25–31; "Apartheid and the Atom: The United States and South Africa's Military Potential," *Africa Today* 23 (July-September 1976), pp. 25–37; "Uranium Politics and U.S. Foreign Policy in Southern Africa," *Journal of Southern African Affairs* 4, no. 3 (July 1979), pp. 281–300; "U.S. Policy and Nuclear Proliferation in South Africa," in *U.S. Military Involvement in Southern Africa*, Western Massachusetts Association of Concerned Scholars, eds. (Boston: South End Press, 1978), pp. 17–30; "The United States and South Africa: Nuclear Collaboration under the Reagan Administration," *Trans-Africa Forum* 2, no. 2 (Fall 1983), pp. 17–30; "United States–South African Nuclear Developments," in Michael Kamara and Salima Marriot, eds., *Perspectives on United States Policy toward Southern Africa: Policy Evaluations and Alternative Proposals* (Baltimore: Morgan State University Press, 1983); with Kenneth S. Zinn, "The September 22, 1979 Mystery Flash: Did South Africa Detonate a Nuclear Bomb?" (Washington, D.C.: Washington Office on Africa and the Congressional Black Caucus Foundation, 1985).

Abbreviations

AEC	Atomic Energy Commission (U.S.)
AFC	Agreement for Nuclear Cooperation
ANC	African National Congress
ARMSCOR	Armaments Development and Production Corporation
CANUC	Campaign Against Namibian Uranium Contracts (U.K.)
CDA	Combined Development Agency
COMURHEX	Société pour la Conversion de l'Uranium en Metal et en Hexaflourure
CSIR	Council for Scientific and Industrial Research
CTG	General Labor Confederation
DIA	Defense Intelligence Agency (U.S.)
DOE	Department of Energy (U.S.)
ERDA	Energy Research and Development Administration (U.S)
ESCOM	South African Electricity Supply Commission
FRG	Federal Republic of Germany (West Germany)
IAEA	International Atomic Energy Agency
IISS	International Institute of Strategic Studies
LWR	light water reactor
MNR	Mozambique National Resistance Movement
MPLA	Popular Movement for the Liberation of Angola
NADGE	NATO Air Defense Group Environment
NATO	North Atlantic Treaty Organization
NGO	nongovernmental organization
NOVIB	International Development Financing Organization
NNPA	Nuclear Nonproliferation Act
NPT	Treaty on Nonproliferation of Nuclear Weapons
NRL	Navy Research Laboratory (U.S.)
NUFCOR	Nuclear Fuels Corporation of South Africa
OAU	Organization of African Unity

OMB	Office of Management and Budget (U.S.)
OSTP	Office of Science Technology Policy (U.S.)
OTA	Office of Technology Assessment (U.S.)
PAC	Pan-Africanist Congress
PRC	People's Republic of China
ROK	Republic of Korea
RTZ	Rio Tinto-Zinc
SAAEB	South African Atomic Energy Board
SACTU	South African Council of Trade Unions
SADCC	South African Development Coordinating Council
SADF	South African Defense Force
SAFARI-1	South African Fundamental Atomic Reactor Installation-1
SAM	surface-to-air missile
SASOL	South African Coal, Oil and Gas
SATO	South Atlantic Treaty Organization
SERA	Société d' Études et de Recherches d'Uranium
SIPRI	Stockholm International Peace Research Institute
SNEC	Subgroup on Nuclear Export Coordination
SWAPO	South West African Peoples Organization
UCOR	Uranium Enrichment Corporation
UNITA	Union for the Total Independence of Angola
ZANU	Zimbabwe African National Union
ZAPU	Zimbabwe African Peoples Union
ZIPRA	Zimbabwe Peoples Revolutionary Army

1
Introduction: The Failure of the Nonproliferation Regime

Most responsible observers believe that South Africa has the capacity to manufacture nuclear weapons or at least should be classified as a "near-nuclear weapons state." That there is still some lingering ambiguity in this assumption is itself an interesting problem. In fact, South Africa has been regarded by the international community as possessing such a potential for a considerable period of time. For example, in hearings before the U.S. Senate Foreign Relations Committee in 1968, the now defunct Atomic Energy Commission listed South Africa as one of those nations that could take somewhat more than ten years, from the point of the national decision to do so, to produce nuclear weapons.[1]

At the 1975 Workshop on Arms Control of the Aspen Institute, George H. Quester's paper was concerned in part with the political problem that "outlaw states'" possession of nuclear weapons presented to the international system, since they are generally regarded as problem states, existing in highly volatile regions of the world. After noting the swift pace of the southward movement of the African revolution bearing down upon South Africa, that nation's position as a threatened state surrounded by hostile neighbors, its status as a nonsignatory to the Nuclear Nonproliferation Treaty, and its nuclear enrichment-related technological advances, he commented on the status and motivation of South Africa to contend in an environment in which it possesses nuclear weapons. Citing the necessity of beginning to openly discuss the strategic problems presented by a South African weapons state, he alluded to the possibility that South Africa, like Israel, might detonate a bomb sometime in the future, because both countries were "threatened with extinction" and did not wish to be "driven into the sea."[2]

Continuing statements by South African government officials support Quester's view. In February 1977, Connie Mulder, then Minister of Information and Interior, made the (oft-cited) statement that if South Africa were attacked, "no rules [would] apply at all," adding that the government would use every means of defense available, and making reference to its nuclear facilities such as the uranium enrichment process and significant uranium reserves.[3]

Nevertheless, the strongest public admission of a South African military nuclear capability has come not from the South African government, but the French. At a luncheon gathering of journalists in Paris, French Prime Minister Raymond Barre said, in defense of the French sale of two 922-megawatt nuclear power generators to the South African government, that, "South Africa already has nuclear military capability." His point was that the additional sales of his government added nothing to the South African capability in this regard.[4]

Of course, the problem of knowing when such a state has in fact produced weapons is difficult, because on the one hand, no country wants to *openly* violate so-called safeguard agreements either as a part of the International Atomic Energy Agency (IAEA), the informal London Agreement of 1975, or bilateral agreements signed as a part of nuclear trade arrangements. On the other hand, to some extent, absolute secrecy defeats the deterrent purpose of developing such weapons, so that countries that develop them are expected to make this fact known in some manner.

Clearly, then, the circumstances under which nuclear weapons are developed compounds the problem of knowing when they will be produced, what kind will be produced, and, therefore, what strategy will be adopted by the producer for their utilization.

Certainly, secrecy itself is part of the strategic decision, not only in the tactic to produce nuclear weapons, but in the ultimate decision regarding their use, as can be seen in the following scenario.

> The Israel nuclear option has every possible quality: its nonexercise can be sold for the thing that really matters, sophisticated conventional armaments, and remain to serve another day; in the meantime the stockpile grows steadily; the transmission of assurance tends to discourage countermoves in Arab countries; and should the conventional balance shift at some future date, the option remains to be exercised at a time when it would make the maximum emotional impact. It is easy to see how the temptation to acquire a nuclear option for these purposes might occur to other powers with difficulties of access to their great power friends: the most obvious example is South Africa.[5]

Under such a circumstance, therefore, it is perhaps, a more practical question to assume that the country in question—once it can be established that it has the economic and industrial resources, the technological skills, research and development activities of significant accomplishment, and linkages to international nuclear commerce—for all practical purposes is a nuclear weapons state. Nevertheless, that such weapons either exist or could be produced quickly should constitute an openly acknowledged danger to the people of South Africa, to those in the region of Southern Africa, and perhaps to others as well. Just as important, concerning those nuclear weapons states professing a concern for nuclear nonproliferation, it is puzzling to discover their resistance to the thesis that, indeed, their continued nuclear trade in materials as well as their provision of technical assistance and financing to South Africa have contributed to its capability, and, thus, render them culpable in the entry of South Africa into the nuclear club, either now or at some point in the future. It is, then, not puzzling that the relationship of the nuclear powers with South Africa has *not* substantiated the corollary thesis that their continued nuclear relations would provide the necessary constraints to make the acquisition of additional nuclear capability by South Africa unnecessary.

In this context and in light of my initial statement, it is not only logical and tantalizing, but probably even urgent to approach this problem from the perspective of a new proposition—that the South African case represents a failure of international nonproliferation policy in particular. The inescapable assumption is that the constraints upon the acquisition of the technology necessary to produce a nuclear explosion do not appear to be working, and that proliferation in this case has defied successful management, forcing a new set of choices upon the major powers concerning their policies regarding both further trade and technical assistance and, of course, the political aspects of foreign policy toward South Africa and the region. It is this thesis and its corollary which are the basis of this book.

Why, it might be asked, is this strong conclusion warranted in the face of such continued ambiguity with respect to South African nuclear capability? I believe that such a thesis is altogether entertainable because the ambiguity may not be real, in that its sources lie in both the technical definition of *nuclear proliferation* and in the political constraints upon the revelation of such a capability.

The ambiguity with respect to the technical question involves, first, the problem of knowing when proliferation has occurred. Within the twenty-five years immediately after World War II, five states exploded nuclear devices and went on to develop a weapons proliferation problem. Thus, *proliferation* in this sense was defined as a power exploding such a device with the intention of testing a nuclear weapon. Then, in 1970, when the International Treaty on the Nonproliferation of Nuclear Weapons (NPT) accord was reached, nuclear weapons states were prohibited from transferring or participating in the manufacture of nuclear weapons or nuclear explosive devices. Likewise, the nonnuclear powers were prohibited from acquiring or manufacturing such weapons or devices. In 1978, the Nuclear Nonproliferation Act was written with the intention of preventing proliferation, not only by inhibiting the transfer of nuclear weapons or devices, but also by effecting the "establishment of more effective international control over the transfer and use of nuclear materials and equipment and nuclear technology for peaceful purposes."[6]

From these concepts it is apparent that the definition of proliferation is shifting to encompass technology and trade in essential nuclear materials and equipment, because of the general recognition that the line between the attainment of civilian and military nuclear capabilities is virtually indistinguishable. In 1974, India exploded a nuclear device, but it is not reported to be pursuing a nuclear weapons fabrication program. On the other hand, Israel has not acknowledged exploding any nuclear device, but is widely reported to have manufactured nuclear weapons. Which is the more dangerous case of nuclear proliferation? Tentative steps to sanction India were made by the Ford and Carter administrations, but were ultimately abandoned for one reason or another. But no sanctions have been levied against Israel, even when it was discovered to have received eighty krytons, essential elements in the fabrication of nuclear weapons.[7] Perhaps it is the fact that no sanctions were levied against either country that has led some observers to feel that nonproliferation of nuclear weapons does not have a high place in the foreign policy priorities of nuclear nations.

Nevertheless, nuclear proliferation theorists have proceeded to fashion strategies for controlling the problem based on the ability of states to "manage" it, given leadership by the nuclear weapons states. For example, in 1977, three important works were published that yielded nearly forty overlapping recommendations aimed at controlling both the capabilities and incentives for countries to "go nuclear."[8] They might be summarized as follows:

1. Weapons states would provide "confidence-building" measures to nonweapons states through scientific and technological cooperation and regional security guarantees.

2. All states would accede to the NPT and the regime of safeguards sponsored by the IAEA; the role of the IAEA would be enhanced by its evaluation of the fuel cycle to find alternatives to plutonium production.

3. Nuclear weapons states should reduce reliance on nuclear power in general, and on nuclear weapons as symbols of status and as means to settle disputes.

4. The United States and the Soviet Union in particular should enter into genuine arms control agreements designed to reduce the number of nuclear weapons and eventually eliminate them.

5. Nuclear weapons states should conduct international nuclear commerce in consonance with nonproliferation objectives, including the orderly and selective provisions of nuclear services.

What appears to be involved in all of the recommended strategies is the application of restraining political criteria to decisions concerning trade, finance, technology, and security problems that take nuclear proliferation into account. Therefore, where nonproliferation fails, it would appear that states that could have made a difference lacked the will to employ the political criteria to decisions, instead elevating the discrete concerns of commerce and finance, or security, over the value of nuclear proliferation, for whatever reason.

These strategies, however, as dedicated as they are to the proposition that nonproliferation can be managed, fail to give adequate attention to the worst case proposition—that regardless of the extent to which nonproliferation strategies are employed, some states will seek to acquire what they perceive to be the ultimate deterrent in order to permanently guarantee the security of their state or regime. Such states will also give priority to manipulating the extent to which others know of their nuclear capability in an attempt to avoid sanctions—thus adding to the existing ambiguity.

Ted Greenwood, Harold Feiveson, and Theodore Taylor have described this phenomenon as "latent proliferation" when there is either precipitous "drift or concerted action toward the actual possession of nuclear explosives" in ways that fall "short of actual diversion of nuclear materials from civilian nuclear facilities but facilitate a possible future decision to acquire nuclear weapons."[9] Then, in an excellent description of the problem, Leonard Spector said that the new "rules of engagement" between weapons states and nonweapons states suggests that weapons states will tolerate "veiled nuclearization" by nonweapons states so long as this capability is kept ambiguous, that "if a country does not openly display its nuclear capabilities or break IAEA rules, it may approach and actually cross the nuclear weapons threshold with virtual impunity."[10] Obviously, this new definition of the state of nonproliferation, in practice, comports well with the drifting target that defines the phenomenon.

What makes the South African situation extremely dangerous is both that the nation is a beneficiary of the new drift toward ambiguity in international nonproliferation policy and practice, and that its nuclear capability exists under critically unstable conditions. I will discuss a major reason for the drift as it relates to the environment of the international competition in the nuclear market, and then examine the regional security situation as a source of the instability of the regime.

The Environment: International Competition in Nuclear Trade

The major elements of the international environment that have provided the backdrop for a developing South African nuclear capability are (1) the passing of the U.S. nuclear monopoly to include other major states as developers and exporters of nuclear power materials and equipment, and (2) the competition among these major powers for export markets of nuclear materials, resulting in an ever widening group of "second-level" powers capable of reproducing these materials and the weapons as well.

It was in the best pragmatic tradition of foreign policy that, in an effort to maintain as much of a monopoly as possible over the technological secrets surrounding the development of nuclear power, the United States began the distribution of experimental nuclear reactors under the Atoms for Peace program in 1953. The increasing proliferation of this technology, both inside and outside of the European alliance, created a situation where, by the late 1960s, a group of eight countries—the United States, USSR, France, West Germany, China, Canada, Japan, and Britain—possessed the technological knowledge and industrial base to manufacture nuclear explosions if they desired; by 1970, all but West Germany, Japan, and Canada had done so.

The second factor in this picture is that most countries in this group have since become active exporters of nuclear technology in their own right, thus breaking the control over the market once exercised by the United States. This situation was evident as early as 1970, but was accelerated by the shock created by the sudden rise in the price of oil in 1973 and 1974. This shock made both major and minor states begin the search for alternative sources of lower-cost energy, causing a ripple effect among states especially locked in oil-dependent relationships with oil suppliers.

As the competition among the major nuclear suppliers increased, sales of nuclear materials went beyond the supply of reactors and fuel to the export of processing plants, complete with agreements to supply the complementary resources that could make some states self-sufficient in this field at some point in the future. By 1974, the United States had called together the suppliers in a forum which came to be known as the London Suppliers Group to address the twin questions of proliferation and orderly marketing which had resulted from the fierce competition. Yet, this did not appear to stem the tide. For example, in 1976, in a $200 million deal, France agreed to construct for Spain the necessary nuclear processing facilities to meet the country's energy needs for the foreseeable future.[11] Then, again, some of the more controversial sales have involved West Germany with Brazil, France and West Germany with Iran, Canada with India, and, of course, France with South Africa, a relationship I will study in greater detail.

All of this was happening amid attempts at the initiation and enforcement of the International Treaty on the Nonproliferation of Nuclear Weapons (which sparked discussions in international forums on such things as the establishment of "nuclear-weapons–free zones" or "zones of peace" and amid discussions about strengthening the IAEA safeguard regime and advocating motives replete with assertions regarding the "peaceful uses" of nuclear energy. It is most striking that these moral and enlightened motives as the basis for curbing nuclear nonproliferation appear to be succumbing to economic interests.

Among the multinational firms and governments that support these firms' activities, participation in the international nuclear materials market is a *business* proposition first; it is this attitude that motivates the struggle for control of lucrative markets in the sale of these materials. Such attitudes among corporations are not unusual, but government interests appear to have been the same. Agreements are made between governments to facilitate this commerce, guaranteeing the supply of materials; multinational corporations are issued licenses; and the sales are often based on financing provided by or guaranteed by government agencies.

In fact, the position of the U.S. government as a leading proponent of nuclear nonproliferation has been a bit precarious. Although not wanting to openly fan the flames of proliferation, at the same time, it is desperate for its firms to succeed in acquiring contracts for nuclear-related services, holding on to some semblance of commercial viability in an ever crowded market. This role raised the activity of government agencies to a new level of aggressiveness, according to one observer, such that State Department officials participated in securing contracts as if they were employees of nuclear corporations, and the Export-Import Bank became a strong competitor through its ability to finance nuclear exports.[12]

This is not the only testimony to the bitterness of West German–American competition at the government level, but it confirms the view that the role of policymakers is to preserve the principle of sustaining market share at all cost. There is a reason for this. The United States has slipped from a position of dominance in the market since 1974. In some prior years, it made as many as twenty sales of nuclear power plants. But after 1974, no additional U.S. orders were made, and only eighteen orders were made outside of the United States.[13]

This situation has been the result not only of such competition, but also of higher energy prices (which have brought slower economic growth and an attendant lower demand for electricity) and of the social factor of citizens groups' effective opposition to further nuclear energy development. In fact, one observer was led to say that the situation thus created led to the "greatest collapse of any enterprise in industrial history," as all of the major supplier states were affected.[14] For instance, the Japanese nuclear energy industry drastically cut back planned nuclear power in the mid-1970s from 60,000 Mw by 1985 to 33,000 Mw. In Britain, electricity demand is severely depressed to the point that its needs have been met from existing sources of water, coal, and oil-fired plants; not one nuclear plant has been ordered since 1973. West Germany also initiated a moratorium on the construction of nuclear plants. This problem produced substantial competition in the Third World, causing Klaus Barthelt, chairman of Kraftwerk Union, West Germany's largest reactor-building company, to suggest that the lack of domestic orders for reactors would make exports impossible, exacerbating the situation in which foreign competition in Third World markets had already degenerated to "hungry dogs" scrapping over the few contracts available.[15]

This situation did not improve between the mid-1970s and mid-1980s, as total reactor orders, especially without the momentum of the United States, fell precipitously to the lowest point in the history of the global industry by the end of 1984. At that time, there were 317 operating reactors on line, 209 units under construction, but only 128 units planned.[16]

In 1978, the four remaining reactor manufacturing companies in the United States (General Electric, Westinghouse, and the smaller firms Babcock and Wilcox and Combustion Engineering Inc.) had a 131-unit backlog. The problem they faced was in the typical six- to ten-year period. Since it normally takes four years for the completion of a plant, it takes eight to ten orders per year for a firm to remain solvent; the declining numbers they were receiving were inadequate. By 1984, these four companies controlled 38 percent of the market for reactor construction, leaving the rest of the field to European and Japanese companies, plus a new entrant of the government of India.[17] Still, the opinion in the industry mirrored that in Europe to the extent that it was felt that the shortfall could be made up by foreign sales—principally to second-level states.

Meanwhile, a similar scenario was developing in reactor services and materials, but it was particularly telling in the case of uranium. However, commercial competition as a factor in the strategic role of South Africa in the nuclear field is also highlighted by its control of perhaps the second largest reserves of uranium in the world. Although I shall discuss the specific dimensions of this capacity later, suffice it to say here that in both reserves and present production activity, South African uranium sales together with those of other countries created a depressed market price for natural uranium "yellowcake." In fact, in 1971, the price per pound dropped to less than $5.00 with a world demand at approximately 26,000 tons and over 100,000 tons available from suppliers. Apparently, this situation was exacerbated by South Africa, which the French believed were consistently underselling other suppliers due to their "desperate need for cash flow."[18]

The answer, therefore, was an attempt to control the price by manipulation of supply among the major producers through an "orderly marketing arrangement," which included representative companies such as Gulf Oil Minerals (the Canadian subsidiary of Gulf Oil in the United States), the

Table 1-1
Uranium Reserves in Selected States, 1976
(1,000 metric tons)

South Africa	462.0
Argentina	20.6
Brazil	10.4
Korea	2.4

Source: *Nuclear Proliferation and Safeguards* (Office of Technology Assessment, U.S. Congress, July 1977), p. 249.

British Rio Tinto-Zinc, and the governments of four countries (Australia, South Africa, France, and Canada) and their corporate representatives (including South Africa's Nufcor and France's Uranex). This in group met several times in 1972, finally establishing, by May of that year, an apparatus which included the setting up of a secretariat in Paris with the cover of exchanging marketing information under the name Société d'Études et de Recherches d'Uranium (SERA). The rules of this club (written one month later in Johannesburg) governed the system of rigged pricing by controlled bidding among the members, the objective being to raise the price a modest 3 percent per year. (This was done without the participation by the United States government, which allowed no foreign-source importation of nuclear fuel until 1977.)

As a result of the cartel's operations, Westinghouse Corp. as a supplier of low enriched uranium to U.S. utilities, was squeezed and provoked a legal battle against the cartel by suing the U.S. member, Gulf Oil. This case revealed the interesting fact of the increasing participation of foreign uranium suppliers in the U.S. market. So strong had this competition for uranium services contracts become by 1985, that European producers of enriched uranium such as URENCO (a British, Dutch, and West German organization with offices in the Netherlands and Britain) and Eurodif (a gaseous diffusion plant in France built by France, Italy, Belgium, Spain, and Iran) are entering into long-term service contracts with U.S. utilities. At the same time, the share of uranium enrichment services provided by the U.S. Dept. of Energy to the European market declined from 90 percent in the mid-1970s to only 35 percent in the mid-1980s, and is projected to drop to 10 percent within the decade.[19]

The result of such competition on the Third World has been striking, in that countries such as India, Brazil, South Korea, China, and Taiwan have become leading second-level nuclear powers. This is reflected in the fact that these countries account for 25 percent of all planned nuclear power to be constructed in the future, and nearly half of such planned construction not counting West Germany and the Soviet Union.[20] A strange paradox to the logic of proliferation theory exists, however, in that such countries as Israel and South Africa (which do not have strong civilian nuclear power programs projected) are, nonetheless, considered to be among the leading countries in nuclear technological capabilities. This feeds the strong suspicions that their capabilities are substantially related, instead, to weapons production.

There continues, nevertheless, to be plaintive concern given to the question of nuclear nonproliferation, despite the furious competition for the dissemination of nuclear materials. As preparation was taking place for the quinquennial NPT Review Conference in 1985, concern was expressed that the two key issues deadlocking the 1975 and 1980 Conferences—the issues of peaceful nuclear trade among signatories (article IV) and the achievement of nuclear disarmament (article VI)—would be deadlocks again in 1985.[21] These issues, which would appear to divide the nuclear weapons states and non–nuclear-weapons states, the states with "civilian" nuclear power programs and those without them, and the signatories and nonsignatories, threaten to disrupt the residual utility of the Nonproliferation Treaty itself. Of course, both Israel and South Africa have special sensitivities to these concerns, due to the fact that in 1984, the twenty-eighth general session of the IAEA passed resolutions condemning Israel for having bombed the Iraqi reactor in 1981, and calling upon all states to end nuclear cooperation with South Africa.[22]

Therefore, even at the level of international realities, there is a grand ambiguity that countenances the expansion of nuclear trade in the developing countries and their politically volatile regions as normal, (especially if fed by the engine of "orderly" competition for markets by the suppliers), while at the same time, entertaining realistic expectations regarding limitations on the ability of such countries to find the means to manufacture nuclear weapons. The evidence, however, suggests that the international environment for nuclear competition has intensified the pressures on suppliers to sell nuclear materials, and the theory of nuclear nonproliferation suggests that if the incentives are sufficient, nonweapons states will buy them to develop a weapons capability. The question is whether or not these incentives to "go nuclear" are stronger than those to limit proliferation, especially without an equally effective deterrent emanating from the more advanced states. I will next examine this question in the context of the perception that South Africa might possess motives to provide the incentive for the development of nuclear weapons.

South African Incentives for the Bomb

The motives that might have pushed South Africa toward the consideration of acquiring a weapons option as part of its insecurity as a nation have many sources, such as the process of decolonization of states in the region and South Africa's domestic racial problems. Both of these will be addressed in turn. The process of decolonization all over the world entailed changing the status of people from being the subjects of other nations and empires to being citizens of sovereign nations. Thus, as Rupert Emerson has expressed it, for many, the end of nationalism was the nation as a "terminal community."[23]

It is known, however, that this was not the only result, for both the antagonisms and cooperation of contiguous states also made citizens of one nation de facto citizens of other states in the region within which their state was set, or part of a "security community."[24] Unfortunately, there is no generally agreed upon concept for the transition between these two types of community, which involves the process of the reconstitution of a former colonial region into a new area possessing autonomous states in what may be considered a "pluralistic" security community. Nevertheless, this is the process that the Southern African region has been undergoing as an extension of the wider decolonization process involving the entire African continent, beginning in the late 1950s. It is one which has steadily dismantled the former British, Portuguese, and South Africans colonial control of the region and, therefore, successively stripped away the colonial authority the British and Portuguese left to the South Africans. Accompanying this process, there are increasing signs of the perception that states in the region must develop effective economic integration, which will afford them greater political independence from South Africa.

In addition, South Africa, an avowedly anticomunist state, is evidently upset by a vision of the future of the region with three Marxist states sharing its borders. This prospect has been the basis of a massive and aggressive campaign of hostile actions against its neighbors, indeed, before there is any definitive evidence of the degree to which they intend to intervene in South African domestic affairs or regional hegemony.

The basic problem, of course, is with the South African system itself. The absence of black enfranchisement and, thus, the absence of the grant of legitimacy by the majority of the population to the white minority leadership means that the normal concept of "nationality" is seriously flawed, since there is little political integration. Practically, it means that the system is held together by force with a constant challenge by the dispossessed to the authority of the ruling white minority. This challenge has become endemic and destabilizing, making it extremely difficult for the rulers of a powerful nation to be confident in the success of either their internal or external future.

Decolonization and Destabilization

The breakup of the old colonial region might be regarded as the process of "subregionalization" or a means of creating the conditions through which the new states came into existence and a new independent region was created, albeit, a region theoretically antagonistic to the existence of the status quo hegemony of South Africa. It is argued that this process creates increasing degrees of insecurity for the South African regime through the elimination of buffer states in three important stages.

The first stage was the elimination of the buffer of the Portuguese territories through the revolutionary movements developed in Guinea-Bissau, Mozambique, and Angola, and the success of the movement in Guinea-Bissau in particular. It was the latter nation that, by 1975, made it clear to young Portuguese military officers who started a coup in their country that the counterrevolutionary war was not only wrong, but destined to fail in the other territories over the long run. So, in 1974, Portugal gave independence to Guinea-Bissau and in 1975, eliminated the buffers of Mozambique and Angola from South Africa and its colonial territory of Namibia, bringing independent states to South Africa's borders. This event would have been a routine occurrence in other parts of Africa, but South Africa began to finance a dissident element called the Mozambique National Resistance Movement (MNR) operating near its borders, in an effort to initiate the kind of havoc that would interrupt the ability of the leaders of the country to govern effectively. At present, even though an agreement has been signed between the South African regime and Mozambique, the rightist guerilla group continues to operate in the southern part of the country, apparently with South African assistance.

The second stage was the elimination of the buffer of Zimbabwe (formerly Southern Rhodesia) through a long war for independence between the white minority regime which broke away from the British colonial authority in 1965, and two black liberation guerilla forces, the Zimbabwe African Peoples Union (ZAPU) and the Zimbabwe African National Union (ZANU). British- and U.S.-led negotiations between these two factions and the South Africans produced an independence agreement and an election in April 1980, which was won by Robert Mugabe of ZANU. The advent of Mugabe's government in Zimbabwe was a critical setback for the South Africans, since historically Rhodesia had been a functional part of the leadership of the ruling system in Southern Africa, especially after the withdrawal of the British government from most of Southern Africa by the mid-1960s, and the final withdrawal of the Portuguese in the mid-1970s. Again, the white redoubt had been broken and the borders of South Africa were more exposed than ever before to a potentially hostile power. The response by South Africa has been to mount a covert operation in Southern Zimbabwe in support of "ZAPU dissidents" opposed to Mugabe's leadership, and to sponsor acts of sabotage and other forms of disruption similar to the MNR's in Mozambique.

The third stage is defined by the current struggle over the independence of Namibia which, when achieved, would mean that three of the four states bordering South Africa (all but Botswana) would probably have Marxist-oriented governments. To the South Africans this would be destabilizing politically, economically, and possibly militarily, since all of these states, including Botswana, are nominally declared opponents of apartheid. Thus, South Africa has waged a desperate military campaign to continue its control over Namibia and to eliminate the opposition guerilla group, the South West African Peoples Organization (SWAPO), by striking at its bases in southern Angola. This military intervention has also served the purpose of its destabilization campaign against the Angola government by supporting the antigovernment guerillas of the Union for the Total Independence of Angola (UNITA) and disrupting Angolan life with a war that has killed many thousands of combatants and civilians alike and destroyed much of the rural infrastructure in the region.

Domestic Instability

The source of domestic instability is the practice of the doctrine of apartheid by the white minority regime. This entails practices so dehumanizing and intolerable, with such catastrophic consequences upon the nonwhite population, that segments of this group and their white allies have taken up various forms of resistance. These acts of resistance include a wide variety of measures, from acts of noncooperation with the system to armed revolutionary warfare. In any case, these acts of resistance define South African internal security as a national, regional, continental, and global problem.

The national dimension of this problem has become the most serious challenge to the regime since 1976, because of the magnitude of the acts of resistance, which cut across all groups—from youths, to community activists, to workers—and have been almost continuous since that time. The forms of resistance have involved every conceivable instrumentality—massive work stoppages, civil rights protests, riots and insurrection, even guerilla bombings at strategic facilities. The level of activity appears to be growing.

Undoubtedly, this scenario of protests against apartheid has caused the regime to intensify its control. The evidence is that it has moved beyond simple police tactics to an extensive utilization of military force. The government has also attempted to contain civil protest through the mass detentions of its leadership. None of this, however, has appeared to effectively decrease the protest, but has had the opposite effect of stimulating an action–reaction cycle with ever greater casualties, both black and white, fostering signs of frustration and instability for the regime.

It is a regional problem since the African National Congress (ANC) and the Pan Africanist Congress (PAC), political organizations with guerilla operations inside the country, were driven underground by the regime in 1961, but have continued to mount what Defense Minister Botha described in the Defense White Paper of 1973 as a "war of low intensity on our borders."[25] By 1976, however, the head of the security police, Brig. C.F. Zietsman, revealed that nearly 2,500 "terrorists" have been brought to trial under the security legislation, saying that the conflict was "no longer child's play," but "an extended onslaught."[26] The ANC and PAC have utilized the environment of serious domestic unrest to intensify the guerilla war, apparently increasing the sophistication of their weapons, as they have engaged the twenty-one battalions of the South African Defense Force (SADF) repeatedly in the Caprivi strip.

The war has made all of the states in the region potential targets of preemptive strikes or "hot-pursuit" military operations by the SADF in an effort to find and eliminate the operations of the guerilla forces. No doubt, the removal of buffer states has raised the spectre that South Africa will have to defend its entire land border from encroachments by guerilla forces.

It is a continental problem inasmuch as African countries to the north, through the Organization of African Unity (OAU) and in international forums, have added to the psychological and political pressure on South Africa. In this sense, the ironic fact that many of these same nations must secretly purchase South African products is of little international consequence. Thus, the African states take the initiative in making opposition to apartheid an international problem as well, with the result that open and formal political or military alliances with South Africa have been shunned by every Western state (though the economic support provided by these states is crucial to the strength of the South African economy, 40 percent of which involves direct foreign investment). Thus, South Africa feels the frustration of having the capabilities of a substantial power, yet not the status of being able to exercise this power in the international system.

The Utility of Nuclear Weapons for South Africa

The foregoing discussion illustrates the growing nature of the regional security problems faced by the South African regime both externally and internally, problems challenging its very survival. This gives the leaders of South Africa added rationale to acquire the ultimate weapon. This factor also provides the rationale for the reassertion of my thesis that the issue of South African nuclear proliferation is beyond "management" according to the general tenets of nonproliferation theory. But if this thesis is accepted, it raises the question of how such weapons would be utilized in the Southern African context, and here, it is necessary to question a growing body of theorists who have addressed this specific question.

Speculation began to occur concerning why South Africa was apparently acquiring such a sophisticated nuclear infrastructure soon after the government announced, in 1974, its domestic uranium enrichment achievement and its plans for a commercial plant as well as a nuclear power plant. John E. Spence, a leading authority on South African military strategic matters, suggested that the acquisition of a weapons capability was unlikely, since it would run counter to the foreign policy objectives of the government at that time. He explained that politically it would mitigate against developing closer relations to traditional allies in the West; strategically, it would represent little addition to the regime's security when balanced against the damage caused to its attempted regional rapprochement, dubbed its "outward-looking" policy; and economically, the regime would have more to gain from cementing nuclear commerce with the West, rather than risking its "opprobrium."[27] He went on to say that the nature of the threat faced by South Africa in the immediate term was from insurgent guerilla warfare, and its emphasis on counterinsurgency made nuclear weapons of dubious utility.

This line of reasoning was apparently influential on a number of other analysts such as George Quester, who argued as early as 1973 that in view of South Africa's clear conventional military superiority in the region, it "hardly seems advisable to change the rules of the game."[28] Also, Edouard Bustin, writing in 1975, agreed, adding that "it is perhaps within the context of South Africa's search for some sort of Western guarantee of its security that the pursuit of nuclear capability can be most validly justified."[29]

Then, there is a body of opinion that moves to a less moderate stance, reaching a midpoint between the clearly conservative opinions just expressed and a more military-oriented end-use proposition. These views are represented by writers such as Richard Betts and John Spence, who admit that South Africa may, indeed, have nuclear weapons, but that a military end use is unlikely; that if they are used at all, it is probable that the target would be either the Soviet Union or its proxy states; but that their greatest utility is symbolic.[30] This view is interpreted by Robert Jaster, Leonard Spector, Kenneth Adelman, and Albion Knight to mean that the possession of a nuclear capability is meant to gain political leverage over the West and to signal the South African regime's invincibility in an effort to blunt challenges to its legitimacy and survival.[31]

In another work, however, Adelman and Knight take a further step by suggesting that given the South African concept of the threat to their security as a "total onslaught" requiring a "total national strategy," there could be many such uses for a nuclear weapons capability, such as a weapon of last resort, defense against large-scale conventional military buildup, tactical battlefield situations, and defense against Soviet proxy forces.[32] Joined in this more extreme view by Pierre Lellouche and Robert Harkavy, agreement is tailored to their special perspective of South Africa as a "pariah state." Here I combine Lellouche's view that the "deterioration of the strategic situation in Southern Africa has increased the purely military value of potential nuclear weapons,"[33] together with Harkavy's view that given this occurrence, "one must consider a range of strategic doctrines—last resort deterrence, deterrence by uncertainty, massive retaliation, or 'trip-wire' doctrines, tactical battle field uses, etc."[34]

Discussion

With respect to the first body of theory regarding the utility of South African nuclear weapons, it is safe to say that time and the pace at which the regime has developed its nuclear capability have brought me to the assumption with which I began this study: that the nuclear program of South Africa is so advanced that only the political decision is necessary for it to possess nuclear weapons, since the technological capability it has accumulated in both the nuclear and military fields means that only a short time for fabrication would be necessary. This assumption obviously contradicts an earlier one that South Africa would probably not, for a variety of reasons, fabricate nuclear weapons.

I have attempted to emphasize what is also a growing consensus that the security problems of the regime are more ominous, both domestically and among states in the region. Thus, there is much greater regime instability and greater motivation for it to have made the political decision to acquire a nuclear deterrent today than ever before. Therefore, those moderate theories of enduse holding that the most critical utility for nuclear weapons possession by the regime would be for symbolism and for the exercise of political leverage against the West must also explain why the regime has so crudely handled the revelation of its explosive capability in an apparent attempt at testing.

I take some liberties here in full recognition of the fact that there is little doubt that in 1977, a test was in preparation at the nuclear facility in the Kalahari. But I will also present a positive thesis for the 1979 nuclear flash in a subsequent chapter. One might understand why a state, having a powerful motive, might once risk an attempt to see if it could test an explosive device without detection. But having been caught, risking detection yet a second time is a sign of a desperate state which has cast the nuclear nonproliferation concept aside in favor of a dedicated nuclear explosive program.

Therefore, I am in agreement with the third body of opinion presented above, embellished by Steve Chan's concept, which holds that among pariah states in volatile regions of the world, rather than holding to a view of "balanced deterrence," they have constructed a decisionmaking scenario based on "assured resistance."[35] The South African government has a low tolerance for challenges to regime authority (legitimacy) because of its minority status, instability, and isolation from immediate assistance by allies. Furthermore, Chan's insight is novel in suggesting that given the security status of South Africa and its long and substantial nuclear technological relationship with the West, resulting in its own nuclear bureaucratic momentum, the decision to develop ultimate nuclear capabilities is a *normal act*. In fact, the abnormality in such a situation would be the decision *not* to develop such weapons.[36]

Therefore, I am persuaded that the balance of existing theory purporting to explain South African nuclear weapons utilization is outmoded, and that an alternative explanation is now necessary. If people assume that South Africa has already made the conscious decision to acquire a nuclear weapons capability, then they can resolve the inconsistencies with regard to such factors as the addition of nuclear power to its electric power capability in the first place, the addition of technologies such as uranium enrichment and information pertinent to nuclear explosions, the maintenance of unsafeguarded facilities, the refusal to become a signatory to the NPT, the lack of response to U.S. attempts to negotiate new status under the NNPA of 1978, the mysterious nuclear facilities and evidence of testing, and the alliances with other presumed nuclear states. Then one may further assume that South Africa has made the decision not to admit that it is seeking a dedicated nuclear weapons program, but has had the difficulty of managing such apparent ambiguity. This task is complicated by the duality of its status as both a pariah state and a client of the West, a role which has given the regime a contradictory set of obligations and political responses. For example, the same activity leading it to test its explosive technology (perhaps in an effort to confirm the direction of its weapons program), if definitely validated, might drive it farther away from the West, at least in the court of international public opinion.

As will be seen, however, Western states may be in no hurry to validate the occurrence of a nuclear test by South Africa. If anything, there has been an expansion in nuclear cooperation between them and South Africa in recent years. Both parties' success in managing ambiguity makes possible continued nuclear commerce and other relations, resolving the contradictions by avoiding challenges to those relationships. So, what in the terms of Imai and Rowen, may look like "muddling along" may actually be a strategy for maintaining essential cooperative relationships with a mutual policy of ambiguous proliferation.[37] This may explain, for example, why the mysterious flashes in both 1979 and 1980 were denied in the United

States by, first, a Democratic and, then, a Republican administration in a tellingly consistent act of foreign policy.

The Solution

My view of the problem dictates that the nonproliferation regime as defined by the five points above can only be marginally useful in dealing with the threats emanating from a variety of sources that are motivating South Africa toward the possession of nuclear weapons. Even a casual familiarity with my exposition in chapter 4 on the forces shaping the regional security environment should buttress the conclusion that South Africa is being pushed past the barriers of technology, and, thus, the answers lie not in that realm, but in the realm of politics—where the answers have always been. In this sense, I agree with Marshall Schulman, that since mankind has come a long way in understanding the technological problems of nuclear proliferation, "we tend to bemuse ourselves with the technological aspects of this problem," but "the technical discussions leave me with the feeling that we are all victims of a failure of political imagination."[38]

The assumptions of nuclear proliferation theory do not deal adequately with South Africa's regional political problems having to do with its increasing political and geographical isolation due to the development of a black-controlled regional subsystem. They also do not deal with the endemic violence and counterviolence caused by the struggle for control of power within the state, a struggle spilling over into neighboring states, which are the real source of the regime's constant fear of survival. The reasons for the inadequacy of this theory is that it underplays both the legitimacy and the increasingly explosive regional dynamic of conflict in the reaction of the black and nonwhite majority peoples of South Africa to the practice of apartheid by the white minority regime.

An illustration of this principle is that one of the supposed deterrents to proliferation is the extension of security guarantees to South Africa by a patron state such as the United States. Apartheid, however, keeps such states from, at least publicly, developing formal and public alliances, so that the international security value of such agreements is lost to South Africa. Another such example is the maintenance of reliable nuclear commercial relationships with South Africa by a patron state in order to reduce its incentive to construct facilities for its own nuclear services. However, the nuclear relationship is vulnerable to attack by those opposed to apartheid, and as such, even though nuclear trade between the United States and South Africa still exists, it has also been somewhat restricted. Then, there is the question of how the IAEA safeguards regime should function in the case of South Africa, when that body responds to the crime of apartheid by expelling South Africa's representatives, and develops resolutions for other countries to cease nuclear relations with the nation.

So, it is apartheid that ironically stands in the way of the effective functioning of the nonproliferation theory. It is considered ironic because of the reality that the key to breaking the cycles of isolation and violence is in the hands of the South African regime itself through the elimination of apartheid. This, however, will only be possible when it is understood by the government that the initial decision to deliberately construct a nuclear weapon to ensure the survival of its *control* of a nation is not the same as ensuring the security of *the nation and all of its people*, unless control is worth equating with the other factors that define the nation itself. In which case, if the survival of the control of a nation by a minority becomes the same as the survival of a nation itself, and one views the defense of one in terms of the defense of the other, South African whites will ultimately have to answer the question of whether that is a catastrophic price to pay for continued dominance. Nevertheless, this is ultimately the political question embedded in the possession and use of nuclear weapons by South Africa, and all signs point to the fact that they have answered that question in the affirmative.

The following chapters will discuss the implications of this thesis and my conclusions as they relate to South Africa, the African states, U.S. foreign policy, and the wider international system.

Notes

1. "Non-Proliferation Treaty," Hearings before the U.S. Senate Committee on Foreign Relations, July 10, 1968, p. 31.

2. George Quester, "What's New on Nuclear Proliferation," Aspen Institute Occasional Paper (Denver: Aspen Institute for Humanistic Studies, 1975), p. 5.

3. *Washington Post*, February 16, 1977, p. A12.

4. *Washington Post*, February 18, 1977, p. A28.

5. Leonard Beaton, "The International Political Context," in Mason Willrich, ed., *Civil Nuclear Power and International Security* (New York: Praeger, 1971), p. 78.

6. Nuclear Nonproliferation Act, article II, section 2a.

7. *Washington Post*, May 14, 1985, p. A20.

8. *Nuclear Power Issues and Choices: Report of the Nuclear Energy Policy Study Group* (Cambridge, Mass.: Ballinger, 1977), pp. 297–99; Office of Technology Assessment, Congress of the United States, *Nuclear Proliferation and Safeguards* (New York: Praeger, 1977), p. 85; David Gompert, Michael Mandelbaum, Richard Garwin, John Barton, *Nuclear Weapons and World Politics* (New York: McGraw-Hill, 1977), pp. 210–11.

9. Ted Greenwood, "Discouraging Proliferation in the Next Decade and Beyond," in Ted Greenwood, Harold Feiveson, and Theodore Taylor, *Nuclear*

Proliferation: Motivation, Capabilities and Strategies for Control, (New York: McGraw-Hill, 1977), pp. 125–6.

10. Leonard Spector, "Proliferation: The Silent Spread," *Foreign Policy* 58 (Spring 1985), p. 56.

11. *New York Times,* December 20, 1976, IV, 7.

12. Norman Gall, "Atom for Brazil, Danger for All," *Foreign Policy* 23 (Summer 1976), p. 167.

13. Ibid, p. 176.

14. Amory B. Lavins, *Business Week,* December 25, 1978, p. 44.

15. Ibid.

16. *Nuclear Engineering International* 29, no. 360 (October 1984), p. 2.

17. *Nuclear Engineering International,* 29, no. 360 supp. (October 1984), p. 3.

18. *Confidential Report to Irwin J. Landes,* chairman, Corporations, Authorities and Commissions Committee; by William F. Haddad, director, Office of Legislative Oversight and Analysis, New York State Legislature, May 20, 1977/revised, p. 4.

19. *Nuclear Engineering International* 30, no. 364 (January 1985), p. 6.

20. *Nuclear Engineering International* 29, no. 360 supp. (October 1984), ibid.

21. *Nuclear Engineering International* 30, no. 366 (March 1985), pp. 21–23.

22. *Nuclear Engineering International* 29, no. 362 (November 1984), p. 6.

23. Rupert Emerson, *From Empire to Nation* (Boston: Beacon, 1960), p. 96.

24. Karl Deutsch, *Nationalism and Social Communication* (New York, Wiley, 1953).

25. *Defense White Paper,* Republic of South Africa, June 1973, p. 2.

26. *Washington Post,* July 2, 1978, p. A1.

27. John E. Spence, *The Political and Military Framework* (Upsala, Sweden: Africana Publication Trust, 1975), p. 80.

28. George Quester, *The Politics of Nuclear Proliferation* (Baltimore: Johns Hopkins University Press, 1973), p. 801.

29. Edouard Bustin, "South Africa's Foreign Policy Alternatives and Deterrence Needs," in Onkar Marwah and Ann Schulz, eds., *Nuclear Proliferation and the Near-Nuclear Countries* (Cambridge, Mass.: Ballinger, 1975), p. 223.

30. John Spence, "South Africa: The Nuclear Option," *African Affairs* 80, no. 321 (October 1981), pp. 441–52; Richard Betts, "A Diplomatic Bomb for South Africa," *International Security* 4 p. 2, (Fall 1979), pp. 91–115.

31. Robert Jaster, "Politics and the 'Afrikaner Bomb'," *Orbis* 27, no. 4 (Winter 1984), pp. 825–50; Leonard Spector, *Nuclear Proliferation Today* (New York: Vintage/Random House, 1984), pp. 277–307; Kenneth Adelman and Richard Knight, "Can South Africa Go Nuclear?" *Orbis* 23, no. 3 (Fall 1979), pp. 642–43.

32. Kenneth Adelman and Richard Knight, *Impact upon U.S. Security of a South African Nuclear Weapons Capability* (Washington, D.C.: SRI International, April 1981).

33. Pierre Lellouche, in C. Raja Mohan, "Atomic Teeth to Apartheid: South Africa and Nuclear Weapons," *Institute for Defense Studies and Analysis Journal* 12 (January-March 1980), p. 264.

34. Ibid.

35. Steve Chan, "Incentives for Nuclear Proliferation: The Case of International Pariahs," *Journal of Strategic Studies* 3, no. 1 (May 1980), p. 30.

36. Ibid., pp. 37–38.

37. Ryukichi Imai and Henry Rowen, *Nuclear Energy and Nuclear Proliferation* (Boulder, Colo.: Westview, 1980), p. 142.

38. Marshall Schulman, "The Utility of Nuclear Weapons," in Mason Willrich, ed., *Civil Nuclear Power and International Security* (New York: Praeger, 1971), p. 90.

2
Nuclear Weapons Capability

S outh Africa has developed one of the most formidable nuclear infrastructures available to a second-level state in the international system. I will describe some of the facilities comprising its growing capability, emphasizing, of course, those aspects that are directly amenable to the fabrication of nuclear weapons. Accordingly, this description will look at the development of reactors, uranium mining and enrichment, and the Koeberg power plant as the basic weapons-related infrastructure. I will then suggest ways in which weapons fabrication could have been achieved.

In general, the South African nuclear program should be conceived as a part of the Western development of nuclear capability after World War II. President Jan Smuts appointed a Uranium Research Committee in 1946 that resulted in the Atomic Energy Act being passed in 1948, establishing the South African Atomic Energy Board in March 1949. South Africa first exported uranium in 1952 to the Combined Development Agency established by its wartime allies, the United States and Great Britain. This relationship began the uranium-industry–fostering operations devoted to the mining, extraction, and sale of uranium concentrates, as well as mineral exploration, the distribution and control of radioisotopes, and the study of heavy water production.

In 1957, however, the Atomic Energy Research and Development Program was initiated. It was completed in 1958, and adopted by the government at the end of 1959. It envisioned a substantial expansion of nuclear research and development activities, based upon a five-year plan which included scientific concentration upon these activities currently underway, as well as new fields such as electric power production and the more efficient utilization of the country's major nuclear resource—uranium.[1]

Such an expansion, however, could not occur without a major government-financed nuclear research center, so construction began at Pelindaba, near Pretoria, in mid-1961. By July 1963, critical buildings were completed which were dedicated to housing reactor research, chemistry, the accelerator, and water purification. The country's nuclear development did not rest on this facility alone, as research facilities were established for theoretical topics at institutions such as the Southern Universities Nuclear Institute and the government-sponsored Council for Scientific and Industrial Research (CSIR). In addition, considerable scientific expertise existed in the industrial sector where, for example, chemical and metallurgical work were concerned. Then, recruitment yielded a core of expatriate Western scientists who complemented the technical assistance from major Western nations, either directly or through agencies such as the International Atomic Energy Agency (IAEA), of which South Africa was one of the eight founders.[2]

Uranium

Uranium is a fuel mineral mined in its raw state in South Africa, most of which is processed as a by-product of gold mining in the Witwatersrand geological system. The presence of uranite was first noted in 1923, in the Witwatersrand ores; in 1945, ore-testing programs there were associated with the defense needs of Britain and the United States.[3]

In 1967, when the uranium trade between South Africa and the United States ceased, the Nuclear Fuels Corporation (NUFCOR) of South Africa came into existence. NUFCOR was one of the several "parastatal" corporations in South Africa which combined private consortia in a joint venture with the government participating as the controlling interest. This organization facilitated research into more efficient processes for recovering low-grade uranium ores from the gold slimes, sponsored exploration for other mining sites, and developed alternative markets for the product. For example, through NUFCOR, the initial economic feasibility of mining the Rossing uranium deposits in Namibia was established in 1969. Regular production levels were planned by NUFCOR to be reached by 1976 or 1977 at an annual rate of 5,000 tons with a maximum output of 13,000 tons in the 1980s.[4]

The Nuclear Development Corporation, the umbrella government agency created in 1984, took the place of the Atomic Energy Board. It evaluated the country's uranium resources, finding that total assured and speculative recoverable reserves exists at over 2 million tons, second only to the United States in magnitude. Production reached a high of 6,400 tons in 1959, and actually fell in the 1960s and 1970s, only reaching above the 6,000 level again in 1980, this level being achieved through the operation of nineteen plants.

As table 2-1 shows, production fell between 1980 and 1982, rising in 1983, but recently falling again. Nevertheless, it continues to constitute approximately 15 percent of world uranium production.

Table 2-1
Annual Uranium Production in South Africa, 1977–84
(tons per year metric)

1977	1978	1979	1980	1981	1982	1983	1984
3,360	3,961	4,797	6,146	6,131	5,816	6,038	5,694

Source: OECD and IAEA, *Uranium: Resources, Production and Demand* (Paris: OECD, 1983).

The problem of falling production is a response to falling prices for uranium, as the high production levels in the early 1980s created a supply-demand imbalance. The South African aspect of the upsurge in production in the late 1970s was due to the rising price of gold, since the output of uranium is tied to the production of gold at roughly a 3:1 ratio of gold-to-uranium, and there are few dedicated uranium-mining plants in South Africa. (In fact, the price of gold doubled, from the $200 per ounce level in the early 1970s to over $400 per ounce by the late 1970s.)

In most countries involved in various stages of nuclear energy, research and development, program details are protected from the scrutiny of researchers and other interested persons primarily in an effort to withhold what is regarded as sensitive information that would give to a military or commercial competitor undue advantages. In the case of South Africa, nuclear weapons proliferation may be an additional motive for keeping its nuclear data secret; thus, information regarding its uranium production is shielded by Act no. 90 promulgated in 1967. It "imposes severe sanctions on anyone (found) guilty of publishing material relating to the prospecting, production and pricing of uranium."[5]

The full impact of South Africa on the world uranium situation incorporates Namibian uranium. This is important because the combined production of South Africa and Namibia constitutes the largest operation in the world. The Rossing uranium mine, the largest open pit mine in the world, is managed by Rossing Uranium Ltd. and is owned by the British firm Rio Tinto-Zinc (RTZ). The major equity holders of which are the United Kingdom (46.5 percent), Industrial Development Corp. (a South African government agency—13.2 percent), Rio Algom of Canada (a subsidiary of RTZ South Africa—10 percent), Total-Compagnie Miniere et Nucleaire of France (10 percent), and General Mining and Finance Corp. of South Africa (6.8 percent). Through the weighted voting procedure administered on the basis of different classes of shares, and the leverage of the South African government in the collection of corporate taxes, South Africa (as a government and as shareholders) exercises the effective controlling interest in Rossing. In 1983, while estimates for the top producers such as the United States and Canada were 7.9 and 7.5 thousand tons of uranium respectively, the combined total of South Africa and Namibia was 9.6.[6]

This is important, since the increasingly autonomous nuclear position of South Africa will be based on its control of local uranium resources, and this resource is also directly pertinent to its ability to develop nuclear weapons.

Reactors

South African nuclear scientists have over the years received the kind of training and technical assistance in the use of nuclear materials from the United States and other Western powers that has made it possible for them to diversify their facilities. Critical in this regard was the degree to which South Africa took advantage of the "Atoms for Peace" program, begun by President Eisenhower in the 1950s, which emphasized the dissemination of information on such instruments as nuclear reactors.

In 1961, a U.S. light water reactor, later called the South African Fundamental Atomic Reactor Installation (SAFARI-1), was purchased by South Africa from the Allis Chalmers Manufacturing Co. It became operational in April 1965. A somewhat large reactor for research, it could also be utilized for simulations of power plant operations.[7] A second reactor, Pelinduna-Zero, was built and designed in South Africa for research into the building of nuclear power stations. It went into service in 1967.[8] These reactors operated at a low level in relation to power reactors, or at about 20 MWe and 10 MWe respectively. Nevertheless, while Pelinduna-Zero used 2 percent enriched uranium, SAFARI-1 utilized highly enriched uranium in the front end and produced plutonium in the waste material. As such, these plants were formidable instruments in the hands of the growing body of scientists South Africa was accumulating at its Pelindaba nuclear research facility in the 1960s and 1970s.

Uranium Enrichment Plant

A most important facility is the pilot uranium enrichment plant built with the aid of U.S. and West German technology. A.J.A. Roux, former chairman of the South African Atomic Energy Board (SAAEB) and then Prime Minister John Vorster announced in 1970, that South Africa had developed a technique for enriching uranium, an effort begun in 1968.[9] At that time, Vorster was not considered credible when he suggested that South Africa could accomplish such a feat. Nevertheless, as early as August 1973, it was revealed by the government that South Africa had indeed developed this new method for enriching uranium and that *it had produced a few tons of weapons-grade fuel* for its experimental nuclear reactor at Pelindaba.[10] In addition, a report prepared by the newly established Uranium Enrichment Corp. (UCOR) for the SAAEB, covering six months of research in 1973, intimated that the capital investment of the government in the pilot enrichment plant was less than 65 percent of that for a comparable diffusion plant, a fact that appeared to suggest a potentially favorable economic attraction to others interested in the technology.[11]

By November 1975, Minister of Mines Dr. Pieter Koornhof said that the full support of the government was involved in the decision to proceed with building a large-scale commercial uranium enrichment facility.[12] Earlier that year, at the European Nuclear Conference in Paris, South African government representatives announced that the uranium enrichment process had been perfected, and, while remaining secretive about full details of the technology, they described the process as aerodynamic, where the separating element was a stationary walled centrifuge.[13]

While an analysis of the technology of the enrichment process is outside the scope of this book, the description appears to confirm the achievement of their goal of providing enrichment by an efficient process of unique design for later commercial-scale exploitation. While the delegation optimistically suggested that testing would be completed and full operation would be achieved by the end of 1977, their optimism was tempered by the invitations from the government for a "shared approach" to the development of this technology "with friendly countries" participating in an "international venture."[14]

Natural uranium exports by South Africa earned approximately $3 billion in income from 1972 to 1982. However, raw uranium is far less valuable than enriched uranium because of the growing international demand for fuel for nuclear reactors and the few available processing centers. The government moved to acquire adequate financing in 1975, by creating a subsidiary of UCOR which sold shares to the public. This financing was based on the assumption that a new large-scale enrichment plant would be heavily financed from internal sources, have an initial capacity to produce about 5,000 tons of enriched uranium per year, and cost about $4.5 billion totally, while earning about $250 million a year in foreign exchange. These projections pleased both Prime Minister Vorster and Dr. Koornhof, while other analysts noted that the realization of a uranium enrichment capability would challenge the U.S.-European monopoly while adding to the strategic importance of South Africa as well.[15] The lack of international cooperation in the financing of the commercial-scale uranium enrichment plant, however, considerably lowered the scale of the plant and extended the time within which it would become operational. By mid-1986 no public notice had been given on whether a commercial-scale plant had reached final operational status.

Nuclear Power Plant

On the basis of studies carried out by the South African Electricity Supply Commission (ESCOM), SAAEB, the Council for Scientific and Industrial Research, various universities, and the government's Division of Sea Fisheries for Environmental Safety, by 1974, South Africa decided to construct a commercial-size light water reactor (LWR) plant for the production of electricity at Koeberg, near Capetown. Although this decision was made partly due to the safety features of the LWRs used in the United States, criticism of this safety factor by the British nuclear industry shows, again, the competitive responses to market decisions by alternate suppliers.

Nevertheless, South African strategy was to invite nine firms with experience in building LWRs to submit preliminary proposals before October 1974. The government's plan was to select a few submissions, ask the firms to produce a detailed proposal, and then hope that after selecting the firm, construction would start approximately in 1976, with the facility to be in operation in 1980.[16] This strategy was interferred with by the uproar created when groups in several countries discovered that their multinational firms were bidding on a contract that would result in South Africa having access to a mature nuclear power capacity. This, however, did not stop a French consortium of companies led by Framatome from winning the primary contract for construction of two 925-megawatt reactors; Alsthom Atlantique provided the turbine generators and Spie Batignolles provided the general engineering services. Of Westinghouse design, the plant was originally estimated to cost $1.2 billion, but the doubling of steel and power costs has pushed the cost nearer to $2.3 billion.[17]

Koeberg 1 had been scheduled to come on line in 1984. The first delay was caused by an explosive device planted by the military wing of the African National Congress, Umkhonto We Sizwe, on December 18, 1982, which caused a fire at the construction site and required extensive repair.

Table 2–2
Spending by South Africa on the Koeberg Station, 1976–84
(*$ millions*)

1976	$ 74.4
1977	103.2
1978	181.2
1979	254.4
1981	241.2
1982	156.0
1983	93.6
1984	60.0

Source: *Nuclear Engineering International* (September 1977), p. 48.

Then, there was the scramble to find fuel for the reactors. South Africa had signed a long-term contract with the U.S. Dept. of Energy to supply the highly enriched uranium fuel for operating Koeberg reactors until the South African uranium enrichment plant could become operational. However, in 1978, the new U.S. nuclear export policy required that all South African nuclear facilities be put under the international safeguard inspection system of the IAEA and that the nation sign the NPT. Because South Africa refused, this supply agreement was not honored. The fuel was purchased by South Africa, nevertheless, on the spot market by two U.S. firms—Edlow International and Swuco—acting as brokers. Koeberg-1 finally went critical on March 14, 1985, and was scheduled to reach full power by July. Koeberg-2 was scheduled for fuel loading in September of the same year.[18]

The close proximity to the start-up date of the Koeberg plant had sparked some debate in the South African Parliament concerning costs, safety, and plans for additional nuclear facilities. It was the task of Fredrik de Klerk (director of ESCOM, which operates Koeberg) to reply to one question with the statement that "the construction of other nuclear power stations cannot be excluded."[19] While Parliament was somewhat pleased by the fact that costs had dropped during the past few years of construction, internal critics of Koeberg have seized upon the problem that no suitable waste disposal sites have been located and that Koeberg was built upon an earthquake fault. The task of dealing with these technical questions has been handled partially within the framework of a new nuclear regime Parliament created in 1982, establishing an Atomic Energy Corporation, a Council for Nuclear Safety, and criteria for the licensing of nuclear activities.

This debate, however, did not include another issue—the release of radioactive airborne effluents from Koeberg which would move out from the coast over Robben Island, the site of the infamous prison containing hundreds of blacks. When the Koeberg site was chosen, the CSIR meteorological experiments with wind behavior in the Cape region clearly showed that

> a release of airborne effluent from Koeberg into the land breeze layer would move out over the sea towards Robben Island, to be returned to land in the Cape Town area by the increasing NW component of the surface winds south of Robben Island.[20]

The essential question here appears to be how far the effluents travel near Robben Island since the scientific experiments performed by CSIR indicated that sea breezes would move from the approximate area of Koeberg out over the Robben Island region.[21] Moreover, charts of the wind patterns clearly show Robben Island in the path of the wind system from 30 to 60 percent of the year. Given that medical science has established a causal connection between exposure to radiation and incidence of cancer, this aspect of the Koeberg plant operation would appear to pose a great hazard to the inmates of Robben Island, as well as, perhaps, to the Cape Town population.

Nuclear Weapons Capability

As noted, data on aspects of South African nuclear capability have been released at times and in quantities to signal scientific achievement in research and development. No doubt, these disclosures were directed toward the political objective of making possible estimates of the regime's capability to produce materials for nuclear explosions based on extrapolations which consider their level of technological development thus far, and the normative utilization of material to which they have access. The route to the acquisition of necessary materials of weapons grade is varied, but some observers estimate South Africa's stockpile of nuclear weapons to be as high as 40 or more.[21] The possible scenarios below attempt to examine how this may have been achieved.

Plutonium Production

The use of either South African or U.S. fuel in SAFARI-1 is safeguarded under a tripartite agreement among the two countries and the IAEA. Nevertheless, South Africa could have abrogated this agreement and stockpiled the spent fuel rods until an appropriate time for reprocessing of weapons-grade plutonium by a third country, or it could have reprocessed the spent fuel itself, extracting and stockpiling the separated plutonium.

The 20-MWe SAFARI-1 research reactor utilizes 90 percent enriched uranium, and was operated at 5 MW from the time it began in 1965 to April 1968, when it was boosted to its full operational capacity of 20 MW, operating at that level from February 1969 to mid-1986 (with occasional shutdowns). Since it began operation, the United States has supplied 104 kilograms (230 pounds) of enriched uranium to the facility. If it is true that this reactor could produce enough plutonium to construct one atomic bomb every three or four years (at 10 MW), as one observer says, then it would appear to have the capacity to construct twice that amount.[22]

Less is known about the capacities of Pelinduna-Zero, which is reputed to be much smaller than SAFARI-1 and built by the South Africans themselves. The most likely source of enriched uranium fuel for Pelinduna-Zero would be locally produced fuel, since the use of U.S. fuel for this reactor would involve safeguards.

The largest reactors, however, are those at the 1,844-MWe Koeberg nuclear power plant, which will be both the largest consumer of low enriched uranium and the largest producer of spent fuel as a consequence. It has been established that a 2,000-MWe reactor electricity-generating capacity also produces 400 to 600 kgs. of plutonium in one year. Highly concentrated plutonium-240 is usable for fabrication of nuclear weapons once reprocessed from spent fuel, and estimates are that theoretically fifty bombs per year, depending upon the technology, might be produced.[23]

My point concerning whether or not South Africa actually has weapons-grade plutonium is obscured by the lack of information regarding its access to reprocessing facilities required for the extraction of plutonium from spent fuel. In 1976, Myron Kratzer (then deputy assistant secretary of the Bureau of Oceans and International Environmental and Scientific Affairs at the U.S. Dept. of State) testified before Congress that the U.S. government did not allow South Africa to build up large stocks of enriched uranium, supplying it "as needed" on a "common sense basis." But he also indicated that "After irradiation, we *encourage* it to be returned to either the United States or some other country for reprocessing" (emphasis added).[24] Indeed, an inspection of the imports of high enriched spent fuel waste from South Africa to the United States for reprocessing indicates an episodic record, leading to the conclusion that either such waste material is being reprocessed in other countries or it is being stockpiled in South Africa.[25] In fact, testimony from the congressional hearing referred to above indicated that other nations may reprocess the fuel and return it to South Africa without the direct oversight of the United States government.[26] Given the notoriously faulty monitoring system of the IAEA, it is possible that materials from South Africa have not been subject to a rigorous system of materials accounting. Therefore, despite the IAEA agreement between South Africa and France, for example, so much of the system of inspection of materials depends upon South African notification of IAEA officials that exports or imports of materials are occurring that IAEA's monitoring capability is highly suspect.

There remains the possibility that South Africa itself is capable of reprocessing spent fuel, given the sophisticated state of its chemical industry and its chemical research facility at Pelindaba. Indeed, experts suggest that reprocessing might be accomplished without large capital outlay. "There seems little doubt that almost any state with a modest chemical industry could on its own build a reprocessing plant large enough to supply plutonium to a small explosive program."[27] Nevertheless, it was the specific view of officials at the U.S. Energy Research and Development Administration (ERDA, now the Dept. of Energy), that, "a country with a technical infrastructure such as South Africa possesses has the capability of at least constructing a laboratory of pilot-scale reprocessing facility."[28]

These officials went on to question whether or not sufficient incentive existed for South Africa to expend resources for such a facility. Other experts indicate that, inasmuch as the technological variations of systems designed to achieve reprocessing range from the relatively inexpensive to the more expensive (depending upon reactor design, degree of purity of plutonium required, amounts needed, and so forth), the problem for a country such as South Africa is more one of incentives than costs.[29] I will attempt to show that the political incentives for South Africa have consistently outweighed economic costs.

Enriched Uranium

Despite the possibility of the plutonium route to nuclear weapons fabrication, experts agree that enriched uranium constitutes the most likely source. U.S. officials have, in the past, asserted that there are no stockpiles of enriched uranium in South Africa from U.S.-supplied materials. However, the fact that South Africa does not allow complete on-site inspection of its nuclear facilities by anyone mitigates against such certain statements. In addition, since the above discussion suggests that South Africa has not been subject to strict materials accounting, the possibility exists that after more than a decade of receiving supplies of highly enriched uranium from the United States, some imports could have been diverted to a stockpile for the production of nuclear weapons.

Within this category, however, it is probable that South Africa has had access to its own stores of enriched uranium since its pilot enrichment plant became operational in 1974, and especially since 1976, when the enrichment process was announced to have been "perfected" by government officials. In any case, the nation has supplies of raw uranium and an unsafeguarded pilot enrichment plant. Although the capacity of this process only enriches uranium to a level of 3 to 5% with one pass-through, it could enrich uranium to weapons grade with multiple recycling of the material. Given more than a decade of operation, the regime could have developed a considerable stockpile of enriched uranium for a weapons program. It should also be noted that if such a stockpile exists, it is probably dedicated to weapons fabrication, since the government might have purchased low enriched uranium on the open market for Koeberg's first fuel loading to avoid revealing the existence of its own supply.

Again, the lack of complete information about the South African nuclear program should prevent one from simply assuming that it automatically has to use 90 percent enriched uranium in a weapons program. It has been suggested that a weapon may be fabricated from as little as 10 percent enriched uranium, although the standard practice is to enrich it nearer to 90 percent. It should also be noted that the kind of enrichment

process chosen by South Africa is considered to be comparatively unde-
manding in the production of weapons.

> The South African aerodynamic processes are probably least demanding
> in manufacturing capabilities and capital requirements, and this would
> seem to be their major advantage over the centrifuge for small scale weap-
> ons manufacture.[30]

The exact capacity of the enrichment plant to be built at the Koeberg
site has been shrouded in secrecy, although it is known that in February
1978, Minister of Mines Fannie Botha said that the pilot plant would be
converted to a "relatively small" uranium enrichment production facility
which would "eventually" have the capacity to meet South Africa's needs.[31]
Reputable estimates in 1985 placed plant capacity at 300 metric tons (sepa-
rative work units), suggesting that the plan is "due to be commissioned by
the second half of this decade."[32]

One reason for the government's caution may be its declining ability to
obtain long-term financing in general. In the 1970s, long-term investments
in South Africa began to dry up. Since it had already borrowed heavily on
the international market, the burden of the costs of more expensive domestic projects would increasingly be left to local capital sources.[33] In any case,
the drastic reduction in the scale of the enrichment plant doubtless affected
its initial revenue projections and its status in the market. It should also
effect projections of nuclear explosive devices possible per year, given the
eventual capacity of the plant.

Another important, though admittedly remote reason for such caution
and the reduction in the scale of the plant may have been a decision by the
government not to invest too much in current technology when more efficient methods of uranium enrichment are on the horizon. This can only
explain why in the last few months of 1976, South African government
representatives made inquiries at several scientific laboratories in the United
States about laser isotope technology applications in uranium enrichment.[34] For more than a decade, private and government agencies in Israel,
France, and the United States have conducted research into laser enrichment methods and have concluded that considerable cost savings could be
achieved through the employment of such a technology. Normally, the
aerodynamic technique requires about two thousand successive stages or
"cascades" to produce enriched uranium of weapons grade, while the laser
process accomplishes the same task (or nearly so) with only a single pass-
through. Thus, the resulting cost saving is the source of the momentous
decision recently made by the U.S. Dept. of Energy to switch entirely to
laser enrichment technology.[35]

Alternative Sources of Explosives Production

Although nuclear explosions are usually made from uranium or pluto-nium, they can also be produced from oxides of these materials, though they do not perform as well as explosions made from the "parent" mate-rials. Nevertheless, it is assumed that such a bomb would be of sufficient explosive power as to yield an effective weapon in an area where the absence of a counter nuclear capability would lessen the drive for maxi-mum efficiency. It is important to note that there are a number of fuel cycles employing thorium (including the light water reactor) because of such advantages as the plentiful supply of thorium in nature and its com-patibility with other fissile isotopes.[36] Since it is, therefore, possible to use thorium in a nuclear weapons program, evidence that South Africa has used this material in experimental nuclear research might suggest an attempt to diversify its explosive capability. On October 29, 1973, a license was issued to the Kerr-McGee company for the export of 183.4 pounds of thorium to South Africa.[37]

Delivery Systems and Supporting Technology

The point has been well made that apart from the ability to explode a nuclear device, the credibility of this capability as a weapon rests in the ability to deliver it accurately to a chosen target. The growing sophistica-tion of tactical nuclear weapons makes possible this delivery by small mis-sile launchers such as a 155mm Howitzer, normally a conventional military weapon. The manufacturing capability of the South Africans is such that the production of this weapon has just been announced. It should be remembered that such an advanced cannon (with a range of 75 miles) and shells were surreptitiously exported to South Africa by the Space Research Corporation (U.S. defense contractor headquartered on the Canadian border) in 1977 and 1978.[38]

Otherwise, the consensus suggests that South Africa has possession of viable aircraft such as the Canberra B(I)12, which is regarded as a light bomber with a maximum range of 2,000 miles. This would put most targets in southern and south-central Africa within its reach. In addition, Dr. Frank Barnaby of the Stockholm International Peace Research Institute (SIPRI) has summarized other possible nuclear-capable delivery systems to include: the U.S. A-4 Skyhawk, F-104 Star-fighter, F-4 Phantom, Honest John, Lancer, Pershing, and Sergeant; the French Mirage 5; the British Canberra and Buccaneer bombers; the Soviet Ilyushin 28, Scud, and Frog missiles; and the Israeli Jerico missile.[39] Of these systems, South Africa has a version of the French Mirage, the Canberra and Buccaneer bombers, and the Jerico missiles, plus missiles of its indigenous development.

An analysis of South African missile development by SIPRI indicates that extremely close relations with West Germany have produced a functional capability in this area. In 1963, an initial contact was made by Herman Abs, a West German banker, offering cooperation in nuclear research, the outcome of which was the establishment by the Lindau and Harz Group of a rocket research center and an ionosphere station in Namibia at Tsumeb. Then, in the same year, it was announced that "South Africa was engaged in research to develop military rockets of an unspecified nature," and

> when the Rocket Research Institute was established one year later, Professor A.J.A. Le Roux said that South Africa had been *forced by events in Africa* to enter the missile field. That same year the Cactus project began in France (emphasis added).[40]

In 1968, the South African Defense Department in cooperation with a West German firm constructed a missile range at St. Lucia, 100 miles north of Durban and 40 miles from the Mozambique border. On December 17, 1968, it began test firing the first missiles. The system produced, in 1969, the Crotale, adapted from the French Cactus ground-to-air missile and manufactured under French license.[41] By 1973, the Propulsion Division of the National Institute for Defense Research was established for work on the various phases of missile development, including warheads.

The above picture relative to missile development also includes a companion project called Advocaat, a radar communications project developed largely in cooperation with West German scientists, who supplied the materials and technology. For instance, the $25 million project facilities were installed by Siemens AG and AEG-Telefunken, with Siemens delivering $3 million in equipment in 1970 alone. The project equipment consisted of shortwave transmitters, relay stations, telephone and telex stations, and computerized data processing capability; its major location is at the Cape Town central headquarters; regional headquarters are at Port Elizabeth, Durban and, Walvis Bay in Namibia.[42]

Advocaat is apparently quite versatile, assisting the South African government in its internal security by monitoring the identity and movement of the nonwhite population and also monitoring naval traffic (including Soviet submarine movements) in the South Atlantic and Indian Oceans. It has also been suggested that Advocaat supplies down-range clearance information for missile guidance and tracking, making it an indispensable part of the strategic inventory of South Africa.

It should be noted that the "events" to which Dr. Le Roux referred in 1963, were probably the founding of the Organization of African Unity and its strong declarations against apartheid which provided the stimulus for the development of the missile program of South Africa. But it is just as rational that they may also have accelerated the decision to acquire nuclear weapons. Further evidence of the farsightedness of the South Africans can be seen in the development of the SASOL oil-from-coal project (South African Coal, Oil and Gas), which anticipated the nation's vulnerability to supply dependence on oil.[43]

Israeli arms sales to South Africa also provide a context for missile cooperation, as the Gabriel missile has been sold to South Africa. Although normally a surface-to-surface missile, it will be used mounted on patrol boats. Also, the relatively small Lance missile may be a candidate for sale to South Africa, a possibility made likely by the sale of 200 Lance missiles to Israel by the United States in 1975. One weapons expert has suggested that "it would not be too difficult for Israel to develop an atomic warhead to fit into the relatively small Lance missile," a one-kiloton weapon with a range of 70 miles and a payload of 1,000 lb.[44] However, the Jerico, which Israel has already sold to South Africa, carries a larger payload of 1,200 pounds.

Finally in 1983, Fred Bell, managing director of the Armaments Development and Production Corp. (ARMSCOR), announced that the missile testing range at St. Lucia in Natal was being replaced by a new land acquisition in the southern cape coast. The new facility would cover 243,000 acres and was described as equalled only by more advanced facilities in the Soviet Union or the United States. Suggesting that this was a response to the arms embargo, Bell indicated that ARMSCOR had affected a "planning horizon" of at least twenty years in which to respond to the demand for more advanced weapons systems traveling greater distances. The development of the range was projected to be completed by the 1988–90 time period, and would undoubtedly give South Africa the capability to test missiles that could reach military targets considerably beyond the Southern Africa area.[45]

The Neutron Bomb

In 1979 and 1980, flashes in the sky off the southern coast of South Africa led to speculation that there had been a nuclear explosion. Some felt that the explosion's effect resembled that of a neutron bomb. Scientists suggested that the paucity of verifying evidence such as radioactive fallout might indicate that a neutron bomb had been exploded and that it might have been the result of a collaboration between Israel and South Africa. One reason for this conclusion was that both countries were known to have been engaged in fusion research; in fact, for some time, the South African Atomic Energy Board has taken "an active interest in controlled thermonuclear or fusion energy and hence plasma research."[46]

The South Africans have constructed a medium-sized tokamak, used in plasma research, named Tokoloshe, and have been involved in an experimental program of attempting to produce satisfactory controlled thermonuclear reactions by the fusion technique since 1980. South African scientists speculate that the rationale for the government's entry into this form of research is based on the existence of advanced programs in other countries, which, if successful, will greatly effect the economic position of fission reactors and the uranium market upon which South Africa depends. Although this is entirely possible as a motive, the South Africans still might have advanced to the point, especially in collaboration with other countries such as Israel, where a program of fission research is also in operation, and where testing of an explosive device produced by fission reaction has occurred.

Conclusion

Chapter 1 strongly inferred that South Africa had a major motive for balancing its future security interests with the acquisition of what it considered to be the ultimate weapon—a nuclear weapons capability. This chapter has provided statements by South African officials to the extent that events of the early 1960s on the African continent (including, presumably those inside South Africa as well) *forced* the regime to consider the development of weapons systems such as missiles. In this connection, the point was made that it would be folly to consider that they would dismiss the objective of planning to develop armaments for those missiles of the most destructive explosive power available.

Therefore, this chapter has concentrated on the nuclear infrastructure of South Africa, concluding that, in the terms of a 1977 report of the Office of Technology Assessment (OTA), South African facilities enable it to meet the objective criteria of a nation capable of rapidly developing nuclear weapons.[47] It has made the investment and, thus, satisfied the OTA criteria of *cost*; it has *rapid access to special nuclear fissile materials* such as enriched uranium and plutonium; and it has the *military technological capability* to fabricate weapons. Furthermore, in an attempt to sharpen the connection between resources and the routes to weapons production, I have shown that critical South African facilities for the production of special nuclear materials (such as its pilot enrichment plant and a research reactor) are unsafeguarded. Also, regarding the pressures under which the regime considers itself to be existing, the possibility has not been excluded that current safeguard agreements covering SAFARI-1, the Koeberg nuclear power plant, or the use of U.S.-supplied highly enriched uranium would be abrogated in a covert operation to manufacture nuclear weapons.

One argument that has always made South African motivation for entering into nuclear power development suspect to critics is that it was necessary for the production of electricity in the future. Despite the fact that South Africa experienced electricity shortages as recently as Winter 1981, the question has remained why it has chosen nuclear power over other forms of energy. In a work treating the development of South African nuclear capability more extensively than I have attempted to do here, Barbara Rogers and Zdenek Cervenka suggest that the South Africans wanted to preserve their considerable coal resources, the third largest in the world, for export.[48] In particular, the initiation of Koeberg was viewed as a response to the oil shock of OPEC at the end of 1973, and as an additional means to counter dependency upon imported oil. In his study of South African electrification, Renfrew Christie supports this view, adding that another motive for the initiation of the uranium industry was strategic and that the expansion of the nuclear industry in the 1970s, was to maintain access by industry and privileged individuals to the cheapest electricity in the world. This cheap energy was in large part made possible by apartheid wages paid to black workers in the labor-intensive mining industry.[49] The result of this pattern of energy development is that South Africa now exports several kinds of energy resources.

Such an understanding puts into perspective the sentiments expressed by South African government officials such as Dr. Louw Alberts, vice president of SAAEB. In a lecture in Grahamstown, South Africa in 1974, Alberts said that this resource puts South Africa in a powerful bargaining position.[50] One year later, this concept was supported by Pieter W. Botha (then defense minister), who, in an interview with *Der Spiegel* published in South Africa on South African military power, added that South Africa "theoretically" had the ability to produce an atomic bomb as a result of its level of nuclear technology, but that it would use its resources for "peaceful purposes."[51] These sentiments, however, should be balanced by the belligerent statement of a cabinet minister in 1977 hinting at the use of nuclear weapons in the ultimate defense of South Africa.[52] The point to be made by such statements is that South African officials have been aware for some time of the capability given them by twenty-five years of nuclear development. Should analysts of the international politics of Southern Africa continue to presume that the ability to manufacture nuclear weapons by the regime is merely potential and not as well-established fact? Perhaps the following analysis of the attempted testing of nuclear explosives will give additional credibility to the extent of the development of this capability.

Notes

1. *Pelindaba* (South Africa: National Nuclear Research Center, South African Atomic Energy Board, 1964).

2. Barbara Rogers and Zdenek Cervenka, *The Nuclear Axis* (New York: New York Times Books, 1978).

3. S.A. Finney, "Recovery of Uranium as a By-product in the Processing of Gold Ores," SM-135/28 (Vienna: Atomic Energy Agency, 1971).

4. *Mining Magazine* (July 1977), p. 9.

5. Leonard Beaton, "The International Political Context," in Mason Willrich, ed., *Civil Nuclear Power and International Security* (New York: Praeger, 1971), p. 78.

6. *Uranium: Resources, Production and Demand* (Paris: OECD/IAEA, December 1983), p. 30.

7. *Mining Magazine* (October 1977), p. 333.

8. John Spence *The Political and Military Framework* (Upsala, Sweden: Africa Publication Trust, 1975), p. 219.

9. A.J.A. Roux and W.L. Grant, "Uranium Enrichment in South Africa: Nuclear Energy Maturity," *Proceedings of the European Nuclear Conference*, Paris, April 21-24, 1974.

10. A.J.A. Le Roux, W.L. Grant, R.A. Barbour, R.S. Loubser, and J.J. Wannenburg, "Development and Progress of the South African Enrichment Project," a paper presented at International Conference on Nuclear Power and its Fuel Cycle, International Atomic Energy Agency, Salzburg, Austria, May 2-13, 1977.

11. *The Times* (London), August 20, 1973, p. 1.

12. Ibid, p. 7.

13. Ibid.

14. Ibid.

15. "Uranium Stake Offered by State," *The Star* (Johannesburg), June 11, 1975, p. 3; "South Africa Capable of Making Atom Bomb," *The Times* (London), April 8, 1975, p. 5.

16. Marais Malan, "Research Backs S. Africa Claim of N-Reactor," *The Star* (Johannesburg), August 2, 1974, p. 18.

17. *Nuclear Engineering International* (September 1977), p. 48.

18. *Nuclear Engineering International* 29, no. 355 (May 1985), p. 6; *Nuclear Engineering International* 29, no. 356 (June 1985), p. 11.

19. *Nucleonics Week* 23, no. 8 (February 25, 1982), p. 8.

20. D. van As, D.E. Norden, and P.S. Botha, "Who Knows Where the Westerlies Blow?," *Nuclear Active* 25 (July 1981), pp. 8-11.

21. Ibid.; Leonard Spector, *Nuclear Proliferation Today* (New York: Vintage/Random House, October 1984), p. 305.

22. Frank Barnaby, "Africa and Nuclear Energy," *Africa* 69 (May 1977), p. 92.

23. Frank Barnaby, "Nuclear South Africa," in *United Nations International Seminar on the Implementation and Enforcement of the Arms Embargo against South Africa* (London: United Nations Center Against Apartheid, March 1981), p. 6.

24. "U.S. Policy toward Africa," *Hearings, Subcommittee on African Affairs, Subcommittee on Arms Control, International Organizations and Security Agreements, Committee on Foreign Nations*, U.S. Senate, May 27, 1976 (Washington, D.C., U.S. GPO, 1976), p. 290.

25. Ibid, p. 317.

26. Ibid.

27. Ted Greenwood, Harold Feiveson and Theodore Taylor, *Nuclear Proliferation* (New York: McGraw-Hill, 1977), p. 18.

28. "Resource Development in South Africa and U.S. Policy," *Hearings, Subcommittee on International Resources, Food and Energy, Committee on International Relations*, U.S. House of Representatives, May 25, June 8, 9, 1976, appendix 6, p. 293.

29. O.J. Wich, ed., *Plutonium Handbook: A Guide to the Technology*, vol. 2, (New York: Gordon and Breach, 1967).

30. Greenwood et al., p. 25.

31. Fannie Krueger, "France in Nuclear Deal?," *The Star* (Johannesburg), February 14, 1978, p. 17.

32. *Uranium: Resources, Production and Demand*, p. 257.

33. "France in Nuclear Deal?," op. cit., p. 17.

34. Testimony of Ronald Segal, "U.S.-South Africa Relations: Nuclear Cooperation," Hearings, Subcommittee on Africa, U.S. House of Representatives, June 30, 1977, p. 21.

35. *Nuclear Engineering International* 29, no. 355 (May 1985), p. 6.

36. *Nuclear Proliferation and Safeguards*, op. cit., pp. VI, 15.

37. "U.S. Policy toward Africa," op. cit., p. 321.

38. "Enforcement of the United States Arms Embargo against South Africa," Hearings, Subcommittee on Africa, Committee on Foreign Affairs, U.S. House of Representatives, 97th Cong., March 30, 1982 (Washington, D.C.: U.S. GPO, 1982), appendix, pp. 41-92.

39. "Africa and Nuclear Energy," op. cit., p. 68.

40. Stockholm International Peace Research Institute, *Southern Africa: Escalation of a Conflict* (New York: Praeger, 1976), p. 143.

41. Ibid, p. 131.

42. Ibid, p. 134.

43. Ibid. p. 119.

44. *New York Times*, January 24, 1975, p. 6.

45. *The Citizen* (Johannesburg), March 24, 1983, p. 6.

46. E. van der Spuy, "Rationale for Plasma Research," *Nuclear Active* 24 (January 1981), p. 13.

47. *Nuclear Proliferation and Safeguards*, op. cit., pp. VI-15.

48. Rogers and Cervenka, *The Nuclear Axis*, op. cit., p. 163-65.

49. Renfrew Christie, *Electricity, Industry and Class in South Africa* (Albany: State University of New York Press, 1984), pp. 165-93.

50. *The Times* (London), July 12, 1974, p. 7.

51. *The Star* (Johannesburg), February 5, 1975.

52. Jim Hoagland, "S. Africa Within 2 Years of Atom Bomb," *International Herald Tribune*, February 17, 1977, p. 1.

3
Nuclear Weapons Testing: The September 22, 1979, Case

The testing of nuclear devices through the production of explosions is the most decisive sign of a weapons capability and a sure signal that a country has entered into the ranks of states possessing such military instruments. Testing, however, is not important to the use of nuclear weapons; it is well known that the bombs dropped over Hiroshima and Nagasaki were not tested before their use. However, testing may be important to establish the credibility of a different scale or variety of nuclear weapons technology by states such as South Africa which may not have the capability to conduct a nuclear program the size and standards of the major nuclear powers. Testing may also provide important political benefits over adversaries by signaling that proliferation has occurred and that a country has reached a certain stage of military power and sophistication sufficient to deter attack by others. In any case, testing should be regarded as something done *after* a weapon or device has been fabricated and, therefore, a signal that a state does, indeed, possess such a device. In fact, in the case of the 1977 nuclear testing facility discovered in the Kalahari Desert, Murray Marder and Don Oberdorfer of the *Washington Post* reported that, considering the advanced state of South African nuclear development, Carter administration planners proceeded on the assumption that "what was being built could be used."[1]

During the Carter administration, at least three such incidents came to public attention, providing observers with the strong suspicion that South Africa possesses a nuclear device. On August 8, 1977, the Soviet press reported that their satellites had detected a nuclear test facility on the ground in the Kalahari Desert near Namibia, a fact confirmed by the U.S. SR-71 satellite. There was substantial discussion among Western allies; then public pressure was brought to bear upon South Africa to dismantle the facility, to which the South African government eventually agreed. Then, on the night of September 22, 1979, the U.S. Vela satellite picked up the distinctive flash of a nuclear explosion in the Indian Ocean-Antarctic region near the coast of South Africa. After considerable monitoring and analysis, the scientific community disagreed as to the exact nature of this event, though credible sources still maintain that a nuclear explosion occurred.[2] Finally, on the night of December 16, 1980, another mysterious flash occurred in the approximate region as that of September 1979.

Is it possible that all of these indications of nuclear testing are false? The scientific verifications of these events have ranged from "99 percent sure" in the case of the test facility of August 1977, to "technically indeterminate" in the case of the September 1979 flash, to an apparent consensus inside the government that a meteoroid caused the December 16, 1980 event. The ambiguity of the verification of these incidents has caused predictable ambiguity in U.S. nuclear policy toward South Africa. Since the 1977 incident has been rather thoroughly discussed, perhaps one can examine the 1979 mysterious flash in an effort to understand whether or not the source of such ambiguity is entirely scientific.

The Vela Incident

Additional evidence of nuclear testing is found in reported events surrounding the September 1979 "mysterious flash," despite the reluctance of U.S. government officials to admit that South Africa had possession of a nuclear explosive capability. The public first knew that on September 22, at 3:00 A.M. (South African time), there had been detected the distinctive flash of a nuclear explosion by monitoring devices, on October 25, when John Scali of ABC News broke the story of this incident, which apparently had been leaked to him. The Dept. of State immediately issued the following statement:

> The United States Government has an indication suggesting the possibility that a low-yield nuclear explosion occurred on September 22 in an area of the Indian Ocean and South Atlantic including portions of the Antarctic Continent, and the southern part of Africa. No corroborating evidence has been received to date. We are continuing to assess whether such an event took place.[3]

Later that same day, a "high government official" was reported to have said to Congressman Steven Solarz (Dem. N.Y. and chair of the House Subcommittee on Africa) that U.S. monitoring instruments had detected an event consistent with known data characterizing a nuclear explosion. The next day, Secretary of State Cyrus Vance said that air sampling in the 4,500-mile area of the suspected explosion had been undertaken, but that nothing had yet been found, and that the development of a nuclear weapon by South Africa "would be a destabilizing and dangerous step forward."[4]

While the U.S. government appeared tight-lipped about the incident, the South Africans were ready with possible explanations. For example, the head of the South African Atomic Energy Board branded the reports of such an explosion "complete nonsense." Vice Admiral A.C. Walters, chief of the South African navy, suggested that they were investigating the possibility that an accident had occurred on board a Russian nuclear submarine then in the area.[5] The Soviet Union, of course, disagreed with the South African report involving what the Soviets called an "unidentified" nuclear submarine, suggesting instead that South Africa was "attempting to distract attention from itself."[6] Then, a chemist in the nuclear physics division of South Africa's Council for Scientific and Industrial Research (a government agency conducting nuclear research) stated that the incident was perhaps the result of the explosion of a missile of undetermined origin which was observed to have landed in the suspect area sixteen years earlier![7]

The information supposedly verifying the fact that a nuclear explosion had occurred was obtained from a U.S. government satellite, the Vela, one of two then in orbit that were specifically designed to detect nuclear explosions. (Since 1963, six pairs of Vela satellites had been launched into orbit; forty-one times the Vela had detected the double-pulse of intense light signaling a nuclear explosion. Furthermore, although the current satellites had been in orbit since 1970, the sensors had been calibrated just one week prior to the important sighting.) Since the Carter administration had lost the Strategic Arms Limitation Treaty partly on the strength of the perception in the Senate that it could not be verified, Secretary of State Cyrus Vance was quick to add at his initial press confrontation on this issue, "I would point out that within a period of an hour or so, the information picked up from the satellite had been reported back and we knew about it. So, the equipment which we had worked perfectly."[8]

Perhaps in response to ABC's public disclosure of the nuclear flash, a panel of experts was hastily established by White House Science Advisor Dr. Frank Press, who conducted the first series of two meetings on November 1 and 2. At this point, there were seven experts on the panel whom the White House refused to identify, but by the time of its final report, the group had grown to nine: Jack Ruina of MIT (chair), Luis Alvares of University of California at Berkeley, William Donn of the Lamont-Doherty Geological Observatory, Richard Garwin of Harvard University, Riccardo Giacconi of the Harvard-Smithsonian Center for Astrophysics, Richard Muller of Berkeley, W.K. Panofsky of Stanford University Linear Accelerator Center, Allen Peterson of Stanford University Research Institute, and F. William Sarles of MIT. They had been charged with the responsibility of examining alternative explanations for the Vela sighting, including possibly a "superbolt" of lightning, meteoroid events, or other such natural phenomena, and even whether or not the Vela had malfunctioned in some way.[9]

The major task of the press panel was to evaluate the growing evidence. For example, subsequent press reports indicated that immediately after the mysterious flash, the Air Force Technical Applications Center and the CIA reported finding acoustic soundings from listening posts in widely scattered areas of the world.[10] Then, on November 13, the New Zealand Institute of Nuclear Science at Gracefield (near the capital city of Wellington) reported detecting an increase in the measurement of radioactive fallout—possibly from a nuclear explosion with the force of between two to four kilotons—saying, "we've searched for other causes of this fallout but can find nothing else."[11] The increased radioactivity appeared in the samples of rainwater which were collected from August 1 to October 28, 1979, and which contained trace elements of three fission products of nuclear explosions. So convincing was the new evidence that by early January 1980, some experts on the White House panel were suggesting that a nuclear explosion had occurred. Especially suggestive at the time was another report of findings in January by the Arecibo Ionospheric Observatory in Puerto Rico that a team of scientists had observed in the ionosphere a ripple or wave moving from south to north at a time that could associate it with a possible nuclear explosion. This new finding was viewed by panel member Richard Garwin as the most believable piece of evidence that a nuclear explosion had occurred, although even this did not constitute confirmation.[12]

As the pattern of evidence began to provide dramatic confirmation that a nuclear explosion had occurred, the suddenness with which the credibility of the evidence became undermined was just as dramatic. For example, the acoustical data discovered by the Air Force and the CIA was withdrawn as having probably been "random background noise" in November 1979. Also, on October 26, 1980, the United Nations General Assembly requested the secretary general to make a report on this incident. In the secretary's report issued one month later, the South African government indicated that its Atomic Energy Board had discovered no evidence of radioactive fallout in its regular monitoring activities; the United States reported that the only evidence it possessed was the Vela sighting; and most important, a reanalysis of the New Zealand data on radioactive fallout by that government's National Radiation Laboratory revealed "no statistically significant levels of fresh fission products," all of which cast doubt on the credibility of the original findings. Inexplicably, the New Zealand report went on to make the amazingly strong statement: "It is clear from these reports, that scientific evidence and research in New Zealand does not verify reports that South Africa, or any other country, detonated a nuclear device in the southern hemisphere on or around 22 September 1979."[13]

The Arecibo evidence suffered a similar reduction of credibility after vigorous criticism by members of the White House panel. Garwin, who at first suggested the data to be a strong candidate for verification of a nuclear explosion, also said he personally doubted that so strong a ripple could have been made at such a great distance from the supposed scene of the explosion. Richard Bhenke and Lewis Duncan of the Arecibo Observatory, however, remained confident of their findings and expressed annoyance that their presentation before the panel was "an exercise in mass confusion," believing that the panel was unfamiliar with the capability of their method or the sophistication of their facility. The method of observation they were using had only been employed for two weeks before the event; it was pointed out that the Arecibo radar picked up such signals when the more traditional ionospheric monitoring instruments (which were also in use at their facility) recorded nothing at the time. Duncan in particular was reportedly surprised "that people have tried as much as they have to discredit [the findings]," since the panel proceeded to also find fault with calculations regarding the speed at which the ripple was travelling.[14] In the end, not even Duncan and Lewis, despite their belief in their own data, could associate the Arecibo findings with the possible nuclear event, although all agreed that it was "a piece of the puzzle."[15]

Despite the fact that it could be reported in January 1980 that the panel disagreed as to the nature of the event (which its report described as "technically indeterminate), the report was not released at that time because evidence continued to materialize. For instance, the CIA had speculated that South Africa and Israel were possibly involved because of previous levels of nuclear and military cooperation between the two countries. Indeed, the CIA reported to a congressional committee in January that a fleet of South African warships were conducting night maneuvers in the area of the suspected blast on the night of September 22.[16]

CBS News reported on February 21 that Israel in cooperation with South Africa had exploded a nuclear bomb near the coast of South Africa in September of 1979.[17] The *Washington Post* reported that the contents of a book to be published by two Israeli journalists stated that Israel had been making nuclear bombs for at least ten years; that it first had an offer from South Africa to test them in 1966; but that it did not accept this offer until September 22, 1979.[18] They also said that the Israelis had been cooperating with South Africa and Taiwan in the development of missile delivery systems, a fact which they said was confirmed by intelligence sources.[19] These reports which focused on the strong possibility of a joint effort between Israel and South Africa made the matter, in the words of Congressman Clement Zablocki (D-Wisc.), chair of the House Foreign Affairs Committee, "extremely delicate" and caused him to defer to the White House investigation.[20] The CIA information had also been shared with Congressman

Steven Solarz (then chair of the House Subcommittee on Africa), who had promised to hold hearings, but demurred perhaps for the same reason.

The Navy Investigation

It is quite possible that, although the press panel had reached a decision on the incident, the continuing intelligence reports uncovering new aspects and potential evidence constituted the wrong environment for the public to receive the panel's report with the desired credibility. Therefore, Dr. John Marcum of the White House Office of Science Technology Policy (OSTP) contacted Dr. Alan Berman, director of research at the Navy Research Laboratory (NRL), and requested a study of the Vela sighting that would take into consideration both the Arecibo data and other ionospheric data relevant to the event. Perhaps reflecting sensitivity to new reports regarding the possible involvement of Israel and South Africa, Marcum's request appeared urgent, inasmuch as he focused on the point that the Arecibo data was the only evidence supporting the veracity of the Vela sighting and, thus, confirmation of it was important, since "resolution of the origin of the September 22 signal is an important matter which has major foreign policy ramifications."[21]

Berman immediately proceeded to obtain the necessary clearances within NRL concerning such aspects as security, media relations, relations with other non-Navy agencies, and method of reporting between NRL and the White House OSTP. He established the study framework which consisted of (1) examining available experimental evidence, (2) formulating and evaluating hypotheses, (3) undertaking necessary computations, and (4) preparing pertinent reports on the data for transmission to appropriate users. He projected the study to be completed by May 15, 1980.

The first task was to confirm whether there had been a high-altitude or a low-altitude burst, because of the utilization of different data-gathering strategies based on these assumptions. The best evidence that there was not a high-altitude burst came from the Coast Guard's Omega Project which evaluated electromagnetic signals on various station paths. Recorded data from the triangular paths from Liberia, to Argentina, to La Reunion, to Liberia were examined at the purported time of the event; no evidence of any irregular signals was discovered. Thus, the researcher was able to say that "this implies that the effective dimensions of the wave-guide were not changed significantly or abruptly by a high altitude nuclear burst. . . . However, it is also well known that near-earth bursts . . . do not seem to produce observable effects on Omega phase data."[22] This appeared to confirm the negative results from the Air Force samplings of the upper atmosphere for radioactive fallout debris taken shortly after the Vela sighting.

The Los Alamos Scientific Laboratory had made inquiries to NRL about its study and any available data. To forestall additional inquiries, Dr. James Goodman, the NRL project manager, visited the lab in late February and talked with James Walker and Lewis Duncan, researchers at the Arecibo facility. They indicated that they were holding firm to their findings (the data having been recalculated), but they could not prove that there was a relationship between their sighting and the Vela sighting. Nevertheless, since their data continued to potentially corroborate the Vela sighting, NRL moved on to the assumption that there had been a low-attitude burst.

On March 5, Goodman examined data from a military satellite experiment by the Air Force for the time in question, and discovered that the satellite sensors had picked up evidence of an enhanced high-frequency radio wave which he reported as a "large-scale, low-amplitude disturbance."[23] He felt that this finding might be related to the Arecibo event because the high-frequency wave was not caused by a natural event, but through enhanced terrestrial noise, since it was observed at more than one frequency.

Both the Vela and the DMSP satellites were in good position to "see" the event in question at the time indicated. However, other weather satellites also showed storms in the immediate vicinity of Arecibo, Puerto Rico, at the time, all of which made Goodman feel that the ionospheric disturbance sighted by the observatory was caused by atmospheric gravity waves generated by Hurricane Eloise.[24] In addition, a researcher at NRL had indicated through computations that signals arriving at Arecibo from a one-kiloton nuclear burst would be too low to be detected. All of this weakened claims that the Arecibo data were related to the Vela flash, since Richard Garwin of the White House panel had argued the same thing. It should be remembered, however, that Duncan had argued that the sophistication of the Arecibo facility allowed it to detect such subtle ionospheric effects. So, NRL still had the impression that something had happened, but that it was not necessarily detected by the instruments at Arecibo. Where it had happened was still in doubt.

The thesis that the nuclear explosion occurred near water gained credence within the lab, based on findings supporting evidence from radio waves, from confirming studies of the lack of fallout in the upper atmosphere, and from another interesting source—a hypothetical model calculating the behavior of acoustic waves from a low-altitude, low-amplitude nuclear burst. The NRL researchers found that the results were "consistent with the model" in that the "wave period agreement appears good."[25] Thus, in connection with preparations for a naval expedition to the suspected area of detonation for samplings (Prince Edward and Marion Islands, owned by South Africa, 1,500 miles off its southern coast), the firmness of this assumption could be noted in the statement of an NRL investigator, who said that, "it is presumed that the device was detonated at the sea surface, probably on Natal Bank, a sea mount occurring on the shelf enclosing Prince Edward Island."[26] Further analysis of various sources of data through May continued to set the September 22 data apart, and caused NRL researchers to reach the conclusion that "the 22 Sept. event is still unique."[27]

With this rather firm evidence from several sources appearing to confirm the Vela sighting as having been a nuclear event, the NRL report was closed out and sent to the White House on June 30, 1980, even though all of the data requested had not been received. It was, therefore, of the most urgent importance to NRL researchers when the Marion Island acoustic records were later received and analyzed; they appeared to confirm previous findings. Goodman's view, presented in a memo to Berman, was that "some rather striking anomaly is in evidence in the Marion Island record," extending from 0045 universal time (ut) on September 22, 1979, to about 0230 ut, or the exact time of the Vela observation.[28] Goodman was careful to consider such "oscillations" in the ionosphere after midnight in this region as normal occurrences, but he did not consider normal what he described as a "bite-out," or a short empty space in the recorded acoustical signal tracings. He explained that:

> It is known that a ground level nuclear burst will produce a shock which will propagate through the ionosphere, elevating the temperature and changing the chemical reaction rates. . . . A 1 kiloton burst would produce a very slight increase in the free electronic loss rate . . . thus producing a slight hole [in the signal tracings].[29]

Berman immediately transmitted this data to Marcum of OSTP, and further indicated that "no similar effect was observed in ionosonde (acoustic) records which were taken at the same time at Johannesburg, Kerguelen and Grahamstown."[30] There appears no discoverable public response by the White House to this critical finding, perhaps since it shows a growing trend to reverse the initial statement of government officials that there was "no corroborative evidence" for the Vela sighting. At this point, there were the Vela sighting, the DMSP sighting, and acoustic records, all actual evidence confirmed by theoretical calculations.

Evidence of Fallout

New evidence supporting the Vela sighting was reported in a letter of September 25 to Berman from Dr. L. Van Middlesworth of the Dept. of Physiology and Biophysics, at the University of Tennessee College of Medicine. He said that for the past twenty-five years, he had examined cattle and sheep thyroids from Australia on a routine basis and that he believed that his samples for November 12 and 13 contained unusual levels of radium, a full six times above normal levels. He also explained that his report of this finding was late, inasmuch as he only discovered it nine months after the fact when additional funds made possible a reexamination of the set of samples for the entire year. Obviously, he believed this to be important, since he confessed to have never before discovered radioactive iodine in sheep thyroids.[31]

A reanalysis of the data by NRL confirmed the Middlesworth finding, although at a somewhat lower rate of five times higher than normal levels, while at the same time expressing a possible linkage between this data and the NRL's own findings. The problem here was the source of the iodine. The findings could have been easily explained if the source had been from normal facilities in the urban areas such as scientific laboratories, industrial plants, or health facilities. However, since these samples were taken from sheep grazing in the rural areas, the probable source was from grass contaminated by radiation from rainwater.

Berman felt the new data to be significant confirmation of the conclusions in the previous study, so he sent the Middlesworth data to Marcum as an annex to the NRL study, on November 3. But he also suggested a hypothesis concerning how the fallout could have been transported to Australia, consistent with the view that "NRL believes that there are significant indications that a nuclear detonation may have taken place on 22 September 1979, in the vicinity of Prince Edward and Marion Islands."[32] Berman reported the findings of NRL scientists showing that a "footprint" of the fallout trajectory would have taken it from the suspected site of the detonation to Australia in the region of the provinces of Victoria and Tasmania between September 26 and 27. The thought was that a radioactive cloud could have travelled this route and deposited the fallout in the grasslands where it could have been ingested by the sheep.

The team that prepared this hypothesis was headed by Dr. L. Ruhnke, who went on to explain the theory by observing that on September 22,

a major cyclone approached Marion Island and moved eastward. It could have been followed by satellite data as well as conventional weather maps until it reached Australia 6 days later. A trajectory analysis showed that a possible radioactive cloud was caught by this storm and stayed with it at least to September 28, 1979.[33]

Thus, this earlier study by Ruhnke appeared to provide a possible explanation for the transport of the radioactive material.

It should also be noted at this point that the early reports of fallout from New Zealand were also from a rainwater source, and although the Institute of Nuclear Sciences Lab at Gracefield (which reported the original finding of radiation in the rainwater) and the National Radiation Laboratory of New Zealand both finally concluded that their reanalysis of the data showed no evidence of fresh fallout, there are two remaining curiosities. One curiosity is that the Gracefield Lab conclusions are somewhat ambiguous, since they agree with the National Radiation Lab, but in doing so, they explain that the original samples must have been contaminated, while admitting, "we are still not certain what this radioactivity is" or how the contamination occurred.[34] The second anomaly is that the scientific data submitted to the United Nations by New Zealand appearing in the United Nations Report seem to indicate that the original findings of radiation in rainwater by the Gracefield Lab were based on rainwater samples taken from a period covering August 1 to October 28, while the subsequent analysis performed by the National Radiation Laboratory was based on samples taken from the month of October only.

Reviewing the evidence for the hypothesized trajectory analysis, the meteorological data show that, in fact, a weather system had deposited substantial amounts of rain on the Australian provinces in question on September 26. Second, if the trajectory of NRL were adjusted so that it began nearer to South Africa from the Antarctic and travelled the southern coast of Australia, it could possibly cover both the Australian province of Tasmania and the New Zealand areas in question. Third, Ruhnke gives the existence of the storm system and its "capturing" of radiation produced by the explosion as the main reasons why no radioactive debris was discovered by air force search teams sent out soon after the Vela sighting. He concluded that "a 2 kt explosion on 22 September 1979 under the prevailing meteorological conditions could not be detected more than 5 days later by airborne sampling methods, and under average meteorological conditions could not be detected at the existing sampling network."[35] Finally, Berman presented data to Marcum showing that (1) levels of cerium 144 found in surface air at the South Pole monitoring stations were at the highest levels in three years; (2) the gross gamma activity measured in surface air in October 1979 over Santiago, Chile, was the highest in three years; and (3) that levels of strontium 90 reported at the Santiago, Chile, monitoring station were the highest in four years.

While Berman felt that a strong case existed on the basis of his lab's analysis of the data, Marcum requested another opinion of these findings by the Dept. of Energy (DOE), which came to different conclusions. For example, in its report, DOE suggested (while not disputing NRL's finding regarding cerium 144) that another element, 95/Zr, would have been a better indicator of fresh fission, but no evidence of this was found; that the report of gross gamma concentrations in the air over Santiago had suffered "a typographical error of a decimal point," making the levels "well within the normal observations;" and that the evidence for strontium 90 was "weak" based on the absence of 95/Zr and the fact the half-life of strontium

90 is so long that for significant increases to occur, the theorized burst would had to have been much nearer the Chilean station.[36] Then, a DOE analysis of the sheep thyroid data suggested that the increase had been only *one* standard deviation from the norm. By February 1981, the statistical differences between the two agencies were resolved at 3.1 standard deviations; at this level, an NRL researcher was led to conclude: "a signal of this magnitude is unfortunately in a middle ground where it cannot be dismissed as a frequent occurrence nor can it be claimed with certainty to be different from background."[37]

Although the findings of DOE appeared to reduce the credibility of the NRL data concerning radioactive fallout and the evidence from sheep thyroids, it is important to keep in perspective that their findings *do not constitute a direct refutation of the NRL findings*. Rather, DOE raises indirect challenges to the veracity of the data on many points. It should be noted that the arguments over statistical methodology neither obliterated the uniqueness of the Middlesworth finding (especially considering his long experience with sheep thryroids) nor, therefore, the probability that evidence of fallout was discovered.

The Aftermath

The NRL investigation is covered here in some detail since, because the reports of other agencies have remained classified and withheld from public consumption, more is known about this analysis than many others, even though its full report to the White House was similarly withheld from the public. Still, from all accounts, there was a wide-ranging investigation of the Vela sighting by many agencies, which testifies to the significance accorded the event by the administration and the scientific community. Illustrating those groups' involvement in the ongoing investigation:

1. the Los Alamos Lab continued to analyze the Vela sighting;
2. Arecibo researchers reanalyzed their data and sought other confirming observations;
3. the Air Force Technical Applications Center continued to request data on the event;
4. the Arms Control and Disarmament Agency requested information on the NRL study;
5. the Livermore Lab requested data on the event.

Doubtless, there were many other individual private and government agencies interested in this phenomenon, but not all of them issued statements of findings. One agency that issued such a statement was the Defense

Intelligence Agency (DIA), which on July 14, 1980, said that the flash sighted by the Vela satellite on September 22 was probably a clandestine nuclear explosion.[38] Basing its finding on an analysis of the "optical flash" recorded by Vela, the DIA results were particularly interesting in confirming the accuracy of the instrument's performance. In this light, it was instructive that the long-held report of the White House Panel was released the following day and contained conclusions that appeared to cast doubt on this very point—the interpretation of the Vela sighting data itself.

In what was regarded by the press as a sanitized version of its final report, the press panel said that it met three times in reviewing all data and came to the following conclusion:

> Based on the lack of persuasive corroborative evidence, the existence of other unexplained zoo events which have some of the characteristics of signals from nuclear explosions, and the discrepancies observed in the September 22 signal, the panel considers it more likely that the signal was probably not from a nuclear explosion. Although we cannot rule out the possibility that this signal was of nuclear origin, the panel considers it more likely that the signal was one of the zoo events, possibly a consequence of the impact of a small meteoroid on the satellite.[39]

The basic reasoning given for the panel's ambiguous conclusion was that while the signal recorded by Vela was roughly characteristic of previously recorded low-yield nuclear explosions, this signal varied in that the twin flashes of light were not recorded with equal intensity by the sensors ("bhangmeters") aboard Vela. The sighting is shown on a graph as a double-humped signature, and since one hump is slightly smaller than the other, this feature, different from previously recorded signals, was enough to cast doubt upon the sighting as emanating from a nuclear explosion. The sighting was, therefore, classified as a "zoo event," meaning that of the thousands of Vela sightings of flashes from various sources, one such accidental source was probably the cause of this particular flash.

The reaction to this finding ranged from caution to incredulity. Some reports indicated that such zoo events had been detected by the Vela thousands of times before, but none had so closely resembled a nuclear explosion as this one.[40] Others reported that the panel's finding that the Vela sighting could have been triggered by a speck-sized meteoroid hitting the satellite as it flew by its sensors at a high rate of speed "strained credibility" and was considered statistically so small as to be one in a billion.[41]

With regard to the possible corroborative data, the panel results agreed with the NRL findings that the disturbances sighted at Arecibo were probably unrelated to the Vela sighting. It also found that an acoustic signal discovered at one site in the Northern Hemisphere was probably unrelated and that a low-yield burst would not have been detected in that region. However, it appeared to attack the NRL hydro-acoustic findings, suggesting that it was "a very preliminary analysis," that in one case, "176 signals occurred above background during a 156-hour period," and that as a consequence, "This entire study is still too incomplete to apply to the event because no determination of background signal amplitude and occurrence have been furnished to resolve the question of ambiguity in signal identification and source location."[42] In other words, given the variety of unusual signals involved, since the NRL could adequately distinguish neither what had caused it, nor the point and specific direction from which it emanated, the entire study was incomplete!

Berman publicly countered the White House panel's view that his three-hundred-page study was "incomplete," saying that "it was the only comprehensive and original analysis commissioned by the government," to which NRL had assigned a staff of seventy-five people. He also pointed out that the panel had come to its conclusions before the completion of the NRL study and its transmission to the OSTP. He further indicated that NRL had searched the log of hydro-acoustic signals thirty days after the September 22 event, and could find no signals comparable to the one they discovered that may have been caused by natural phenomena. (In addition, NRL had found one strong signal and one weak one, which might explain the way in which the Vela sighting was detected, and thus may provide some additional correlation for the event.)[43] Asked by one reporter from the *Washington Star* why the White House had "lied" when it indicated that his study was incomplete, Berman said:

> A group of distinguished people [the White House panel] had come to an independent conclusion. The fact that their conclusions may have differed in some respects from ours was indicative of the fact that the quality of the data would have not allowed a conclusion to be achieved which was beyond alternative interpretations.[44]

Given the fact that the White House scientific advisors appeared to work very hard at opposing the credibility of findings from the various centers sharing the view of NRL (the DIA, the Los Alamos Lab, the Sandia Lab, the CIA, and others), it is worth examining whether the ambiguity was substantially determined only by the quality of the data or was a product of other considerations as well.

Questions and Implications

The possibility that the White House was working hard not to produce positive findings of a nuclear explosion is raised by the following questions:

1. Why did the White House put together a panel under its control and not request scientific studies by government agencies in the first place?
2. What accounts for the extremely hostile attitude of the panel to the Arecibo findings?
3. Why did the White House hold up its panel's report and then issue it one day after the DIA statement supporting the Vela sighting as a nuclear burst?
4. Why was there an apparent pattern of reevaluating the initial data supporting the Vela event, resulting in subsequent negative findings?
5. Why did the White House OSTP say that the NRL study was "preliminary" and "incomplete"?
6. Why did the panel come to such an implausible conclusion when a body of evidence still remains unrefuted that points equally to the possibility of a nuclear explosion?
7. Why did OSTP not update the panel findings in the light of NRL's Marion Island acoustical report of July 1980?
8. Why did Dr. L. Van Middlesworth's findings not have standing as valid corroborative evidence, even at the finally determined level of 3.1 standard deviations?
9. Why has there never been a congressional investigation of this case?

These questions and many others point to the strong conclusion that there was political interference from the White House in the conduct of this investigation, with the intention of preventing any clear and conclusive evidence from emerging that suggested that there had, in fact, been a nuclear explosion in the Indian Ocean-Antarctic region by either South Africa, Israel, or both of them working together. The obvious reason for the seductiveness of such a hypothesis is that offered by Dr. John Marcum himself when he said to Dr. Alan Berman that the undertaking of a study of the Vela event was a matter with significant foreign policy implications. One Department of State official said that it would substantially affect U.S. relations with South Africa and Israel if it could be determined "conclusively that either had tested a nuclear bomb," that it made him "terribly nervous" to seriously consider the probability.[45] Another Department of State aide explained that it would become "more difficult to negotiate and enforce nuclear nonproliferation pacts" if such countries were considered to be secretly making weapons.[46] But the most graphic statement came from a government scientist reported to believe that the Vela event was nuclear in nature:

> The crux of the matter is that the White House is afraid that if the [Vela Report] is true, its nuclear nonproliferation policy would be shot to hell.

So they said, let's convene a panel and ask them to find a technically feasible explanation other than this, because we don't want to have to face it.[47]

The foregoing opinions find immediate claim to credibility in that 1980 was an election year, so it is highly unlikely that President Carter, already consumed with the negative domestic implications of the Iranian hostage crisis, would have wanted to entertain publicly another intractable problem if it could be avoided. The administration, on the other hand, was deeply engaged with the British in attempting to gain a foreign policy victory through its diplomatic involvement in the independence of Zimbabwe, and events were at a critical stage in this period.

The first period was the settlement of hostilities whereby the Lancaster Conference, convened on September 12, 1979, bore fruit with the signing of the Rhodesia Act by the British Parliament on November 12 and the passage of an act by the Rhodesian Parliament restoring British authority on December 1. Then, in early December, the British representative, Lord Soames, arrived in Rhodesia. By December 28, a cease-fire had been declared. In the second period, a new government was formed, with the months of February and March 1980 taken up by parliamentary elections and the rest of the year by determining the government's functioning.

In this delicate period, the South African government had more than once signaled that it was a factor in the negotiations, since it had maintained a close relationship with Rhodesia for nearly a century. In fact, it was discovered that South African military units had crossed over bordering Beit Bridge into southern Zimbabwe during this process of transition, but it is also quite plausible that a nuclear test in September 1979, could have been calculated to send a powerful signal to all concerned, communicating South Africa's regional military superiority. Such a message might have been meant especially for an avowedly Marxist government coming into power at its very borders.

Moreover, it is true that one of the recognized achievements of the Carter administration was the passage of the Nuclear Nonproliferation Act of 1978 (NNPA) which established new criteria for U.S. export of special nuclear materials. One criterion, South African agreement to the international Treaty on Nonproliferation of Nuclear Weapons, had been the stumbling block in negotiations between the United States and South Africa, and as a result, nuclear exports to South Africa were halted. Nevertheless, the new act was consistent with the previous Agreements for Nuclear Cooperation in the understanding that the detonation of a nuclear device on the part of a country that was at the time or had been the recipient of special nuclear materials was ground for the cancellation of the nuclear agreement altogether. Furthermore, even though the law provides that the president may waive this provision should he find continued relations to be in the U.S. interests, there would be a national debate and inexorable political pressure for compliance with the basic sanction of cutting off nuclear cooperation.

Next, official admission by the United States that it had credible evidence that South Africa had exploded a nuclear device would, undoubtedly, have been construed to indicate a violation of the 1977 Mandatory Arms Embargo against South Africa sponsored by the United Nations. Point 4 of Resolution 418 of November 4, 1977 says that "all states shall refrain from any co-operation with South Africa in the manufacture and development of nuclear weapons." Since it is well known that the United States has assisted South Africa in the development of its nuclear capability, it would no doubt be implicated in such a violation. The pressure would also spread to states such as West Germany, which assisted South Africa in the development of its uranium enrichment process, and so would also be found guilty of such violation.

In fact, the pressure on U.S. allies also arises out of the NNPA of 1978, which says that in the event it has been determined that one of its recipients of special nuclear materials has exploded a nuclear device, it would initiate consultations with its allies in an attempt to arrive at a program of multilateral sanctions for violation of the agreement. But it is also highly probable that pressures of a general sort would be stimulated in all of the Western countries for more general sanctions against South Africa, beginning with a halt in export of nuclear trade, but including other trade sanctions as well, since the provisions of the International Nuclear Nonproliferation Treaty would also shape the actions of member Western states toward South Africa.

Finally, the U.S. response to the pressure would have important ramifications in two ways. First, a precedent would be set for third world nations similarly poised to enter into the zone of nuclear experimentation. Second, a passive attitude toward officially acknowledged proliferation on the part of South Africa would provide further motivation for others to proceed with such experiments. While such a problem would have widespread implications, it would be of special relevance to the volatile situation in the Middle East where Israel and the Arab states have established a pattern of nuclear rivalry.

The question of Israeli intervention is also significant in view of the fact that the U.S. intelligence community suspects its involvement in the September 22, 1979 event. As previously suggested, Israel is widely believed to have developed a sophisticated nuclear science capability at its Dimona research facility, leading to production of nuclear weapons which Israeli scientists have wanted to test. Similarly, an official acknowledgment that Israel had participated in a nuclear weapons test with South Africa would provide added incentive for other Arab states such as Egypt—the other large recipient of U.S. military assistance—to acquire an offsetting nuclear capability. Thus, the existing tensions in that region would become more highly politicized and even more dangerous than at present.

A final political motive for the ambiguity in the data rests with the fact that at the very moment of the blast, a South African delegation was in Washington attending the tenth meeting of the Antarctic Treaty of which it was one of the twelve original signatories (along with Argentina, Australia, Belgium, Chile, France, Japan, New Zealand, Norway, the United Kingdom, the U.S.S.R., and the United States, with Poland signing in 1977). The meeting, held at the Department of State September 17 to October 5, 1979, affirmed the purposes of the Treaty as expressed in the Final Communique:

> One of the most important results of the Treaty system is that it has established Antarctica as a zone of peace. The Treaty provides that Antarctica shall be used exclusively for peaceful purposes. Military activities, including establishment of military bases and fortifications, the carrying out of military maneuvers, or the testing of military weapons, are prohibited in Antarctica. The Antarctic Treaty, there, represents a landmark development in the field of arms control. The Treaty also prohibits nuclear explosions or the disposal of nuclear waste in Antarctica.[48]

In view of the fact that on this occasion a South African delegation was guest of the U.S. government for a three-week period, there existed additional motives to withhold announcement of the discovery of the flash until at least after October 10, and given the scientific nature of the delegation, there may well have been opportunities for the U.S. to consult with them regarding it. Further speculation is prompted by the fact that both South Africa and Israel established research stations on Antarctica in December 1979, and while this might have been done in anticipation of the Antarctic Treaty activities, it might also have been in response to further monitoring of a nuclear blast.[49]

Conclusion

Detecting nuclear weapons testing is vitally important in accurately determining whether or not a country has crossed the threshold of possessing nuclear explosive capability and, thus, nuclear weapons. To begin with, the demonstrated vulnerability of U.S. test detection capability with respect to the September 22 event should have been seriously called into question by policymakers and scientists, at least as it related to the wider questions of arms control—the SALT II Treaty having just been rejected by the Congress on the grounds of verifiability. But there was little attempt to pursue this case on such a basis, although it is highly questionable that the arms control community should be concerned about verifiability where the Soviet Union is concerned and unconcerned about lesser countries also developing the means to engage in nuclear destruction. This is an important question, since it is unlikely that countries with the capability to fabricate and test nuclear weapons will cooperate with those wishing to detect such tests, but will more likely seek to do so, as I have suggested, in a manner that makes detection difficult.

It is, of course, very likely that one of the major reasons the data were considered ambiguous in this case is that South African and/or Israeli nuclear experts *deliberately designed it* to achieve that result. It is clear from the record of the White House panel evaluation and other government studies that the scientific assumptions guiding the attempt to detect a low-yield, low-altitude nuclear explosion were based on normative measures of other similar tests; therefore, slightly different degrees of significance in the data were enough for some observers to invalidate the Vela sighting, the sheep thyroid radium, and the hydro-acoustic data—all important sources of verification. The question the lay person naturally raises is why these observations did not allow for the possibility of variations in the nuclear technology employed by the perpetrator, which may have accounted for such small variations in measurements. Apparently, some observers are of the opinion that variations in the South African nuclear program objectives could affect the measurement of testing.[50] Is enough actually known about the South African and Israeli nuclear programs that observers may rule out unique developments in their technology sufficient to cause variations in test results?

In fact, South African scientists had undoubtedly gathered quite significant data on nuclear tests to enable them to anticipate detection methodologies. As early as 1958, South Africa participated with the United States in monitoring a low-yield nuclear explosion at the Cape Town Anomaly; in the early 1970s, South Africa cooperated with the French in monitoring its atomic tests in the Pacific; and shortly before the suspected test in question, South African naval and defense attachés had made inquiries of the U.S. National Technical Information Service about the availability of literature on nuclear explosions and the seismic detection of nuclear explosion, plus, importantly, information concerning flight plans, predicted orbit plots, and operations of the Vela satellite.[51] Therefore, a pattern exists of South Africa acquiring data on monitoring nuclear blasts similar to the blasts it is suspected of conducting.

Ultimately, the participation of the U.S. government in the process of ambiguous proliferation robs responsible decision makers of the ability to make critical choices about such issues as whether or not continued nuclear trade with South Africa and Israel is contributing to their ability to manufacture weapons of vast destructive power in highly volatile regions of the world where the United States has vital interests. The lack of vigilance which comes from a lack of information means that the American people are robbed of the ability to prepare for the possible consequences. In an interview with Walter Cronkite in March 1981, Dr. Leonard Weiss of the Senate Subcommittee on Nuclear Proliferation said that he did not think that it was possible, on the basis of the White House report, for people to forget about this incident "and go to sleep."[52] In this regard, it should be noted that in November 1980, the U.S. Geological Survey observed a strong "earthquake" in the region of Prince Edward Island, near the site of the suspected September 1979 nuclear detonation; then, in the early morning hours of December 16, 1980, satellite sensors picked up radiation caused by a heat source in the same area. In the latter case, the Reagan administration's Dept. of Defense and intelligence sources classified this sighting as a "meteoroid" as well. The American people have demanded no answers to the serious questions surrounding these events from the responsible decision makers. To slumber in this regard could have most disastrous consequences. Utilizing a political and military strategic frame of reference, I will next examine some of these consequences.

Notes

1. *Washington Post,* August 23, 1977, p. Al.
2. *Christian Science Monitor,* December 3, 1981, p. 14. For example, Dr. Edward Teller, father of the hydrogen bomb, was a member of the CIA panel which believed that a nuclear explosion had occurred.
3. For a review of the 1977 test facility in the Kalahari Desert, see Barbara Rogers and Zdenek Cervenka, *The Nuclear Axis,* (New York: The New York Times Books, 1978), pp. 207–18; Dan Smith, *South Africa's Nuclear Capability,* (New York: United Nations Center against Apartheid, February 1980), pp. 10–11.
4. *Washington Post,* October 26, 1979, p. Ald.
5. *Department of State Bulletin* 79, no. 2033, p. 24.
6. *United States Foreign Broadcast Information Service,* ME/6257/B/6, October 29, 1979.
7. *United States Foreign Broadcast Information Service,* SU/6259/A5/2, October 31, 1979.
8. *United States Foreign Broadcast Information Service,* MR/6258/B/4, October 30, 1979.
9. *Department of State Bulletin,* op. cit.
10. *Washington Post,* November 2, 1979, p. A23f.
11. Ibid.
12. *Washington Post,* November 14, 1979, p. Alc.
13. "Policies of Apartheid of The Government of South Africa," United Nations General Assembly, A/34/674/Add.1, November 26, 1979, Annex, p. 1.
14. Quoted in, Eliot Marshall, "Scientists Fail to Solve Vela Mystery," *Science* 207 (February 1, 1980), p. 505.

15. Ibid.

16. *Washington Post,* January 30, 1980, p. A16.

17. See also "CBS Evening News with Walter Cronkite," *CBS News,* 6, no. 52, February 21, 1980, pp. 4–5.

18. *Washington Post,* February 22, 1980, p. A6a.

19. Ibid.

20. Ibid.

21. Letter, Marcum to Berman, January 31, 1980, Office of Science and Technology Policy, Executive Office of the President.

22. Memo, F.J. Kelly to Files, February 26, 1980, NRL.

23. Memo, J. Goodman to Files, March 5, 1980, NRL.

24. Ibid.

25. Memo, J. Gardner to T. Coffey, April 9, 1980, NRL.

26. Memo, Donald Strasburg to Alan Berman, April 21, 1980, NRL.

27. Memo (telephone conversation), Hooten-Dave Evans, May 7, 8, 1980, NRL.

28. Memo, Goodman to Berman, July 23, 1979, NRL.

29. Ibid. Also, see appendix to this book.

30. Memo, Berman to Marcum, July 24, 1980, NRL.

31. Letter, Middlesworth to Berman, September 25, 1980, Memphis, Tennessee.

32. Memo, Berman to Marcum, November 3, 1980, NRL.

33. Memo, Ruhnke to Berman, June 9, 1980.

34. "Policies of Apartheid of the Government of South Africa," *United Nations,* op. cit., p. 12.

35. Memo, Ruhnke to Berman, op. cit.

36. Memo, Dr. Julio Torres (Office of International Security Affairs, U.S. Dept. of Energy) to John Marcum, December 3, 1980, DOE.

37. Memo, K.W. Marlow to Berman, February 26, 1981, NRL.

38. *Washington Post,* July 15, 1980, p. A7f.

39. "Ad Hoc Panel Report on the September 22 Event." (Washington, D.C.: Executive Office of the President, Office of Science and Technology Policy, July 15, 1980).

40. "Blowup?" *Technology Review* 83 (October 1980), p. 78. See also "Clandestine Nuclear Test Doubted," *Avionics* 113 (August 11, 1980), pp. 67–72 for a discussion of the scientific problem involved.

41. "Debate Continues on the Bomb That Wasn't," *Science* 209 (August 1, 1980), p. 572.

42. "Ad Hoc Panel Report on the September 22 Event," op. cit., p. 3.

43. "Navy Lab Concludes the Vela Saw a Bomb," op. cit., p. 997.

44. Memorandum, "Conversation with John Fialka of the *Washington Star,*" Berman to File, August 7, 1980, NRL.

45. Stephen Talbot, "The Case of the Mysterious Flash," *Inquiry* (April 21, 1980), p. 10.

46. "White House Brushes Off Report of Israeli A-Blast," *Science* 207, no. 4436, March 14, 1980, p. 1185.

47. Eliot Marshall, "Navy Lab Concludes the Vela Saw a Bomb," *Science* 209, August 29, 1980, pp. 996–97.

48. "Antarctica: 10th Meeting of Treaty Consultative Parties," *Department of State Bulletin* 79, no. 2032 (November 1979), p. 23.

49. Records indicate that they established such stations, but the site is somewhat ambiguous. Memo, "Project Status Report," Goodman to Berman, March 21, 1980, NRL.

50. Kenneth Adelman, *Impact Upon U.S. Security of a South African Nuclear Weapons Capability* (Arlington, Va.: Strategic Studies Center, April 1981), pp. 72-73.

51. Barbara Rogers and Zdenek Cervenka, op. cit., pp. 207-10; "CBS Evening News with Walter Cronkite," March 6, 1981; *Washington Post*, November 14, 1979, p. A1c.

52. "CBS Evening News with Walter Cronkite," ibid.

4
Politicomilitary Scenarios

As I proceed with the discussion of South African nuclear capability, in an effort to be true to the assumptions of the previous passages, I will address yet another level of skepticism concerning the possession of weapons by the regime—or the question of how could they be used. Skeptics have concluded—utilizing conventional deterrence theory—that since there is no comparable conventional military power, let alone nuclear power in Africa, South Africa would not invest in the development of such weapons and, in any case, their use would appear to be superfluous under any conceivable military circumstances faced by the regime. However, such reasoning has always substituted objective calculations of the threat to South African security for that threat which the South Africans themselves perceive to be the reality. People are, thus, led to assume the existence of scenarios that, no matter how objectively "unlikely," may, in fact, be credible in the eyes of the South Africans who are probably considering the use of such weapons under some circumstances.

My approach to this question will be to suggest the dimensions of the threat to South African security, and, then, the South African response to each dimension, including an assessment of the possible role of nuclear weapons. In this regard, let me put forth a theoretical proposition with respect to the course of the crisis, in the following terms.

1. The guerilla struggle of the African National Congress (ANC) (operating within the country of South Africa) and the South West African Peoples Organization (SWAPO) (operating with Namibia) represents the basic threat to the national security of South Africa at the present time.

2. To the extent that generalized civil unrest inside South Africa becomes endemic, it merges with guerilla tactics of Umkhonto We Sizwe (ANC) to form a significant threat to white South African internal security.

3. The retaliation of the South African white authorities to the internal security situation has been to increasingly militarize their response,

thus causing many casualties and heightening the internal resistance of the black and other nonwhite population in an upward cycle of violence.

4. The retaliation of the South African white authorities to the guerilla struggle has been to attack both the national and regional units and centers of the ANC/SWAPO operation. But to the extent that they attack the regional locations of the guerillas, they antagonize the host states, thus increasing the likelihood of a conventional war.

5. The attacks of the South African authorities against the regional host states of the guerillas have two motives. One is to destroy the base operations of the guerillas; the other is to destabilize Southern African states in general because of their objectionable Marxist ideology and consequent political, economic, and military alliances with the Soviet Union, the extant manifestation of which they contend to be the Cuban troops in Angola.

6. The military destabilization of the region has wider consequences which involve the interests of other states on the continent and which may ultimately attract the involvement of major extracontinental powers, either in the direct protection of their interests or in the indirect protection of those interests by protecting the security of an allied state.

Based on this proposition, there are two broad types of threat to South African security—a guerilla war and conventional war, both of which have major subcategories. For example, the guerilla war has an "in-country" manifestation which includes civil unrest, but it also has a regional scenario in the host countries of Southern Africa. The conventional war category has a regional scenario and an extraregional scenario, both of which are unrealized at the moment, but whose possibilities will be discussed.

Guerilla Warfare: The "In-Country" Scenario

It is a widely shared consensus that the most obvious and immediate threat to the security of South Africa is the military activity of the African National Congress guerilla units in the cities, townships, and rural areas. What provided a new and dramatic intensity to these activities was the increase of civil unrest, especially since the 1976 Soweto uprising, characterized by Nadine Gordimer, an accomplished white South African writer, as "a stage of revolution."[1] Gordimer meant, of course, that the degree of civil violence has escalated since 1976, involving the organized sectors of society such as labor unions. In 1976, the South African Council of Trade Unions (SACTU), with its growing militancy, had a series of major strikes which spurred the challenge to the government; in 1980, there were further massive strikes; and in 1984, the industrial sector of South Africa was paralyzed by two days of nationwide strikes. These strikes have led to demonstrations at work sites where workers were killed, but in 1984, at least fifteen thousand workers were dismissed, adding further fuel to the fire. The strike demands are becoming increasingly political. They included, on this occasion, the demand for the withdrawal of the army and police from the townships, the resignation of all local town councilors, and the release of all political prisoners and detainees.[2]

Labor demonstrations have often been accompanied by school boycotts and political demonstrations by students, who are in many ways the engine of the domestic movement. For example, the students were in the forefront of protest against the school system in 1976, but their grievances have since become more political. In 1980, 1,000 students boycotted schools. The protest against the new constitution on September 3, 1984 turned into a nationwide demonstration in which 800,000 students stayed away from school.[3] Then, a few days later, rent increases announced by the government triggered the festering sentiment against the new political regime, and widespread revolts erupted. At the end of the day, 31 people had been killed and 358 were arrested.

During these years, the guerillas' campaign increased inside the country, as they sensed the truth of South African Minister of Defense Magnus Malan's statement that there was a "new tendency of active internal support" for the ANC guerillas.[4] Bombings and raids intensified. Targets included railway lines, police stations, and government administrative agencies. An increasing boldness led to military-style confrontations between the guerillas and the government security units. In 1980, for example, there was a spectacular raid by the ANC upon a police station in the center of Johannesburg involving rocket launchers and grenades, and on June 1, the strategic facility South African Coal, Oil and Gas Corp. (SASOL), was bombed.

Attacks on military installations also increased. In 1981, there was a bombing at the Durban Defense Force recruiting office and a bold attack on the Voortrekkerhoogte Military Base. In 1982, among the many raids, the Koeberg nuclear power station under construction was bombed, so construction was set back. Then, in 1983, a car bomb severely damaged the South African Air Force military intelligence agency in downtown Pretoria.[5] Such activity is becoming more frequent. Most important is the fact that attacks upon the police (especially black police, who are considered "collaborators") and police installations are apparently now part of the popular resistance and not the sole activity of the ANC. Thus, civil opposition and military opposition have begun to merge; with this merger, the character of the internal struggle changes.

An increase in these events involves the greater mobilization of the domestic nonwhite population of South Africa into activity directed against state authority, threatening the ability of the regime to continue normal activities by disrupting industrial, educational, social, government, transport, military, and police institutions and, forcing the regime to make decisions regarding how to respond.

The Border War

Ever since the late 1960s, when units of the ANC and SWAPO began to infiltrate across the borders of South Africa and Namibia to conduct operations inside the countries, the South African defense force (SADF) has concentrated upon militarizing the border in an effort to make such penetration costly. Sections of the border with Mozambique, for example, are mined and electrified. Nevertheless, this entire 3,000-mile border cannot be fully protected from penetration. The South Africans have attempted to interdict such infiltration routes and thereby, have entertained skirmishes with ANC and SWAPO troops on the southern borders of Angola, Mozambique, Zimbabwe, Botswana, and along the borders of Swaziland and Lesotho. Thus, in the 1973 White Paper on Defense and Armament Production Minister of Defense Pieter Botha said:

> I do not wish to spread alarm, but I must state unambiguously that for a long time already, we have been engaged in a war of low intensity and that this situation will probably continue for some considerable time to come.[6]

Pauline Baker has suggested that the expansiveness of the border, the direction of the infiltration routes into the industrial area of South Africa, and the existence of only 20,000 regular troops all pose areas of vulnerability for South Africa in such a situation.[7] But the Pan Africanist Congress, one of the two main liberation groups, has considered the effect of these vulnerabilities and decided to formulate them into comprehensive strategy, suggesting that the "Azanian [South Africa] revolution can develop from a guerilla type of war in the countryside, extending its area of authority and then surrounding and taking over the cities."[8] The effect of such a move would be to create two fronts of battle, which the PAC says that even with 300,000 men, the South Africans would find difficulty managing successfully.

Then, of course, the impending independence of Namibia could mean the opening of another 500 miles of border to defend, adding to that of Mozambique, Rhodesia, and Botswana. Certainly, the effect of having to fight on two or three fronts could severely strain the manpower resources of the South African military, a situation the White Paper admits is unsatisfactory.

Considering the massive South African raids into southern Angola in 1980 and 1982, the SWAPO has shown amazing resiliency, as in 1982, when a well-armed unit of 100 soldiers penetrated the southern Angola border for 95 miles into Namibia and carried out ambushes in a white farming district.[9] Also, guerilla forces were reported by South Africa to have shot down a military helicopter, killing 15 airmen in a battle near the border. They did not confirm the SWAPO report, however, that a South African base at Omahenene in northwest Namibia had been attacked by SWAPO.[10]

The border war between SWAPO and the South African forces has continued for nearly nineteen years, and the ANC has conducted its campaign for twenty years. While the South African forces may be said to have temporarily contained the guerilla forces, it is also obvious that they are fighting a war of attrition in which the rate of infiltration is increasing as the casualties increase. Therefore, it is fitting to ask what tactics South Africa will adopt when it becomes clear that, in fact, its border war is not effective in preventing a growing infiltration of guerillas into the country.

The South African Response

Many analysts do not understand what William Gutteridge discovered in his analysis, that "successive Defense White Papers in 1977, 1978 and 1979 have demonstrated that planning is being based on the 'worst case' in which the [South African] Republic would be subjected to a violent assault from inside and outside at the same time."[11] No doubt, such a scenario which envisioned the simultaneous maturation of both the internal and external threat to the security of the regime, or "total war," was the basis for its adoption of the concept of "total strategy," made famous by French General André Beaufre in his 1963 work *An Introduction to Strategy*. Describing the possible stages of war in Southern Africa based on examples from Vietnam and Algeria, he inferred that the government would mobilize a counterinsurgency operation, but failing this, it would employ the threat of political or economic retaliation against regional states with guerilla bases, then possibly direct intervention, including "the possibility of the use of nuclear weapons."[12]

Thus, in Beaufre's threat-escalation scenario, one sees elements of outside intervention (envisioned to be by the Soviets or other forces sympathetic to the insurgents by the provision of arms and men; the implementation of economic and/or political sanctions; and, finally, military intervention which could include nuclear weapons). While some analysts might consider this scenario extreme, based on an objective calculation of the situation faced by South Africa, there is little doubt that just as Beaufre's concept of defense against these threats considers "creating the largest possible number of deterrents to supplement the overall nuclear deterrent," so has the South African concept of "total strategy" followed Beaufre's logic.[13]

Just as important, one sees from Beaufre's writings the value placed upon the psychology developed to employ a concept of total strategy. It is one based on the fact that South Africa faces the long-term possibility of preponderant force, a presumption that places upon its deterrence a burden of being most credible in the eyes of any potential adversary. This means that the capacity of South Africa to threaten must be demonstrated at some level. So, at the level of guerilla war, there have been strikes into adjacent countries (ostensibly against SWAPO and the ANC), and, at the conventional war level, there has been unclear evidence of various "nuclear tests," giving evidence of ambiguous proliferation. The sum total of this activity may be characterized by the well-known concept of cold war or, in the words of observer Sean Gervasi, "permanent limited war."[14]

While Gervasi, a researcher at the United Nations, explains that in such a war, South Africa uses its power selectively or even "invisibly," the aim is the use of all of the instruments of destabilization, especially to prevent neighboring states from becoming stable bridgeheads of opposition to the regime, either by serving as hosts to anti-South African guerillas, or by themselves becoming powerful enough to directly intervene. Nevertheless, as shall be seen below, it is the escalation of the regime's military offensive both internally and externally that is driving the degree of violence to a dangerous level.

The In-Country Scenario

Writer Richard Leonard, has looked carefully at South Africa's 1982 Defense White Paper and concluded that the recent activities of the South African Defense Force "reflect the escalation of its conflicts and how South Africa has become a nation at war."[15] Without an involved discussion of his analysis, Leonard quotes a policy statement in the White Paper particularly illustrating his point that "in order to support the civilian infrastructure of the country the Defense Force has become 'increasingly involved in assisting other security forces and civilian organizations.'"[16] Leonard suggests that this reference was to the fact that the military has spent considerably more time in supporting a growing number of counterinsurgency operations protecting "national key points," distinguishing the internal defense posture from previous years when the "low level" guerilla operations even on the borders and in the rural areas were considered "police actions".

Because of the escalating attacks upon police personnel (especially black police) and installations, and because of the broad level of civil unrest in recent years, there has been a growing pattern of utilizing military troops. In fact, the security police which have shouldered the main responsibility for dealing with "terrorism" have had to reorganize, such that Johan

Cotzee, head of this unit, said in 1979, that a special "antiterrorist task force" had begun patrolling the northern borders of the country.[17] This was a far cry, however, from the response to the internal unrest caused by the implementation of the new constitution in September 1984, which ended with seven-thousand armed military troops backed by heavily armored vehicles cordoning off three black townships.[18]

The authority for the use of SADF troops, of course, resides in the 1957 Defense Act, which indicates that the troops may be utilized to counteract "terrorism" or to prevent "internal disorder." As such, as early as 1980, military personnel were deployed into action at the State Committees and through the State Security Council, while senior military officials were becoming more influential in national decision making.[19]

The Border War

As I have suggested, the security police had earlier begun to escalate their operations on the border as a response to increased infiltration of guerillas. However, they were realistic, inasmuch as Police Minister Jimmy Kruger indicated in 1979 that South Africans should accept the fact "that infiltration of terrorists will increase."[20] The increased infiltration of guerillas has placed heavy strains on the security objectives of the South African government with respect to the so-called Homeland areas, some of which (Transkei, Bophuthatswana, Venda, and Ciskei) have undergone a transition to pseudoindependence with the South African government retaining control over defense. Evidence of Kruger's assertion materialized in 1981, showing that there had been 11 attacks upon police stations since 1976, and a 200 percent increase in sabotage from 1979 to a similiar period in 1980. This caused General Constand Viljoen, chief of the South African Defense Force, to say:

> Anti-Republic of South Africa terrorists . . . operate countrywide in South Africa in widespread actions that make far greater demands on the security forces as far as manpower levels are concerned.
>
> The drawn-out, widespread and fluid nature of revolutionary terrorist warfare is aimed at over-taxing the country's security force base and thereby its economic power base as well.[21]

The Bantustan or "Homelands" policy of the government has been directed to the alleged social undesirability of whites being forced to live with blacks in common areas, the economic fact of whites having homeland reserve areas for surplus black labor and the political fact of whites rejecting the participation of blacks in a common electorate and designating these areas only for nominal black political activity. As the guerilla campaign has intensified, however, these areas took on added significance in that they also provided some relief from the possibility that whites would be overwhelmed from a close-in township such as Soweto. This relief came from moving blacks away from the main concentrations of white populations. Indeed, the resettlement policy has concentrated upon eliminating the so-called "black spots" as a mopping-up activity; over 3.5 million people have been relocated since the mid-1960s. Nevertheless, the fact is inescapable that the geopolitical objectives merge with military factors in the sense that target populations have also been created in the Homeland which lend themselves to military control.

It was "inevitable" to Deon Fourie, senior lecturer in strategic studies at the University of South Africa, "that the defense of South Africa was to include the defense of the Homelands," since, it was obvious that the infiltrating guerillas found useful cover in the quasi-independent areas from which they could operate. Thus, in 1978, at the commissioning of a completed airbase in Venda in the Northern Transvaal (now one of the so-called independent states), Major General G.J. Boshoff, chief of staff (logistics), described the facility as one which would aid South Africa in moving men and material speedily to the northern borders.[22] Also, in that same year, P.W. Botha (then defense minister) announced the government's intentions to build a new army base at Palabora in the northeastern Transvaal (50 km from the Mozambique border) and a new air base at Hoedspruit 40 km farther south near Kruger Park.[23]

Strategic *defense* of the Homelands, however, under circumstances where they could become major areas for internal war by guerillas against the white redoubt, might easily turn into strategic *offense*. This might become the case especially where vital strategic South African outposts were overrun by the guerillas and the white regime came to feel that it had no further investment in these areas worth protecting.

Moreover, in 1978, Parliament gave the SADF special authority over a six-mile–wide "barrier" along the border for the South Africans to attempt to create a "cordon sanitaire" with the support of local white farmers, to whom the government was offering bonuses for returning to farms near the area. The fact that so many have left due to the guerilla attacks illustrates some measure of success by the antigovernment forces, and must increasingly raise the question of the posture of the regime since it appears to be slowly losing control of the border altogether.

Certainly the government forces are following the classic counterinsurgency tactics of creating strategic hamlets for protection of loyal groups and creating "free-fire zones" in an effort to develop legitimate target areas. However, if conventional arms are rendered ineffective in destroying the bands of infiltrators, then low-yield nuclear weapons might be utilized with the objective of eliminating all hostile populations in the target area. An attendant objective in the utilization of at least an initial weapon might be to demonstrate its effectiveness and, as such, cause some deterrent effect in terms of guerilla strategy and their host country support as well.

The obvious comparison, perhaps, should be made between the Southern African situation and others where guerilla warfare has been fought, such as in Southeast Asia. U.S. military authorities considered the use of tactical nuclear weapons in Vietnam in an effort to create the loss of life, the destruction of tunnel bunkers, and defoliation, as well as to demonstrate the power of U.S. forces. In the end, such weapons were not used for several reasons, some of which were related to the weight of international public opinion and the option of withdrawing from the war altogether without the further loss of American lives. The South African situation, however, is different in that the native government does not consider the weight of public opinion to bear as gravely upon their decisions, as illustrated by their maintenance of apartheid and colonialism in both South Africa and Namibia. Also, they consider that they do not have the option of withdrawal, and so they possess greater motivation to use ultimate nuclear weapons in defense of their way of life. In this sense, one must discount to some extent the normal restraint that might be anticipated in other situations due to worry over radiation fallout or other disabilities involved in the use of such weapons.

There is also the positive psychological motivation of the guerillas given the success of other guerilla movements, such as one in the immediate area conducted by ZANU and ZAPU in Zimbabwe. They are well aware that a guerilla war is exceedingly winnable, despite the odds of confronting disproportionate South African military power. Various recent incursions have displayed a new guerilla boldness which partly stems from a knowledge that the South African military is not invincible. The most demonstrative case of its vulnerability was not, however, in guerilla war, but in a conventional confrontation with Cuban troops in 1975 in the Angolan civil war. Nevertheless, it is unlikely that even given the eventuality that South Africa might resort to the use of nuclear weapons in such a situation, the guerilla forces would be deterred, and so deterrence may well be unworkable and would give way to the actual use of such weapons in such a situation.

Conventional War

In the wake of the increasing militarization of the conflict between South Africa and the guerilla forces, the defense posture of the regime has shifted from the necessity to engage their enemies essentially at the level of counterinsurgency warfare to increasing preparations for conventional war. Defense Minister Botha, for instance, has felt that the "small wars" the regime was constrained to fight against the guerillas constituted but one stage in the strategy of the communist powers, and that (as Beaufre had also suggested) if defense against them failed, the final stage would be a conventional war.[24] There have been increasing incursions of the guerillas and two or three significant conventional-style battles the SADF has waged against the Angolan government and Cuban troops with sophisticated weaponry in southern Angola since they lost the first encounter in 1975. One obvious conclusion is that since these encounters were not all won by the South Africans, in the future, they would have to be prepared to defend against "a fairly heavy conventional attack."[25] Thus, the regime began to conduct large-scale conventional warfare exercises and to purchase more sophisticated weapons such as advanced artillery, armored cars, and mortor units. "Clearly", Robert Jaster writes, "South Africa's heightened threat perception has led it to prepare for a worst-case contingency: a substantial conventional attack from the north."[26] While Jaster asks the rhetorical question of whether such a threat perception is warranted in view of the potential reality, he nonetheless concludes, in effect, that South Africa is but following the dictates of "total strategy" which call for total deterrence. In this case, the first line of defense against any serious conventional attack would appear to be in the region, and in this regard, one might examine the South African regional strategy.

The Regional Strategy

South Africa is aware of the fact that a successful conventional threat to its security depends upon the extent to which the regional states either make viable hosts for guerilla forces or develop the capacity to intervene directly, perhaps in alliance with other African states. Its xenophobia is heightened, however, by the fact that the Portuguese (an old ally in the region) are gone, and now South Africa is alone in attempting to enforce its version of colonial order upon the region. The critical difference lending a ferocity to its preemptive military operations against adversaries in the region is that, whereas with the Portuguese as a resident colonial power, the pacification of the region was conducted for a wider set of stable Western colonial interests, today, South Africa is fighting directly for its own survival with those interests as a subsidiary concern. Therefore, the regime has developed a regional strategy that apparently depends upon a demonstration of its willingness to remain permanently in the region using its military strength to deter attack from either guerilla or conventional military units operating from neighboring states. Secondly, the regime is attempting to utilize the pressure thus created by military action to achieve political settlement of the status quo by signing nonaggression pacts. I will briefly review the progress of this strategy.

In the process of implementing its regional strategy against guerilla war, South Africa undoubtedly has in its historical memory the role played by the front-line states (Mozambique, Angola, Botswana, Tanzania, and Zambia) in the independence of Zimbabwe, and the capacities of this group now that Zimbabwe is included. It will be remembered that Tanzania, which exercised the leadership of this group, also provided military assistance to the Zimbabwe Peoples Revolutionary Army (ZIPRA) in the form of funds, bases, and military training.[27] Zambia came close to economic disaster in closing its border and, thus, stopping its trade with Rhodesia, and at one point it declared itself to be in a state of war with Rhodesia, appealing to all friendly nations to assist in the defense of its 449–mile border.[28] Mozambique followed a similar course to that of Zambia, as they were also host to ZANU and ZAPU political headquarters, respectively. While Botswana, because of its constant pressure from South African and Rhodesian security police and armies, could offer only passive support to ZAPU and ZANU, Angola could also do little for the Zimbabweans because of its own civil war with UNITA antigovernment guerillas. Still, Angola was vexatious to South Africa because of its support for SWAPO.

Since the events cited above, the South Africans have carried out a broad pattern of military operations against most of these states in the region, ostensibly under international law which allows "hot pursuit," a doctrine the regime has interpreted to permit pursuit across an international border of any party that has carried out an attack against it.[29] The United Nations, for example, reported that between March 27, 1976 and June 11, 1979, 612 Angolans, 198 Zimbabweans, and three South Africans had been killed in such raids.[30]

Thus, South Africa has attacked Angola upon the rationale of General Malan that the loss of Namibia would "move the operational area from the Okavango River to the Orange River" (on South Africa's northwestern border).[31] Most important, it has been engaged in a *conventional war* in Angola, using sophisticated weapons and thousands of troops in standard military operations with combined ground and air combat units. Between February and mid-April 1985, when South Africa announced the completion of its withdrawal of troops, 2,000 troops had been involved in an operation that had driven 100 miles into Angola.[32]

In 1985, South Africa launched strikes into both Lesotho and Botswana aimed at destroying ANC headquarters. However, it was unclear from published reports that those killed, for example, in Botswana's capital city of Gaborone were even ANC members.[33] Then, there is also Zimbabwe which shares a border with South Africa and which, for that reason, was considered to be a geopolitical threat. This is evident by the fact that in January 1980, during negotiations for the independence of the country, South Africa had intervened with over one-thousand troops and heavy weapons in a bid to wage conventional war to impose its own chosen outcome upon the situation. By 1982, evidence was discovered that South African counter-insurgency units were operating in southern Zimbabwe.

The threat from Mozambique has been considered particularly keen by the South Africans, as a Treaty of Friendship exists between the Soviet Union and Mozambique which, among other things, says that,

> in the case of situations tending to threaten or disturb the peace, the two countries will enter into immediate contact with the aim of coordinating their positions in the interest of eliminating the threat of reestablishing peace.[34]

This treaty, however, does not allow the kind of direct military intervention as does the treaty between the Soviet Union and Afghanistan, while the shipments of weapons to Mozambique stored at Nacala and Beira were more symbolic than representative of major Soviet intervention.[35] Nevertheless, for these reasons, South Africa began to provide financial aid and training for the Mozambique National Resistance movement (MNR), an antigovernment guerilla group operating in southern Mozambique, once the white Rhodesians had ceased to do so in early 1980.[36] In January of 1981, Pretoria launched a direct attack with mortars, rockets and grenades on suspected ANC headquarters in the capital city of Maputo.[37] Then, in March of the same year, South African troops fought a significant battle along the border near Ponto do Ouro with Mozambican troops.[38] The pressure caused by these disruptions in southern Mozambique eventually grew to the point that the MNR began to seriously disrupt government operations, causing President Samora Machel to agree to a treaty of non-aggression with South Africa on March 16, 1984, signed at Nkomati, a railroad crossing in South Africa.

In fact, the South Africans' attempt to exact such nonaggression treaties is evident by statements of General Magnus Malan, who warned South Africa's neighbors that they would "lose any war," advising them instead to sign such nonaggression pacts with his government, since the buildup of arms in southern Africa by "the Soviets" could lead to conventional war.[39] Swaziland announced, for example, on March 31, 1984, that it had signed a nonaggression pact similar to the Nkomati Accord two years earlier with South Africa. Lesotho and Botswana are also under pressure to sign such an accord.[40] Then, on February 20, 1984, South Africa concluded a disengagement treaty with Angola which specified, among other things, a timetable for the withdrawal of Cuban troops.

It is instructive to note that both the Angolan and Mozambique treaties are in trouble, as the Mozambique government has accused South Africa of failing to restrain the MNR, but, rather, continuing to provide assistance, while South African troops were discovered in northern Angola on a sabotage mission against Gulf Oil, a U.S. multinational company, whose investments helped finance the Angolan government, after the supposed withdrawal of South African troops. It is possible to agree with the conclusion that the regional strategy of South Africa is in disarray, and as such, the pressures on the regime to prepare for conventional threat from the regional states increases as a consequence.[41]

What is the nature of the potential military threat to South African security from the front-line region? The six front-line states are double South Africa's size in total population. Moreover, while the total mobilizable manpower of South Africa is said to be about 400,000, it would appear to be even greater among these neighboring states, since South Africa would only have the 3 million whites to draw from, not its entire population of 26 million. This raw population advantage translates into a manpower advantage in that, whereas South Africa maintained 83,000 troops under arms in 1985, the combined armies of the regional states totaled 157,000. This also indicates the significance of Zimbabwean independence, since in 1976, South African military manpower amounted to 60 percent of those in the region, but by 1985, it amounted to 52 percent, giving evidence of an erosion of the military manpower in nine years.[42] Nevertheless, South Africa has maintained a clear superiority over the front-line states in advanced military weaponry and in the capability to produce arms. The regime has substantially more advanced aircraft with more fighter squadrons possessing modern jets and more advanced missiles and artillery. It has also developed armored personnel carriers to fit the terrain.

In any case, even at this stage, the combined armaments of the front-line states look significant in that they have an important capability in short-range field artillery with surface-to-air (SAM)s. They also have some Soviet-supplied MIGs. However, even this capability is diminished by the lack of a supportive spare parts industry, all of which makes South Africa clearly the superior force in terms of technology. Yet, the front-line states may be catching up, inasmuch as the increase in South African defense spending from 1976 to 1985 was 34 percent, while the increase in spending by these states was 85 percent. Certainly, in the long run, economies of scale will place severe restrictions upon the extent to which one state can expand defense spending as opposed to six states. I am, thus, in agreement with Walter Barrows, who suggests that:

> The slow unsteady but nonetheless measurable improvement of the front-line states' military capabilities will in time likely narrow South Africa's formidable advantage. South Africa will enjoy military superiority over its neighbors for at least the next decade and probably well into the next century, but as its lead slowly diminishes, one present constraint on front-line support for anti-South African guerillas will relax.[43]

Barrows continues to suggest that as a result of this relaxation, both the crossborder activity of anti-South African guerillas will increase and the states themselves will feel more confident of their conventional military capabilities vis-à-vis South Africa, especially if these capabilities are wielded together in an effective regional multinational force. With the erosion of the military advantage South Africa enjoys in the region, it must eventually face the prospect of the loss of its frontiers and a maturation of the threat to its outlying areas. In its version of a "forward defense" strategy accompanying its "total strategy" concept, an already serious military confrontation would have escalated at this point—which may be the very point at which the regime considers the use of its nuclear deterrent. In such an event, Robert Jaster says, although Pretoria does not consider a conventional attack imminent, it does, nonetheless, regard it as a real possibility for which it may have acquired

> the ultimate deterrent—a nuclear weapon. The acquisition of such a weapon would be consistent with the leaders' perceived need to be capable of deterring a conventional attack and with their defiant go-it-alone defense posture. It also would be compatible with their commitment to assure the survival of the Afrikaner people.[44]

With this scenario in mind, I will proceed to discuss the even wider problem of the threat to South African security and the probable circumstance that might elicit a nuclear response. For example, it is instructive that South Africa has not attacked Tanzania, which also is a host for antigovernment guerilla forces. It may well be that South Africa is sensitive to the powerful political symbolism of Tanzania in the rest of Africa beyond the region, and has avoided directly challenging this level of potential military involvement.

The African Theater

The Pan African Defense Force

Any objective assessment of the military threat to the South African regime in 1963 would most surely have concluded that the nation had little with which to be concerned. However, the view from Pretoria could have been so different as to cause the regime to initiate long-term plans for the acquisition of an ultimate weapon, especially if one took into consideration the fact that in 1962, Umkhonto We Sizwe was set up as a sabotage arm of the African National Congress, and that in December, it began the guerilla war by exploding its first bomb. But the tension was surely heightened when in that same year, both the charters of the radical Casablanca Group and the more moderate Monrovia Group included provisions for a "Joint African High Command" along the lines first proposed by President Kwame Nkrumah of Ghana in a June 1962 speech. Therefore, when the Organization of African Unity (OAU) was established in 1963, the stage had been set for the adoption of the Defense Commission, the objective of which was to protect the territorial independence of African states and assist the liberation movement. In the memorandum setting forth its rationale, it was stipulated that South Africa was the chief enemy and that "confronted with the prospect of a showdown with a well coordinated and determined African force representing the collective moral and material force of all African States," it would change its policy of apartheid.[45]

The first major test of the Defense Commission came in 1965, when Ian Smith, head of the Rhodesian Front, made the Unilateral Declaration of Independence from Britain. A plan drawn up for African military intervention in Rhodesia attracted pledges to send troops from Ghana, Egypt, Algeria, Nigeria, Sudan, Ivory Coast, Congo, and Ethiopia. Not only was this plan later aborted, but practical and political difficulties made the Defense Commission little more than a dead letter. The only body to carry on at least the anticolonial program of the OAU was its Liberation Committee, headquartered in Dar es Salaam, Tanzania; in January 1973, its revised strategy specifically indicated that African states were "to be ready for collective military and economic assistance to any OAU State in case it becomes the victim of aggression from Portugal, Rhodesia or South Africa."[46]

In 1977, Nigerian Head of State Obasanjo, in his speech to the July 4 OAU summit, urged states to pay their assessment to the Liberation Committee with the suggestion, "Let us ensure that at least in this regard our actions conform to our slogans. 'Armed struggle is the only solution to the South African problem.'"[47] The international intervention into Zaire that year nevertheless provides a model of some of the political and logistical difficulties involved in collective armed responses to intervention.

In April 1977, General Mobutu Sese Seko of Zaire, faced with a challenge to his government from the Front for the Liberation of the Congo (which had captured several towns near the Angolan border in Shaba province), appealed to the West for assistance.[48] He received assistance from powers outside the continent. The United States sent $15 million worth of "nonlethal" supplies, West Germany sent $3 million of equivalent aid, Belgium airlifted small arms, Japan rescheduled some of Zaire's pressing debts totaling $3.8 million, South Korea contributed $2.2 million in supplies, and even China supplied 30 tons of military equipment.

The most direct great power assistance, however, was received by Zaire from the French government, which provided transport to 1,500 troops, 170 French officers, and 40 tons of equipment from Morocco in ten Transalls and a DC-8. In addition, Egypt sent a military mission, and Senegal sent tons of medicine. Uganda and Sudan also sent nominal assistance.[49]

Then, again, in May 1978, the Congolese National Liberation Front invaded Zaire's Shaba province, attacking the mining town of Kolwezi, killing about 700 people (approximately 200 of whom were from the community of 2,500 Europeans). In response to the attack on the European community (including 100 Americans), Belgium and France sent troops which were eventually replaced by 1,500 Moroccans ferried by 11 U.S. C-141 troop transport planes. The United States again made available 29 C-141s and one Lockheed C5 aircraft, communication equipment, fuel, and $20 million worth of nonlethal equipment.[50] In the aftermath of this second invasion, attempting to fashion a permanent solution to the protection of foreign mining interest in Shaba, the United States proposed the establishment of a "pan African" defense force supported by major Western powers. In early June, however, several major Western states such as Britain and West Germany rejected the idea at a meeting of NATO members in Washington, D.C.[51]

The results of the Washington meeting could possibly have been influenced by the late May meeting in Paris of twenty-one African heads of state and representatives (largely from the former French territories), who considered the proposal of a joint force. This proposal failed, as did the formal resolution to thank France for its intervention into Zaire.[52] Nevertheless, there was strong sentiment among fourteen of these former French colonial states for a continued defense relationship with France, and the six members of the West Africa Economic Community agreed to work to transform their nonaggression pact into a true defensive alliance.[53]

Subsequently, in July 1978, the matter of an African defense force as a weapon against outside intervention was taken up at a regular OAU meeting. Because of the obvious differences between those states that wanted continued defense linkages with major powers and those wanting moderation of outside intervention from all quarters, there was no resolution of the problem, and the idea of an African defense force was sent to the oblivion of a committee for "further study." Still, there was the strong sentiment for the idea that Africa had a right to solve its own problems without outside intervention, while each state should retain the right to call whatever patron state it wished to assist in its defense—a contradictory set of ideas.[54] Yet there was also much support for the idea that if an African defense force should be created, it should be done only under the legitimacy of the OAU.

Then, it should be noted that the OAU summit of 1978 evinced no willingness to settle the problem of South Africa by force. Rather, it urged support for an economic strategy of an oil boycott, the traditional approach of sanctions.[55]

These events, however, do not rule out the possibility of the eventual creation of such an all African defense force, probably initiated by some cataclysmic event by South Africa. Thus, I will proceed to make a brief analysis of the opposing defensive forces.

According to data from the International Institute of Strategic Studies (IISS), Africa has access to about 1,800,000 troops (as of 1984–85), counting troops from all continental member states, but the largest contingent of troops are from states such as Algeria (130,000), Ethiopia (306,500), Egypt (460,000), Nigeria (133,500), Morocco (144,650), Sudan (58,000), Tanzania (40,350), and Zaire (26,000).[56] This listing, however, is illustrative of the fact that Arab African states make up a large proportion of these troops, and may, because of their important military involvement with the Middle East, be somewhat more reluctant to commit troops and material in combating apartheid than those black states to the south. This raises the question of the extent to which their contingent might be counted upon in a formidable military operation against South Africa.

Also, many of those nations listed in the IISS data (such as Malawi, Gabon, and the Central African Empire) maintain nominal troop strength at a level of 2,000 to 5,000. Such troops are utilized, as are many of those in the large nations, substantially in the fulfillment of domestic tasks in the absence of effective internal police forces, and as support for government authority where there are military regimes in power. Thus, their utilization essentially as fighting forces is questionable, and the picture is further compounded by the likely political conflicts which may at any one time eliminate commitment of numerous troops to any one operation, even an operation in Southern Africa where the use of the armies by some black states would be subject to the influence of major Eastern or Western powers.[57]

In practical terms, therefore (keeping in mind that the total nonwhite contingent of troops is inflated by the inclusion of reserves), it might be realistic to expect the commitment of 10 to 15 percent of the total African troop strength—approximately 200,000 to 270,000 troops, an amount about the size of the likely Southern African white forces. The South Africans boast to be able to mobilize 500,000 troops is highly suspect in view of its manpower vulnerabilities overall. Moreover, there is a serious problem of attrition among the white military-age youth in South Africa due to emigration, which is related to low morale, a problem of motivation lamented by the various South African Defense White Papers.

South African Vulnerabilities

This problem of low white motivation stems from the twin pressures of affluence and unlimited mobility on the one hand, and on the other, whites in South Africa being outnumbered in their own settings and fighting internationally unpopular and perhaps unwinnable wars waged in liberation movements. In addition, it is an open question whether the black and colored soldiers and policemen in South Africa and Namibia would fight "for the last white man" or at some point change sides, as happened in the Algerian revolution and other conflicts.

The white South African numbers shrink even more, however, not only because of the conceptual problem raised by the liberation movements' posing the "two-front" challenge, but because of the present internal antagonisms between the growing military needs of the white-controlled state and the simultaneously growing need for labor to maintain and expand industrial development. In South Africa, for example, this problem has led to the half-hearted cooperation of employers with military training programs.[58] This "third front" then, may be the most affected of all, and severely cripple the ability of South Africa to effectively maintain the necessary logistics to wage effective combat in a conventional setting on multiple fronts.

The basic "third front" dilemma for the whites is the question of whether they are able to leave for war entrusting their industry to the 8.5 million blacks needed to keep it running, or whether the main force will stay and trust the major portion of the war effort to the blacks. Since white South Africans have always manifested a negative attitude toward arming blacks, there are relatively few trained black troops, while the police force is 50 percent black and 10 percent colored. The obvious choice would be for the whites to shoulder the burden of fighting.[59] Meanwhile, the urban black population has reached an estimated 5 million, almost equal in size to the total white population of 6 million, and this would make control of the urban areas in a wartime situation extremely difficult, even with the Commando Force and the Citizens Force to augment the regular Defense Force, since a sizeable percentage of the whites are in the rural areas.[60]

With these limiting factors, it is possible to deduce that since the regime will have fewer troops available for actual combat operations, the dilemma may be so destabilizing as to increase the pressure for South Africa to substitute military technology and explosive force for manpower it lacks.

Irrespective of the problems of the South African regime, as noted in the analysis of the front-line states, they have clear superiority over the continental armies of Africa in the area of military equipment and technology. The intervention in Zaire showed, in a public way, the vulnerability of the Zaire army to attack in a relatively small war, due to the inability of the Zaire government to airlift a sufficient number of troops to the battle scene, thus making necessary the U.S. C-141 transport planes. This situation (together with the lack of other vehicles that would make up a modern air force) plagues nearly all African states with the exception of Egypt, which has over 200 MIGs, an assortment of other naval aircraft, and a variety of other types for a total of 500 combat aircraft. The same deficiency applies to heavy artillery and air defense material such as missiles. Nigeria, for example, has just over 40 combat aircraft and only few SAM missiles.

In constrast, South Africa has more than 300 combat aircraft, sufficient ground transport capability, and a sophisticated air defense force, including modern radar and missiles. This capability, of course is augmented by a sizeable arsenal of civilian aircraft. Such air power is important in their strategy, which has an outer perimeter that is forward of the country borders (often called the "forward defense perimeter"), while the second line of defense (the "inner circle") is manned by light aircraft, light antiaircraft weapons, and missiles.[61]

The All African Defense Force, combined with the more limited regional armies of the six front-line states, nevertheless, are assumed to be involved here in a frontal assault, precisely the situation that has provided the strongest rationale for the utilization of nuclear weapons. One observer says,

> The possibility of using tactical nuclear weapons against troop concentrations instead of a counter-city strike in reaction to a conventional attack against South Africa, could possibly also contribute to deterrence should such a situation arise.[62]

An additional opinion comes from Professor Onkar Marwah and Ann Schulz, who say,

> As a deterrent against conventional attack, nuclear weapons might be effective if we hypothesize a frontal drive by African forces against the South African territory. Such an offensive would obviously have to involve forces other than those of the neighboring black states, and would presumably take place under OAU or other collective auspices with a minimum of two of Africa's largest military powers (e.g. Nigeria, Zaire or Ethiopia) as fully committed participants.[63]

Increasingly, African countries are putting more money into defense. Comparing total expenditures and manpower for the military of selected African states (shown in table 4-1) against those of South Africa yields the results shown in tables 4-2 and 4-3.

As can be seen from this data, the changes in the defense spending in a number of selected (and probably representative) African states, together with the increases in the number of men in arms, compare favorably with those of the South African regime. There is every reason to suspect, therefore, that future increases in military spending will result in the ability of African states to deal with the logistical problems involved in large-scale combat operations somewhat distant from their own countries.

In the meantime, as seen in Zaire, the mere expansion of military forces or defense budgets does not mean a corresponding incresae in military effectiveness. For my thesis to be credible, this unquantifiable factor must also increase markedly.

Then, there is the question of African states' political will to mount such an operation, which is still, as described by one observer, "virtually non-exixtent."[64] Yet, I have described the forces that could, at any moment,

Table 4-1
Military Expenditures and Troop Strength for Selected African States, 1973 and 1983

	1973		1983	
	Expenditures (millions)	Troops (thousands)	Expenditures (millions)	Troops (thousands)
Algeria	$ 215	80	$ 1,334	130
Ethiopia	35	50	381	199
Egypt	2,253	390	2,679	447
Libya	371	20	4,223	68
Nigeria	1,194	305	1,723	222
Morocco	145	65	1,318	135
Sudan	121	35	180	86
Tanzania	44	25	122	43
Zaire	105	65	82	42
Total	4,483	1,035	12,042	1,372
South Africa	757	40	3,132	77
Sub-Sahara Africa	3,800	933	16,900	1,526

Source: *World Military Expenditures and Arms Transfers, 1985*, U.S. Arms Control and Disarmament Agency, Publication 123 (Washington, D.C.: August 1985), pp. 47, 52–88.

Table 4-2
Military Spending for All African States, Selected African States, and South Africa, 1973 and 1983
($ millions, current dollars)

	1973	1983	Percentage Increase
Selected African states[a]	$4,448	$11,661	61%
South Africa	757	3,132	75
African states[b]	3,800	16,900	77

Source: *World Military Expenditures and Arms Transfers, 1985*, Washington, D.C.: U.S. Arms Control and Disarmament Agency, August 1985. See table 10.

[a]Includes Algeria, Egypt, Ethiopia, Libya, Morocco, Nigeria, Sudan, Tanzania, and Zaire (leading military states as of 1973).

[b]Includes only sub-Sahara states.

Table 4-3
Men in Arms for All African States, Selected African States, and South Africa, 1973 and 1983
(millions)

	1973	1983	Percentage Increase
Selected African states[a]	985	1,173	16%
South Africa	40	77	48
All African states[b]	933	1,526	39

Source: *World Military Expenditures and Arms Transfers, 1985*, Washington, D.C.: U.S. Arms Control and Disarmament Agency, August 1985. See table 10.

[a]Algeria, Ethiopia, Egypt, Nigeria, Morocco, Sudan, Tanzania, Zaire, Libya (leading military states as of 1973).

[b]Includes sub-Sahara and North African states.

bring such a unified force into existence. It can, then, be presumed that if the Southern African problem presents a significant threat to the stability of the rest of the independent states of Africa, these logistical problems will be overcome.

Nevertheless, if one assumes such a force, then part of the logistical picture will be the necessity to create regional staging areas, in this case, no doubt, in some of the six front-line states. In fact, the Rabat Summit of 1972 envisioned such a regional defense system complete with a military command structure. Whether or not this system is formalized, it appears that the functional practicalities of the conflict may demand it in any case.

Nuclear Response

In such a situation as that described above, there are probably three graduated types of nuclear responses: (1) an explosion, (2) tactical nuclear weapons, and (3) the use of continental ballistic missiles.

The first assumption of an explosion would have the same effect and objective as in the guerilla war situation, except it would signal to an external force of some magnitude that it could at some point conceivably become involved in a nuclear exchange. This would force the OAU Defense Force to determine the probable point at which this might become a reality and its response to it, given the way in which the retaliatory threat is shaped by the South Africans.

Second, the South Africans could actually deploy and use tactical nuclear weapons. Some obvious targets would be military troops and other strategic targets in the territories immediately contiguous to its boundaries. It could use such implements as necessary across its borders to "hold hostage" certain populations and threaten them with destruction.[65]

With respect to targets, one should, in general, follow Geoffrey Kemp's view that,

> it is preferable to be more explicit about target typologies when examining the options open to medium powers, since their nuclear forces are unlikely to be able to cover all possible combinations of major strategic targets.[66]

Nevertheless, all of the typologies listed by Geoffrey Kemp are considered to be relevant to this study. They are:

1. Military forces and military installations,
2. Major population centers,
3. Industrial structures,
4. Raw materials and energy production centers,
5. Transportation and communications facilities,
6. Agriculture,
7. Educational and cultural centers.

No area on the continent is outside the parameters of the characteristics defined by this listing of possible targets for either conventional or nuclear weapons.[67]

Finally, South Africa could develop and utilize ballistic missiles with sufficient range to reach any one of a number of targets which might include the territory of those states from which the troops come, the headquarters of the OAU itself, land routes used to carry military and/or civilian implements to staging areas, and staging areas themselves.[68]

The objective of the South African government in exercising a presumptive strike using nuclear weapons in this manner would be to demonstrate its military capacity, disrupt the troop delivery system of the African force, and deter as many states as possible from participating in a military operation against it. The consequences of such military action would be of secondary concern to South Africa, since the action is likely to take place from 700 to 2,000 miles from its border, or even farther away.

Notes

1. *Washington Post*, May 27, 1985, p. C8.

2. Jennifer Davis, "South Africa: The Cyclone Is Coming," *Progressive* (February 1985), p. 20.

3. "Four Years after Soweto: Resistance Escalates," *Southern Africa* 13 (June 1980), pp. 2–3.

4. *The Star* (Johannesburg), November 23, 1983.

5. Jeanne M. Woods, "Paper on Five Years of Armed Struggle in South Africa: 1979–1983," North Americal Regional Conference against Apartheid, June 18–21, 1984, New York.

6. *White Paper on Defense and Armament Production*, 1973, Republic of South Africa, Department of Defense.

7. Pauline H. Baker, "South Africa's Strategic Vulnerabilities: The 'Citadel Assumption' Reconsidered," *African Studies Review* 20, no. 2 (September 1977), pp. 89–99.

8. Pan Africanist Congress of Azania, *Report of National Executive Committee Meeting*, September 19–22, 1967, (Moshi, Tanzania: Department of Publicity and Information), p. 13.

9. *New York Times*, April 17, 1982, p. 3.

10. *Afro-American* (Washington, D.C.), September 9, 1982.

11. William Gutteridge, "South Africa's Defense Posture," *World Today* 36 (January 1980), p. 28.

12. Beaufre quoted in *The Star* (Johannesburg), January 29, 1982, p. 17.

13. Ibid.

14. Sean Gervasi, "South Africa's Terrorist Army," *Southern Africa* 16, no. 5 (December 1982), p. 5.

15. Richard Leonard, *South Africa at War* (Westport, Conn.: Lawrence Hill, 1983), p. 101.

16. Ibid, p. 100.
17. *Washington Post*, May 5, 1979, p. A17.
18. Jennifer Davis, op. cit., p. 20.
19. Jeanne Woods, op. cit.
20. *Washington Post*, May 5, 1979, ibid.
21. *Rand Daily Mail*, October 31, 1981, p. 7.
22. *Rand Daily Mail*, December 1, 1978.
23. William Gutteridge, op. cit.
24. Robert Jaster, "South African Defense Strategy and the Growing Influence of the Military," in William Foltz and Henry Bienen, eds., *Arms and the African* (New Haven: Yale University Press, 1985), p. 126.
25. Ibid., p. 131.
26. Ibid.
27. Tanzania allowed a force of two-hundred Cubans to train ZIPRA guerillas.
28. *Washington Post*, May 17, 1977, p. A14.
29. This, of course, is a perversion of the intention of the law of "hot pursuit" as originally applying to pursuit on the high seas, which terminates once territorial waters or land are encountered. See Gerhard von Glahn, *Law among Nations* (New York: Macmillan, 1965), p. 323.
30. *Africa Research Bulletin*, August 1–31, 1979, p. 5373.
31. David Goodman, "How Reagan Blocks Freedom," *New Africa* 213 (June 1985), p. 21.
32. *Washington Post*, April 16, 1985, p. A15a.
33. *Washington Post*, June 4, 1985, p. A20a.
34. *Washington Post*, April 4, 1977, p A1.
35. "Foreign Report," *Economist* (London) 1672, (March 19, 1981), pp. 3–5.
36. *Le Monde*, December 31, 1982, p. 4.
37. *New York Times*, January 31, 1981, p. 3.
38. *Washington Post*, March 19, 1981, p. A25a.
39. "Foreign Report," *Economist*, op. cit.
40. *Washington Post*, October 8, 1984, p. A1d.
41. *Wall Street Journal*, January 29, 1985.
42. *The Military Balance, 1984–1985* (London: International Institute for Strategic Studies, 1984), pp. 74–89.
43. Walter Barrows, "Changing Military Capabilities," in Foltz and Bienen, op. cit., p. 119.
44. Robert Jaster, op. cit., p. 148.
45. Zdenek Cervenka, *The Unfinished Quest for Unity*, (New York: Africana Publishing, 1977), p. 39.
46. Ibid., p. 59.
47. Ibid., p. xviii.
48. Godwin Matatu, "Shaba: Zaire's Armageddon," *Africa* 69 (May 1977).
49. Ibid., p. 24.
50. *Washington Post*, May 21, 1978, p. A1; *Sun* (Baltimore), June 4, 1978.
51. *New York Times*, June 3, 1978, p. 7.
52. *Washington Post*, May 24, 1978, p. A1.
53. Ibid.

54. Karl Lavrencie, "Foreign Intervention Issue Looms Over African Summit," *Christian Science Monitor*, July 19, 1978, p. 4.

55. *Washington Post*, July 23, 1978, p. A1.

56. *The Military Balance, 1984–85* (London: International Institute for Strategic Studies, 1985).

57. See *World Military Expenditures and Arms Transfers, 1972–1982* (Washington, D.C: U.S. Arms Control and Disarmament Agency, April 1984), pp. 95, 99.

58. Ibid.

59. Stockholm International Peace Research Institute, *Southern Africa: The Escalation of a Conflict*, (New York: Praeger, 1976), pp. 119–120.

60. R.W. Johnson, *How Long Will South Africa Survive?* (New York: Oxford University Press, 1977), p. 295.

61. *White Paper for Defense*, op. cit., p. 54.

62. M. Hough, "Deterrence and Deterrence Interaction with Reference to the South African Situation," *Politikon, South African Journal of Political Science* 5, no. 1 (June 1978), p. 8.

63. Onkar Marwah and Ann Schulz, eds., *Nuclear Proliferation and the Near-Nuclear Countries*, op. cit., p. 221.

64. J.E. Spence, *South Africa: The Political and Military Framework* (Upsala, Sweden: Africa Publications Trust, 1975), p. 62.

65. Marwah and Schulz, op. cit., p. 222.

66. Geoffrey Kemp, "Some General Elements of Nuclear Strategy," in Geoffrey Kemp, Robert L. Pfaltzgraff, Jr., and Uri Ra'anan, eds., *The Super Powers in a Multinuclear World* (Lexington, Mass.: Lexington, 1973), p. 149.

67. Ibid., p. 150.

68. Ibid.

5
The Development of U.S. Nuclear Relations with South Africa

W hen National Security Council's Study Memorandum no. 39 was revealed to the public in 1975, it confirmed what many observers had implied—that the United States was following a deliberate policy of closer relations with South Africa.[1] More important was the fact that the National Security Study Memorandum (NSSM 39) also exposed a more extensive underlying rationale for U.S. policy toward Southern Africa. For, although the United States has always been a "verbal" critic of apartheid, at the same time, U.S. investments in the South African economy had continued to grow, while the companies which had so invested have suffered no reprimands from the government for their apparent complicity in the apartheid system. Here, I agree partially with Barnett and Muller that,

> While some of the argument for this change of policy (NSSM 39) was strategic (access to the Indian Ocean) the principal reason was to bring foreign policy into line with a reality that major U.S. companies had created long ago: South Africa under its present hospitable investment climate has a useful role to play in the new world economy.[2]

Now this connection has been noted often, and from the standpoint of the realist-idealist basis of foreign policy, people have understood this type of economic integration to reside within the realistic national interest of the United States and other Western powers. The dominant idea was that the position of South Africa within the Western economy and its European origins formed the basis for its integration into a wider matrix of states that are an extension of Western influence.[3]

I will attempt to illustrate what forces (even unwitting ones) in the United States are involved in this push to integrate South Africa into the West, and the conflict caused by those opposed to such a policy as each group struggles to determine the course of the U.S. involvement in South Africa on this issue of nuclear trade. In doing so, I will discuss the historical outline of the basis for U.S.–South African nuclear cooperation and the aborted sale of a nuclear power plant by General Electric to South Africa. I will examine the impact of imports through a review of the international uranium cartel, and conclude with an investigation of various U.S. legislative policy options pertaining to the problem of South African nuclear capability.

Outline of the Relationship

The U.S.-South African nuclear materials trade began as a result of the United States and British need for raw uranium fuel in their atomic energy programs, specifically in the production of nuclear weapons. On August 19, 1943, the Quebec Agreement initiated the Combined Policy Committee which dealt with the common energy problems of the United Kingdom, Canada, and the United States. From this arrangement the Combined Development Agency (CDA) was formed; it was this agency that negotiated the agreement with the South African Atomic Energy Board in the late 1950s, for the virtual birth of the South African uranium industry.[4] The United States, during this period, was in desperate need of substantial supplies of uranium for its nuclear weapons program. The situation was critical, since, during 1950, 82 percent of its requirements came from the Belgian Congo (Zaire), where production could not be increased. It was, therefore, deemed necessary to develop alternative long-term suppliers, since the uranium industry in both the United States and Canada were in the infant stages of their development.

The 1950 Heads of Agreement negotiations provided for a financing plan on a ten-year basis through interest-bearing loans made directly to the South African mining companies by the U.S. Export-Import Bank and the British government. The total capital investment was approximately $200 million, with $129 million borrowed from the Eximbank and $65 million from the British.[5] This financing made possible the construction of seventeen uranium-processing plants in addition to seven pyrite plants for the production of sulphuric acid. Previously, the mining emphasis had been on gold since, of the twenty-six companies involved in uranium production, only four recovered the mineral as a primary activity, while the remainder recovered it as a by-product of gold mining residues.

The original ten-year agreement made possible the production of 24 million tons of uranium ore annually, with all of this output consigned to the United States and Britain at a fixed price of $11.20 per ton, which was high enough to induce production at very profitable rates. In 1958, however, the CDA negotiated an agreement with South Africa to limit deliveries to 6,200 tons of oxide per year through 1963, with graduated reductions each year, terminating in 1966. By this time, the uranium industry in the CDA countries had shown the capacity to fulfill national requirements.[6]

This closed market for the development and sale of its uranium ore was highly profitable to South Africa. For example, in 1962, production was 5,024 tons and total sales were 4,594 tons, of which 99 percent (4,562 tons) were sold to the United States and the United Kingdom. These sales in one year amounted to approximately $100 million. Nevertheless, after 1967, when all sales under the agreement were terminated, the South African uranium industry went into a period of decline, even though a "stretch-out" program was negotiated to defer deliveries through the extension of its contract to 1973 with the British, and to 1971 with the United States.[7] Yet, of the seventeen processing plants previously in operation in 1960, by 1963, seven had ceased operation; of the remaining ten plants, only five were in operation after 1966. Accordingly, the sales of uranium per pound stood at a level of $4.00 in the mid-1960s, the situation to which an international cartel would address itself in the early 1970s, with South Africa playing a leading role.

Between 1953 and 1971, the United States imported from South Africa 43,260 tons of U_3O_8 (nonenriched uranium) at a value of over $450 million. South Africa also negotiated two long-term, fixed contracts for the import of low-enriched uranium from the United States for its two prospective power reactors at the Koeberg station, at an estimated value of $120 million.[8] Of this amount, South Africa had provided $4.6 million in advance payments by 1976, and had also paid to U.S. firms a total of $1.6 million for other nuclear materials between 1971 and 1975.[9]

The amounts above would have been increased by $200 million in sales if public pressure had not forced the disruption of the award of a license to export two nuclear reactors by General Electric to the South African government.[10] Although the fixed contract with South Africa was large, some indication of the size of U.S. enrichment services may be gained by the knowledge that the South African portion represented only 1.2 percent of such services totaling $10 billion in 1976.

While the Allis-Chalmers Manufacturing Company provided a reactor to South Africa in 1961 at a cost of $450,525, other firms have, since that time, provided other materials critical in South Africa's experimental nuclear activities. For example, special nuclear materials (mainly enriched uranium fuel and plutonium) have been provided by U.S. Nuclear, Gulf Oil, United States Steel, Texas Nuclear, and Gulf General Atomic.[11] Source materials such as thorium and depleted uranium have been provided by Kerr-McGee, Zirconium Corp. of America, and Picker International, while by-product materials were traded by Beckman Instruments and Vernon Craggs. Edlow International was licensed to import materials from the

South African reactor for reprocessing under supervision of the U.S. Energy Research and Development Administration.[12]

The Agreement for Nuclear Cooperation (AFNC)

The original agreement, "Atomic Energy Cooperation for Civil Uses," was signed by the United States and South Africa on July 8, 1957. This document of twelve articles reflected the hegemonic position of the United States over the international nuclear industry in that the agreement contained language illustrating strong U.S. controls—such as the imposition of limits and required clearances upon South Africa in the process of cooperation.[13] The agreement was amended first in 1962, giving evidence of South Africa's intentions to acquire dual reactor capability.[14] The agreement was next amended in 1965, when the IAEA became a third party to the agreement, basically affecting articles X and XI of the original agreement and giving the IAEA a role in the administration of a safeguard system.

Nevertheless, in 1965, the third-party agreement transferring responsibility for safeguards to the IAEA was purchased by the United States for a price. In the first instance, SAFARI-1 operated at 5 megawatts until 1969, when it was adjusted to reach 20 MW, utilizing highly enriched uranium provided by the United States. In addition, the South Africans requested 600 kilograms of low-enriched (2 percent) uranium and 305 tons of heavy water. Johan S.F. Botha (minister of the South African Embassy in Washington) indicated to Dept. of State officials on January 6, that,

> his government had not yet reached a decision on the transfer of safeguards to the IAEA, but he had been requested by Mr. Sole [Donald Sole of the South African government] to inform the Department that it would help "to speed up the process" if South Africa could have, as soon as possible, assurances that the full South African requirements would be met.[15]

In addition, the South Africans informed the U.S. officials at this discussion that, inasmuch as the United States had agreed to supply extra fuel in the amount of 8 kilograms of uranium beyond that needed for the initial loading of the SAFARI-1 reactor, their own calculations came to 9.25 kilograms. The Dept. of State subsequently agreed to these requests made by the South Africans at the end of January, asking that there be no publicity of U.S. fulfillment of these requests due to its efforts to prevent further serious deterioration of the situation in the Congo (another vital source of U.S. uranium).[16] Furthermore, U.S. officials, indicating a delay in deliveries for the reasons mentioned, concluded all arrangements on fuel deliveries in a subsequent meeting in New York between U.S. government officials and Hilgard Muller, minister of foreign affairs for South Africa.[17]

The agreement was next amended in 1967, increasing the percent of uranium enrichment and expanding the quantity limitations exported to South Africa. It also established the idea that quantities of fuel (enriched uranium) in excess of that needed to load the reactor could be held by South Africa by agreement of both parties. Formerly, U.S. approval had been required on a case-by-case basis.[18]

The process of amending the AFNC had previously been to approve modest changes, but the subsequent amendments of 1974, in their scope and direction, set the greatest liberalizing precedents of all on U.S.–South African exchanges in nuclear materials.

In scope, the document has changed from its earlier use as an agreement to guarantee fuel deliveries, becoming an enabling document without supply assurances but of a much longer-term duration. The South African government, for example, requested a 25-year term as the basis of new fuel deliveries for its prospective nuclear power plant, which would become critical in 1982. This period was added to the eight-years the U.S. desired before fuel delivery commitments commenced, thus making the total period thirty-three years for which the agreement was extended by amendment in article I until 2007.

An important caveat was added to the instruction given by the Dept. of State for the intragovernmental decision making concerning 1974 amendments. This caveat resembled that of 1965 in one respect—they were handled in a quasi-secret fashion. One of the instructions counseled: "note that no public announcement will be made by the AEC concerning the amendment and agreement but the Office of Information Services will respond to inquiries."[19] However, in view of the interest and responsibility of Congress in such matters, Congressman Charles Diggs, Jr. (chairman of the House Subcommittee on Africa) and Senator Richard Clark (chairman of the Senate Africa Subcommittee) were notified of the amendments. It was upon this notification as well as the subsequent knowledge of General Electric's prospective sale of a nuclear power plant to the South African government that both Diggs and Clark began to question officials on the matter in 1975. They convened formal hearings in 1976.

The General Electric Case

In connection with his appearance before the Clark Senate Subcommittee on Africa hearings on the General Electric sale of nuclear facilities to South Africa, Mr. James Blake (deputy assistant secretary of state for African affairs) was questioned by Clark concerning whether the sale would be of positive benefit to U.S. policy toward Africa. Blake responded that it would permit the United States to maintain contact with South Africa in an area of cooperative activity which was of obvious importance to them both. Being more explicit, however, Blake stated:

> What I am saying, Senator is that at a time when South African coopera-
> tion and understanding will be important to us in endeavoring to achieve
> the objectives the Secretary outlined in his Lusaka speech, we cannot
> forget the importance of certain things to South Africa itself. *This transac-*
> *tion is obviously of importance to the South African Government. If we*
> *did not go forward with it, I am not saying it would be disastrous in terms*
> *of our dialog, but if we did go forward with it, it is entirely conceivable it*
> *would help that dialog.* (emphasis added)[20]

Senator Clark appeared somewhat taken back by the suggestion that there was some connection between this particular sale and the Kissinger initiatives with respect to the U.S. role in the solution of the political problem of South Africa involving both Zimbabwe (Rhodesia) and South Africa. Therefore, he sought to clarify the response Blake had given by the following question:

> You are saying if we sold them [the South Africans] $200 million in
> nuclear reactors, something as you say which is very important to them,
> that might give us a certain advantage in terms of diplomatic relationship
> with them to help them bring about a solution with Ian Smith in Rhodesia
> or in Namibia. Am I stating your position correctly?[21]

Blake responded:

> I think that is a fair statement of it. But I would like to stress again that
> these are obvious decisions that go right to the very core of South Africa's
> internal and external policy. I am certain they are going to make those
> decisions in terms of their own national interest.[22]

Here is a situation based on an immediate motive which benefits both countries economically but which also has military, strategic, and political objectives projected as the real national interest. It is difficult to tell what the consummation of such a deal would have meant in political terms to the dynamics of the Southern African situation. Nevertheless, one can see that it fits well within the framework of NSSM 39 and what I will show later came to be its economic corollary: the doctrine of "reliable supplier."

The impact of the Nixon administration's policy of cooperation and contact with South Africa upon foreign investment is another important topic, the full discussion of which is largely outside the scope of this book. However, between 1969 and 1972, potential exporters brought intense pressure to relax U.S. restrictions on direct Eximbank loan guarantees to the

South African government. In his testimony before the Clark Senate Sub-committee on Africa in May 1976, Professor John Marcum said,

> In 1969 Secretary of Commerce Maurice Stans, responding to corporate pressure, sent a memorandum to President Nixon, urging a relaxation of restrictions on U.S. loans, arms sales and promotion of exports to South Africa.
>
> Arguing his case, Stans noted that "political objectives may not always accommodate important economic interests." And indicative of which set of interests might prevail in case of conflict, President Nixon, on Secretary Kissinger's advice decided to reverse an earlier (1964) cutoff of direct Export-Import Bank loans to South Africa.[23]

Marcum went on to say that the decision was kept secret and the bureaucracy never informed, and so its implementation took place in ways not likely to attract attention.

Apparently, by 1974, this policy was still in operation as the U.S. government approved the sale of two large computers by the Foxboro Company of Foxboro, Massachusetts, to the South African government, which promptly installed the equipment in their uranium enrichment plant.[24] This sale was approved by the Office of Management and Budget (OMB), Dept. of State, Dept. of Commerce, and the Atomic Energy Commission. Inside the Foxboro Company, it went under the code name "Project Houston" in order to "discourage questions."[25] James T. Lynn, head of OMB, said that the intelligence community was aware of the purpose of the sale before the license was granted by the U.S. government, yet nothing was done to prevent it.

The fact that 28 U.S. banks were involved in providing a loan of $200 million to the South African Electricity Supply Commission through guarantees from the U.S. Eximbank was, no doubt, one of the major considerations in the South African government's decision to initially consider a U.S. domestic firm for the construction of its nuclear power plant.[26]

As early as 1970, discussions involving representatives of the South African government and General Electric relative to building their initial power plants (then assumed to be two 550-megawatt electric nuclear reactors scheduled for late 1977 start-up) reflected the strong desire on the part of the South Africans to deal on the basis of a "turnkey" contract. The other factor involved in General Electric's decision to participate was the attitude of the U.S. government toward prospective financing of a South African nuclear power reactor station. Both of these problems were related to an assured fuel supply (as anticipated in the 1974 amendments to the cooperation agreement) and involved a decision at the highest levels of the U.S. government. By 1976, as reflected in the Diggs Hearings on this sale, the Dept. of State had given its approval.[27]

In light of this approval, the Dept. of State's view of the General Electric sale is interesting. In an exchange with Senator Charles Percy

(R-Ill.) during his testimony before the Senate Subcommittee on Africa in 1976, a Dept. of State official admitted, after a question by Percy as to the role political instability would play in the economic decision to commit the Eximbank, that "political instability would be a factor weighing on the decision on what the credit worthiness would be." Then, Senator Percy asked, "But you have given preliminary approval, is that correct?" Stated Mr. Minikes, "We have given a preliminary commitment, that is correct."

But pressed further by Percy as to the role played by political instability, the department representative said,

> Senator, we issued the initial preliminary commitment in 1974. Our view of South Africa today is that it is a nation which is rich in resources and has an economy which is fundamentally sound. There, of course, is the situation you mentioned, of possible political instability in the long run or short run—I have heard it described both ways.[28]

Thus, although he felt that political instability would play a role in the bank's final decision to approve the loan guarantee, he clearly did not view the situation from any moralistic perspective or any political perspective in line with previous U.S. commitments in the international strategy to combat apartheid. Nevertheless, the public scrutiny and substantial Congressional opposition to this sale caused South Africa to withdraw its tender to G.E. and select the French consortium Framatome instead. Thus, this case provides a revealing look at attitudes in the United States toward growing South African nuclear capability.

The Nuclear Nonproliferation Act of 1978

In April 1977, President Carter released his proposed Nuclear Nonproliferation Policy Act of 1977, amending the Atomic Energy Act of 1954. It was introduced in the Senate as S.1432 by Senator John Glenn, and in the House as H.R.4409 by Representative Jonathan Bingham.

Under article IV, section 404 of the act passed March 10, 1978, the president was directed to initiate a program of renegotiating existing agreements for nuclear cooperation with all countries in an effort to affect compliance with new trade standards compatible with the requirements of the new legislation.

Chief among the concerns expressed in those sections of the act dealing with nuclear export criteria (such as conduct requiring termination of nuclear exports, trade in nuclear components, and peaceful nuclear activities) is a concern with bringing all of the nuclear facilities of a trading partner under the safeguards system of the International Atomic Energy

Agency. South Africa maintains Koeberg I and II and SAFARI-1 under international safeguards through an IAEA trilateral agreement with France and the United States, but neither its enrichment plant for uranium nor the other reactor, Pelinduna-Zero, are safeguarded under any international system. Nor does South Africa accede to the international nuclear nonproliferation treaty.

The U.S. Nuclear Nonproliferation Act of 1978 says, in article III, section 128(a), no. 1, that:

> No such export shall be made unless IAEA safeguards are maintained with respect to *all* peaceful nuclear activities in, under the jurisdiction of, or carried out under the control of such state at the time of the export. (emphasis added)[29]

Since the Agreement of Cooperation then in force only covered safeguards on materials—"equipment and devices transferred to the Government of South Africa"—it was clear that it did not meet all the conditions of the new act of 1978.

According to article IV, section 403(a), no. 5, "No nation or group of nations will assist, encourage, or induce any non-nuclear weapons state to manufacture or otherwise acquire any explosive device." This clause is potentially broader than operative paragraph no. 4 of United Nations resolution 418 (1977), in that it suggests a prohibition on assisting a non-nuclear-weapons state in manufacturing explosive devices, which would appear to cover the neglected area of trade or provision of *materials and technical assistance* necessary in the construction of nuclear explosive devices.

The essence of this legislation is that it provides the president with the initiative in the area of nonproliferation, if he wants to exercise it, but it contains many loopholes and blocking roles for Congress if there is no strong desire to affect high standards of nonproliferation performance by prospective parties to international nuclear commerical arrangements. Such lack of firm leverage in the law gives South Africa considerable room for maneuver in view of the fact, as noted earlier, that many incentives for South African adherence to tough policies of nonproliferation pressure from supplier states are fading due to its increasing status in the field. Part of that maneuvering ability is, as suggested, derived from the current position of South Africa in the market for nonenriched uranium.

The Carter Negotiations

From the passage of the Nuclear Nonproliferation Act of 1978 to the end of the Carter administration, former SALT II negotiator Ambassador Gerard

Smith (representing the U.S. Arms Control and Disarmament Agency) shuttled back and forth attempting to conduct discussions to bring the South Africans into compliance with the NNPA of 1978. As noted, the basic demand was that in exchange for the continuation of nuclear exports, the United States wanted South Africa to accede to the Nuclear Nonproliferation Treaty and accept full-scope safeguards administered by the IAEA. More specifically, the South African government announced in June that it would be prepared to sign the treaty if it could obtain guarantees from the United States for such items as long-term supplies of low-enriched uranium fuel for the Koeberg reactors, supplies of highly enriched uranium fuel for the SAFARI-1 research reactor, and assurance of nonsensitive technology for its new uranium enrichment plant at Valindaba.[30]

In addition, South Africa argued that it would not expose the details of its locally developed uranium enrichment technology to open inspection, and demanded the right to keep these details secret and protected in any safeguards process. But one of the most controversial statements was attributed to Carter's chief nuclear proliferation spokesman, Undersecretary Joseph Nye, Jr. He reportedly suggested that a Washington negotiating tactic is the attempt to encourage nations to accede to the nonproliferation treaty in exchange for the protection of the U.S. "nuclear umbrella" as a disincentive for them to develop nuclear weapons.[31] Speculation was strong, therefore, that South Africa was also engaged in negotiating certain security guarantees in exchange for the abrogation of its ability to manufacture nuclear weapons.

In exchange for the right to continue nuclear exports, the United States wanted, of course, South African agreement to the Nonproliferation Treaty and a little more. The other objective was to obtain agreement from the South Africans that in SAFARI-1, they would utilize enriched uranium of a lower level than had been previously provided by the United States. As I have stated elsewhere, over the years, the United States had provided South Africa significant amounts of highly enriched (93 percent in the isotope U-235) uranium, which is of nuclear weapons grade. But the immediate problem was to get South Africans to accept uranium enriched to levels as low as 35 to 40 percent. But even though it would be more difficult, a nuclear weapon could still be fabricated with materials enriched to this low level.

This attempt was in line with the general policy of the Carter administration which, for example, took a dim view of full utilization of the Clinch River Breeder Reactor facility and the Barnwell chemical reprocessing facility because of the impetus these facilities would lend to the stimulation of a "plutonium economy" in global nuclear affairs. The attempt of the Carter administration to pursue a policy of generally reducing plutonium output with its European allies met with great resistance, a factor which stiffened the opposition of nonnuclear states to the new nonproliferation policy as well.

Nevertheless, the negotiations were ultimately unproductive for this reason as well as the generally hostile climate of relations between the South African government and U.S. representatives such as Ambassadors Andrew Young and Donald McHenry, with respect to the issues of Zimbabwe and Namibia's independence and black political participation in South Africa.

This hostility between the United States and South Africa should not be construed, curiously, to extend to the basic nuclear relations philosophy of the Carter administration. It was the view of the administration, stated in October 1977 and reiterated in March 1978, that it was not the intention of the United States to completely sever nuclear relations with South Africa, and that to do so would only "encourage separate development of South Africa's own nuclear potential."[32] This point of view comported well with the nonproliferation strategy earlier outlined by Dept. of State official Joseph Nye and others inside both the administration and the nuclear industry.

Nevertheless, due to political problems in Southern Africa, during the remaining years of the Carter administration, the attempt to negotiate a valid nonproliferation agreement with South Africa was not productive for assorted other reasons. First, South Africans could afford to be recalcitrant because of their four-year lead time until they would absolutely need fuel for the first loading of the Koeberg reactor. Then, the existence of their pilot enrichment plant gave them the ability to enrich small quantities of uranium in order to keep their research reactors going. But the decisive factor was the knowledge that there existed a considerable competition among nuclear supplier states which would afford them the opportunity to choose an alternate supplier, albeit at a high price. This necessitated a certain flexibility in the U.S. negotiating posture.

It was noted by some close observers of this problem that the United States had asked the South African government to allow periodic inspection of its nuclear plants by the IAEA "on the condition that there would be no inquiry into the amount of plutonium and weapons grade uranium the plants have produced in the past."[33] Such a negotiating posture, while in itself a realistic incentive, was probably part of a package which may have included even the proposal put forth by Joseph Nye, Jr., regarding U.S. nuclear security guarantees. But perhaps this package did not weigh as heavily in the minds of South African officials as did the more immediate political problem created by the imminent independence of Zimbabwe. Ironically, the nuclear talks aimed at securing nonproliferation guarantees from South Africa might have been aborted by the South African perception that an independent Zimbabwe posed a heightened security threat, as illustrated by the difficulty encountered by Britain and the United States in pressuring South Africa to remove thousands of its troops from southern Zimbabwe in early January 1980. Certainly, the dramatic failure of these negotiations and the security context in which they were conducted would have been clear to all if the Carter administration had admitted that South Africa had, indeed, tested a nuclear weapon in September 1979.

Finally, it should also be noted that even though Kissinger apparently operated on the basis of a deal to facilitate the construction of Koeberg in exchange for South African cooperation on Zimbabwe and Namibia, it appears that the successful award of the contract to General Electric would have made little practical difference in the ultimate South African security perceptions or in their response to them.

Conclusion

On the occasion of the release of the Senate Nonproliferation Bill in 1977, Senator Charles Percy singled out South Africa, stating that, "ominous questions have also been raised about [its] nuclear weapons intentions," and citing the need to curb this "extraordinary threat."[34] The rationale has been provided in this book; to reiterate the essentials of the threat, the South African government has:

1. Mined and sold significant quantities of raw uranium from its own and (illegally) Namibian sources, possibly to states under such volatile conditions as Israel.
2. Received substantial supplies of enriched uranium from the United States under long-term agreement for cooperation. These supplies may have been subject to diversion to weapons production or reprocessing for stocks of plutonium.
3. Developed an indigenous nuclear power production capability as well as the ability to enrich uranium to weapons grade.
4. Developed a program for exporting enriched uranium, perhaps to other volatile states in the international system such as Iran, Pakistan, Taiwan, and South Korea.
5. Probably conducted a nuclear test explosion, yielding the strong suspicion that it has developed weapons. Several credible sources openly make this suggestion.
6. Hinted that one of the main areas of probable utilization of a potential nuclear weapon is on the African continent.

Assuming that the factors above constitute much more than a modest confirmation of Percy's sentiment, it might have appeared, at the end of

Carter's term, that an even stronger approach to South Africa was necessary than that eventually set forth in the NNPA (passed in 1978). In the following chapter, we will examine whether or not the Reagan administration heeded the warning offered by Senator Percy, or proceeded to follow a different course in the balance between its efforts to restore U.S. leadership in international nuclear trade and the demands of nuclear nonproliferation.

Notes

1. See Edgar Lockwood, "National Security Study Memorandum 39 and the Future of United States Policy toward Southern Africa," *Africa Fund* 4, no. 3 (Fall 1974); Mohammed El-Khawas and Barry Cohen, *The Kissinger Study of Southern Africa* (Westport, Conn.: Lawrence Hill, 1976).

2. Richard Barnett and Ronald Muller, *Global Reach: The Power of the Multinational Corporations* (New York: Simon and Schuster, 1974), p. 88.

3. Ronald Walters, "The Global Context of U.S. Foreign Policy toward Southern Africa," *Africa Today* (Summer 1972).

4. Ragnar Rollefson, "National Strategy Paper on South Africa," (Washington, D.C.: U.S. Dept. of State, December 13, 1963).

5. Ibid.

6. Ibid.

7. Ibid.

8. "Resource Development in South Africa and U.S. Policy," op. cit, p. 297.

9. Ibid.

10. See Ronald Walters, "The Nuclear Arming of South Africa," *Black Scholar* 8, no. 1 (September 1976), pp. 25–31; "Apartheid and the Atom: The United States and South Africa's Military Potential," *Africa Today* 23 (July–September 1976), pp. 25–37.

11. "Resource Development in South Africa and U.S. Policy," op. cit., p. 31.

12. Ibid.

13. Series 385, "Atomic Energy: Cooperation for Civil Uses, Agreement Between the United States of America and the Union of South Africa," *Treaties and Other International Acts*, July 8, 1957.

14. *Treaties and Other International Acts*, series 5129, June 12, 1962.

15. Series 5880, "Atomic Energy: Application of Safeguards by the IAEA to the United States-South Africa Cooperation Agreement," *Treaties and Other International Acts*, February 26, 1965.

16. Aide-Memoire, Amembassy (American Embassy) Pretoria, January 29, 1965.

17. Ibid.

18. *Treaties and Other International Acts*, series 6312, August 17, 1967.

19. Summary Sheet, "Agreement for Cooperation between the U.S. and South Africa," April 22, 1974.

20. "U.S. Policy toward Africa," Hearings, Subcommittee on African Affairs, Subcommittee on Arms Control, International Organizations and Security

Agreements, Committee on Foreign Relations, U.S. Senate, 94th Cong., March 5–May 27, 1976 (Washington, D.C.: GPO), p. 299.

21. Ibid.

22. Ibid.

23. Ibid, p. 241.

24. *Washington Post*, May 26, 1976, p. A2.

25. Ibid.

26. See notes 1 and 23 in this chapter. See also, Hearings, Subcommittee on Africa, U.S. Senate, op. cit., p. 242.

27. Dixon B. Hoyle, "General Electric Comments on Nuclear Power in South Africa," May 12, 1970; also, "Meeting with General Electric on South Africa, etc.," Note to the Files, Dept. of State, June 8, 1970.

28. Hearings, Subcommittee on African Affairs, U.S. Senate, op. cit., pp. 326–27.

29. *Congressional Record*, February 9, 1978, p. H914.

30. David Fishlock, "S. Africa Seeks Pledge on U.S. Nuclear Package," *Financial Times* (London), June 27, 1978, p. 1.

31. Robert Manning and Stephen Talbot, "Carter's Nuclear Deal with South Africa," *Inquiry* (October 30, 1978), p. 9.

32. *Washington Post*, November 1, 1977, p. A18. See also a reiteration of the Young position by Zbigniew Brzezinski, *Star* (Johannesburg), March 10, 1978.

33. *Nuclear Engineering International* 22, no. 261 (August 1977), p. 13.

34. *Congressional Record*, March 3, 1977.

6
Constructive Nuclear Engagement: The Engine of Proliferation

The Reagan Administration

As a presidential candidate, Ronald Reagan showed a favorable attitude toward South Africa that served as an early indication of his policies as president. Just as important to this analysis, however, is the fact that he was also considerably more lenient than Jimmy Carter on general issues of nuclear nonproliferation. In fact, in an interview with Walter Cronkite of CBS News in early March 1980, Reagan expressed very positive attitudes toward South Africa. More important, he also said, in reply to a question regarding his view on the issue of opposing the development of nuclear weapons by foreign countries, "I just don't think it's any of our business."[1] While he later amended that statement, saying that he favored nonproliferation but saw little chance of its success, this attitude may tell us much about his handling of the second "mysterious flash" which occurred shortly after his election and which was not announced until over one month after he had been officially installed in office.

On February 18, 1981, the (Johannesburg) *Star* newspaper reported U.S. intelligence officials' beliefs that a flash occurring December 16, 1980, over a remote part of the earth near the South African cape, detected by an early-warning satellite, was a nuclear event.[2] Contrary to the earlier flash of September 22, 1979, this time the Dept. of Defense quickly concluded that because its source was not a *light* flash but had emanated from a *heat* source of intense but brief duration, this flash was that of a meteor.[3] Also contrary to the earlier flash, no corroborating evidence was found, nor did the Dept. of Defense release the identity of the satellite having made the observation. Just as important (considering the previous occurrence and the importance such events have for world affairs) was the lack of response from the White House to this incident. It was as though the South Africans had presented the new administration with their first test of loyalty and the U.S. had signaled in the affirmative by ignoring the episode and acting swiftly to stop any speculation. The effect created a unified govermental response along the lines of the official statement to the extent that there was "no disagreement" about this in "expert circles."[4] This response occurred despite "expert opinion" in the case of the 1979 flash, citing fantastic odds against a meteorite explanation, making a second such occurrence appear even more preposterous.

Beside this important initial indication of the Reagan attitude toward South African nuclear politics, the administration came into office under the limitations of the NNPA of 1978 and, therefore, found itself wanting to foster closer relations with South Africa but facing this sizeable obstacle. Important bilateral talks between the United States and South Africa were set for May 14, 1981, at the foreign minister level, covering a series of foreign policy issues. However, even before this meeting, the parties were known to have been engaged in high-level diplomatic exchanges regarding the 1974 contract for the United States to supply $30 million in enriched uranium to South Africa as fuel for the Koeberg station, which had been held up by the NNPA.

Perhaps a month before the talks, South Africa informed visiting representatives of the IAEA that it had fueled its SAFARI-1 reactor with 45 percent enriched uranium which it had manufactured in its own uranium enrichment plant.[5] While this was, no doubt, posturing previous to the talks, it was an attempt by South Africa to demonstrate its own capability in a way that would alleviate some of the U.S. leverage over its nuclear bargaining position. There were two immediate implications of this development: (1) if South Africa could enrich uranium for SAFARI, it could eventually do the same for the Koeberg reactors, and (2) the 45 percent level of uranium enrichment was satisfactory enough to make a crude nuclear explosive device, but an explosive device, nonetheless. This step, together with strong protestations by the South African government that they had expected the approach of the Reagan administration to be more favorable toward them in nuclear matters, set the stage for a concrete discussion between South African foreign minister "Pik" Botha and Secretary of State Alexander Haig in Washington on May 14.[6]

In Spring 1981, sensitive Dept. of State documents containing the essence of likely South African nuclear demands in the May 14 discussions were obtained by Trans-Africa, a black American lobby organization on African and Caribbean issues.[7] In a memorandum from Chester A. Crocker, assistant secretary for African affairs, to Secretary Haig, Crocker sketched the history of the nuclear relationship between the two countries, emphasizing the present dilemma which found the United States hard pressed to supply the fuel for Koeberg "timeously" by a policy that prevented the South Africans from obtaining other sources of supply and that could result in delays to the start-up of Koeberg and serious financial damage to the South African government, damage estimated to be as much as $1.2

million per day. Crocker further indicated to Haig that South Africa was not opposed to the NPT, provided its "basic requirements" could be met; that it would continue to abide by the spirit, goals, and principles of the NPT informally; and that at no time had it tested a nuclear device. The memo went on to state as factual that South Africa was being "threatened by the U.S.S.R. and its associates" (certain African countries with Soviet support), and by the United Nations institutions to the extent that its own security interests were at risk. Under such conditions, it continued, South African officials had apparently indicated to Crocker that they could not afford to sign the NPT and "thus set the minds of our would-be attackers at rest, allowing them to proceed freely with their plans against us."[8] This last statement has the strong hint that the South African possession of a nuclear capability performs a deterrent function, since they themselves established a link between their nuclear designs and their security. The logical implication of this is to suspect that they are actually in a position to utilize a nuclear weapons option.

Finally, the memo deals with those things which South Africa requests of the United States, presenting three options. The first option was that the United States should honor the original agreement, providing the needed fuel for Koeberg by executing the required pending export licenses for delivery of the fuel to France for fabrication into fuel rods for the reactors; second, that the United States should make it known to France that it would relieve South Africa of the binding provisions of the original contract, making it possible for France to supply the fuel; and third, that the Dept. of Energy should cancel the original contract at no cost or agree to postpone its execution until such time as matters between the United States and South Africa permit the resumption of a contractual relationship.

With regard to the first option, Reagan administration negotiators were operating under the NNPA restrictions on nuclear exports, and it was their judgment in the earlier discussions that the public mood as well as the legal and administrative procedures prevented timely provision of the fuel. More likely, the second and third options became the more serious items of discussion; that is to say, for the more immediate problem of supplying Koeberg with fuel for the first reactor core loading, the United States could have encouraged South Africa, with French assistance, to seek an alternative source of supply for the fuel. In fact, one investigator states that a "knowledgeable source" informed him that "the U.S. has suggested that South Africa look elsewhere for enrichment services for Koeberg's first core."[9] This leaves the third option for the long-term supply problem, in the sense that, at some point, DOE can either cancel the original contract or finally work out some solution making resumption of the original supply contract feasible.

Subsequent to and probably as an outgrowth of the May 14 talks, there was movement on all three options in 1981. In an effort to avoid a further complication over the uranium fuel supply contract, in June, DOE suspended throughout the remainder of FY 1981 financial penalties for the late delivery of uranium fuel for enrichment. This allowed South Africa to deliver the 300 metric tons of raw uranium to a DOE enrichment facility at Oak Ridge, Tennesee, in August without delinquency fees. The plan, then, was that the enrichment services would be performed on the fuel, which would then be stored at the site of a new enrichment facility being built at Portsmouth, Ohio, but the fuel would not be shipped to South Africa until there was a successful resolution of their outstanding difficulties.[10]

Movement was also detected on the sticky issue of safeguards which South Africa had refused to entertain, the issue (one of its "basic requirements") being that its enrichment technology must be protected in the safeguards process. In August, a two-man team of South African nuclear scientists from its Atomic Energy Board visited the United States to inspect the Portsmouth, Ohio, enrichment plant under construction. It was one of the most advanced examples of an attempt to design and construct an enrichment facility with safeguard features in mind.[11] Then, the following October, a four-man delegation from the United States visited the Pelindaba enrichment facility at Valindaba, but it was reported that the U.S. group was not permitted to tour the inside of the facility.[12] While the United States had demanded that South Africa accept full-scope safeguards and sign the NPT in exchange for nuclear exports, there was widespread speculation that South Africa would accept the full-scope safeguards and reject the NPT, giving it the status of Spain, Brazil, and Argentina.

South Africa has benefitted to some extent from U.S. training in safeguards procedures, since there is evidence that at least four South African nuclear energy personnel have undergone training in a program provided by the United States, called the "Physical Protection of Nuclear Facilities and Materials," since 1978.[13] One disturbing aspect of this training of South Africans is that a component of the training includes "a field trip to the Barnwell Nuclear Fuel Plant."[14] (The Barnwell plant is a spent fuel reprocessing plant with an advanced system of safeguards.) U.S. assistance in reprocessing technology could assist the South Africans in separating plutonium, a highly fissionable material, from their own spent uranium fuel.

In any case, the U.S. effort has been on such elements of safeguards as physical surveillance, nondestructive assay, and materials accounting, but the IAEA agreements with member countries apply only to verification of accounting data at the expense of sophisticated monitoring and measuring technology. The net effect of the current low status of IAEA-administered safeguards (as confirmed by the GAO, the NRC, and agency experts also) is that the South Africans could agree to full-scope IAEA-administered safeguards that would include their enrichment plant and that would have limited effect on their ability to divert materials for the manufacture of nuclear weapons. Indeed, such sentiments were confirmed in an interview conducted by David K. Willis of *Nucleonics Week* with J.W.L. de Villiers (president of the South African Atomic Energy Board) in late 1981, when Willis asked why South Africa should be the first to put its uranium enrichment plant under full-scope safeguards. He also went on to confirm that Pretoria was exploring with the United States a "nuclear trade-off" which held that South Africa would agree to international safeguards on all of its facilities, including the enrichment plant, if the United States would agree to reactivate the long-term uranium fuel supply contract.[15]

In late October, at the time of the U.S. technical mission to South Africa, John Barratt (director-general of the South African Institute of International Affairs) was reported by the *Christian Science Monitor* to have noticed that with respect to the nuclear fuel issue, South Africa was "noticeably silent" about its need for enriched uranium from the United States. On the other hand, he suggested that the United States was simply trying to hold on to its share of South Africa's nuclear industry.[16] This observation by Barratt was amazingly accurate, because a few weeks later on November 12, press reports from Johannesburg indicated that South Africa had obtained enough enriched uranium fuel for the first loading of Koeberg.[17] Indeed, Framatome had announced in Paris the previous week that the fuel loading of the first reactor would proceed on schedule for June 1982. Immediately, there was intense speculation regarding the origin of the 3 percent enriched uranium, with U.S. officials indicating that China (PRC) was a likely source, a charge which the Chinese government immediately denied as "sheer fabrication."[18] Nor were details forthcoming from either the South African Electricity Supply Commission (ESCOM) or the French nuclear officials, and while U.S. officials showed mild signs of discomfort due to the possible undercutting of U.S. nonproliferation efforts by the French, other observers suggested that the U.S. reaction was mild.

In fact, *Nucleonics Week* said that "The U.S. is not overly disturbed by the ESCOM enriched uranium purchase . . . [since] both Koeberg and any fuel burned in it are under safeguards."[19] They went on, however, to point out the exact source of the uranium: it was purchased by the South Africans from Kerndraftwerk Kaiseraugst, a consortium of Swiss, West German, and French companies building the Kaiseraugst reactor unit in Switzerland. Then the uranium was transferred to Eurodif's Tricastin plant for enriching, and from Eurodif, it was given to Framatome to be fabricated into fuel rods for the reactor core assembly.

One reason for the lack of concern by U.S. officials is not only that the fuel is safeguarded by an IAEA agreement, but that earlier, in Spring 1981, U.S. officials may have encouraged the South Africans to seek an alternative source for the uranium, given their difficulties with the NNPA, to the point where U.S. cooperation was either implied or assured. Certainly, it must be recognized that the strategies employed by the South Africans, if executed with the assistance of the United States, have materially solved the problem of its supply of fuel.

In the acquisition described above, approximately 130 tons of uranium had been purchased, an amount which would be nearly enough for two full loadings for both Koeberg reactors, but the importance of this is that it would allow the operation of Koeberg's two reactors, perhaps at reduced power, until the South African enrichment plant produces enough fuel for subsequent loads. This line of reasoning is mitigated to some extent by the fact that in April 1982, Transnuclear, Inc., a U.S. firm with a South African subsidiary, applied to export 24,252.12 kg of 3.3 percent enriched fuel fabrication.[20] This potential export, however, is also subject to NNPA restrictions, such that one concludes that the export is a long-term back-up move on the part of the South Africans.[21]

About the time it became public knowledge that South Africa had purchased enriched uranium for Koeberg, thus freeing itself from the NNPA strictures, it also arranged the sale of about 5 percent of its enriched uranium held at Portsmouth to the Japanese utility Kyushu Electric Power, attempting to free itself from the total American commitment as well. Since the United States permitted this sale, there is every reason to presume, as did some, that ESCOM "presumably would attempt to dispose of the 2-million swu (80,000 kg) it contracted from DOE to other utilities."[22] The result is that such a strategy has been completed and it is obvious that it was designed to neatly circumvent the NNPA by allowing South Africa to eliminate the source of leverage the United States used against them in order to have them sign the NPT.

Finally, there is the strong indication that the United States may have played a more fundamental role in facilitating the supply of the enriched uranium to South Africa than suspected. U.S. officials had encouraged South Africa to seek alternative supplies in Spring 1981. It was discovered in Spring 1982 that two U.S. firms, (Edlow International of Washington, D.C., and Swuco of Rockville, Maryland) had played a role as brokers in the purchase of uranium from the Swiss consortium for delivery to Eurodif for the South Africans. Whether or not this was done on the direct authority of the U.S. government remains undetermined, but it is clear that some U.S. officials met "from time to time" with representatives of these companies and may have known more about the source of the uranium than was publicly admitted.[23]

In fact, while other "official spokespersons" were reported to be giving out the false information that China was the source of the fuel, James Malone (assistant secretary of state for oceans and international environmental and scientific affairs) appeared before the Subcommittee on Nuclear Proliferation (chaired by Senator John Glenn) a few days after the announcement from Paris, and suggested that the most probable source of the uranium was within the European community.[24] Malone was the person responsible for nuclear negotiations with the South African government at the time of the May 14, 1981 talks.

Senator Glenn's letter to Secretary of State Haig in January 1982 indicated that information had been developed by his staff indicating that the two companies in question were involved to the extent that at one point they actually took title to the uranium from the Swiss consortium for transfer to Eurodif. Senator Glenn took issue with the Dept. of State view that the actions of these firms were outside of the jurisdiction of the United States so they did not have to report the activity. He appeared to base his differences on the moral ground that this activity by U.S. firms undercut the nonproliferation policy of the United States, especially since these firms are beneficiaries of government licenses for trade in nuclear materials.[25] Far more persuasive a case against the companies involved in providing this uranium is found in section 302(b) of the NNPA:

> It shall be unlawful for any person to directly or *indirectly* engage in the *production* of any special nuclear material *outside of the United States* except (1) as specifically authorized under an agreement for cooperation made pursuant to section 123, including a specific authorization in a subsequent arrangement under section 131 of this Act, or (2) upon authorization by the Secretary of Energy after a determination that such activity will not be inimical to the interest of the United States (emphasis added).[26]

Although there is some question as to the accuracy of press reports indicating that the companies actually took title to the uranium at one point, it appears to be beyond dispute that their brokering activity resulted in the production of special nuclear material. They took raw uranium and transferred it to an enrichment facility, the result of which was the production of enriched uranium. It is also beyond question that the NNPA clearly stipulates that "indirect" activity is prohibited—even outside of the United States. There remains, therefore, a gray area with regard to the intent of the law and the permissible "brokering" activity of firms.

There also remains the question of whether or not this activity was legally sanctioned by the Secretary of Energy according to important domestic exceptions, expressly provided for in section 2 of the NNPA. It is, in fact, very possible that these firms were in violation of the law, but despite this possibility, given that U.S. nonproliferation policy was clearly undercut by the activity of the firms, the fact that neither the Dept. of State nor any other official agency voiced condemnation of this activity leaves the strong impression of not only assent but complicity by the government.

In preparation for June 1982 hearings on the improvement of the administration of the NNPA, Congressman Jonathan Bingham, chair of the Subcommittee on International Economic Policy and Trade, asked DOE officials to comment upon some of these problems. At the hearing, James Culpepper (assistant secretary for international security) said:

> As for brokering activities, such as those referred to by the Committee which led to the sale of enriched uranium to South Africa those activities did not involve any of the areas identified in Part 810.7 as requiring a specific authorization, and were not performed in a country on the prohibited list.[27]

Saying, "We do not attempt to control brokering," Culpepper went on to suggest that legislation effecting brokering activities "would not be very practical" because of the manner in which it occurs. In support of his position, he cited four specific reasons relating to the "minimal effect" such an attempt to control brokering would have, including the delays imposed upon U.S. utilities and foreign counterparts, the equally negative effect upon the role of the United States as a reliable supplier, and the additional work load imposed upon nuclear export control staffs. However, while the net effect of this criticism is that the monitoring of brokering activities would be a nuisance, the control over U.S. firms involved in the type of brokering that runs counter to stated U.S. foreign policy objectives in the nuclear field would appear to be in the national interest. It is, therefore, again surprising that, while officials of the U.S. government state that there was no official involvement in the Edlow-Swuco sale to South Africa, there was no finding by the secretary of energy that such a "deal" was, according to his legal mandate under the part 810 authorizations, "inimical to the national interest."

Such a "commerce-oriented" view comports well with the general approach of the Reagan administration to nuclear policy. In both July 1981 and late July 1982, the president's spokespersons signaled the intentions of the administration to follow a policy which would, for example, put reprocessing and uranium enrichment in the hands of private companies and sever the government control, make possible the export of plutonium technology, construct and operate the Clinch River Breeder Reactor, and develop closer nuclear commerce with South Africa.[28]

With regard to the last point, what was described as a "policy shift" was revealed in a letter from the Secretary of Commerce Malcolm Baldrige to Senator Charles Percy. The letter was reported by the *Washington Post* to have announced a more "flexible policy" by the administration, liberalizing the approval of export licenses for so-called dual-use nuclear materials and equipment, especially where "health and safety" uses were the avowed purpose.[29] The importance of such a policy is that while exports related to the production of special nuclear materials are regulated by the

Nuclear Regulatory Commission and the Dept. of Energy through the NNPA, exports that may also be used to manufacture a nuclear explosion, but that are common items of industrial commerce in many cases, may be permitted export licenses by the Dept. of Commerce. Then, despite the fact that an interagency body known as the Subgroup on Nuclear Export Coordination (SNEC) (the Depts. of Energy, State, Defense, and Commerce, plus the Arms Control and Disarmament Agency and the Nuclear Regulatory Commission, chaired by a Department of State representative) monitors such exports, it has allowed, for example, the sale to South Africa of five separate nuclear-related items since 1978. (See table A–1 for additional sales.) Also, although under the Carter administration SNEC held up the sale of a powerful Cyber 170/750, which is capable of modeling a nuclear explosion, eventually the Reagan administration allowed the Dept. of Commerce to export the computer to the Council for Scientific and Industrial Research, a South African government agency with strong technological ties to its nuclear development program.[30]

While a member of SNEC admitted their inability to certify that computers would not be used "to perform runs for the South African nuclear program," officials at the Dept. of Energy emphasized their view that a more flexible export policy would increase U.S. influence in nuclear proliferation matters.[31] W. Kenneth Davis (deputy assistant secretary in the Dept. of Energy) said that the United States had exercised world leadership in nuclear affairs because of its dominant position in nuclear trade, and that this leadership was lost when the Carter administration policies destroyed the credibility of U.S. efforts to maintain its supply and service commitments.[32] He seems to suggest that U.S. ability to contribute to the control of the spread of nuclear weapons was based on its prominence in nuclear commerce. However, his colleague Eugene Rostow, former director of the Arms Control and Disarmament Agency, pleaded that the NNPA approach to proliferation was based on "the nostalgia for an epoch of monopoly that is gone."[33]

Missing from both of their assessments is the fact that nearly thirty years of nuclear commerce (which the policies of the Carter administration attempted to restrain too late) has helped to provide important nuclear capability to states such as South Africa, and that trade has, therefore, been the *engine* of nuclear proliferation.

At issue here is the question of whether or not the long-utilized doctrine of "reliable supply" is, as the Ford/Mitre study suggested in 1977, "an effective nonproliferation argument."[34] This concept, which finds it roots in the Atoms for Peace Program, was the fundamental premise of the Agreements for Nuclear Cooperation consummated by the United States with other countries before the NNPA of 1978, and was carried forward by Carter administration officials as the basis of their policy as well. Most important, however, if it is stripped of its ability to be an effective deterrent to the acquisition of nuclear capability, especially nuclear weapons capability, the doctrine amounts to a public relations theme for U.S. access to the marketplace in nuclear materials or, in other words, normal commercial competition.

It is perplexing that South Africa has never appeared to be particularly motivated by strategies that assumed that there would be "assurance of supplies" of any given commodity, since it has been made acutely aware of the international hostility to the character of its government and the many relationships which flow from it. In fact, I have shown the contrary, that it has assumed unreliability in its relations with other states, including the United States. What rational incentive would such a state have to invest a high degree of confidence in assurances of any state that it would maintain normal commercial relations in any given area? The expectations that a state such as South Africa would have such confidence, when all signs indicated that, in fact, it did not, places the pursuit of such a policy under the most serious suspicion. In fact, it is possible to conclude that such formulations, together with the burden placed upon ineffective safeguards, appear to be rationalizations for nuclear commerce rather than effective strategies to deal with nuclear proliferation.

The essentials of the argument is that by serving as a "reliable supplier" of nuclear materials, states would forgo the decision to acquire full fuel cycles themselves, depending instead upon supplier states such as the major powers. In turn, such supplier states, by becoming reliable, would gain important leverage over the nuclear activities of states consuming nuclear materials. Yet, if this concept were valid, then the international system would not have witnessed the development of so many second-level states having nearly acquired basic facilities of the nuclear fuel cycle and, thus, having reached the point of ambiguous proliferation.

Dr. Albert Wohlstetter's point below is valid in that the question of the possession of that elusive substance "leverage" is, at best, confusing. The United States often disclaims significant political leverage, while at the same time basing nuclear export policy on the need to retain economic leverage over the politically based proliferation desires of customer states, although this leverage is seldom if ever utilized. He suggests that,

> Such reliable supply [the Dept. of State] claims, will enable us to influence the importers. [This is] exactly the opposite of the truth. Importers will be influenced to stay away from stocks of explosive material only if it costs them something not to do so, and only if our threats of sanctions are taken seriously.[35]

An example of this point may be found in the 1977 congressional hearings on South African nuclear development. Joseph Nye, Jr. (deputy to the under secretary for security assistance), while supporting the use of export controls to address the problem of proliferation, said,

> We simply do not have the leverage to exact compliance with sweeping new provisions, insistence on which could be seen by many of our nuclear partners as a breach of our supply commitments. They could decide to take the route of developing their own indigenous facilities.[36]

Without such leverage, South Africa could still make the decision to continue to trade with the United States, and even then, the pledges required under the new legislation would not deter South Africa from continuing to develop its nuclear facilities—facilities that would be adaptable to dual utilization, should the need arise. In addition, it is extremely questionable, since the threat to security is endemic in the case of South Africa, that Nye's description of the process of nuclear development may lead to unintended nuclear proliferation, or such a thing as "innocent progress toward the bomb." This condition is purported to exist where a country is dedicated to the development of nuclear energy for electricity, discovers a threat in the course of its development, and decides to manufacture nuclear weapons.[37]

Despite the record of closer nuclear cooperation with South Africa, the Reagan administration protests that it has made an effort to regulate nuclear exports through the instrument of the SNEC. The SNEC, meeting on the average of every three weeks, inspects the requests for exports related to nuclear developments with regard to the items on the Nuclear Referral List (a listing of prohibited export items) and compares these applications with the data from intelligence agencies concerning the nuclear program in the countries under question and the stated end use of the export.

In the case of South Africa, from the time this monitoring procedure has been in effect to mid–1986, there have been nearly four-hundred nuclear-related exports, of which only 3 percent were rejected for nuclear reasons.[38] The large number of nuclear-related exports to South Africa and the low level of rejections throws additional light on the apprehension of those who charge that despite the NNPA, there is a need for additional legislation that would also cover the licensing activities of the Dept. of Commerce. This would affect the new policy of closer nuclear cooperation announced by Secretary Baldrige, whose policy related to the health field. But even there, it is known, for example, that mass spectrometers, while used primarily for health purposes, also have some uses in aspects of nuclear explosives.[39] As a Dept. of Commerce spokesman said:

> If we make a determination in consultation with all appropriate agencies and the intelligence community that the end use will be in the health field, then we would approve that export to a country that is a non-signator of the NPT, like South Africa.[40]

The secretary's view, then, would appear to confirm the determination of the administration to push ahead with dual-use nuclear exports despite the risk that they may also be used in a nuclear weapons program. That is why, in addition to legislation proposed by some members of Congress concerned with the general problem this poses for nonproliferation, legislation has also been introduced with the specific intent of prohibiting certain aspects of U.S. cooperation with South Africa in the nuclear field. This effort has involved, for example, the persistent initiative Congressman Charles Rangel (D-N.Y.) began in the 96th Congress with his H.R. 7220 to prohibit U.S. nuclear cooperation with South Africa.

The administration provided a rather comprehensive description of U.S. nuclear policy toward South Africa during congressional hearings on the Rangel bill which prohibited "cooperation of any kind" in the nuclear field with South Africa.[41] While Dept. of State officials appeared annoyed that sufficient credit had not been given the administration for refusing to export nuclear fuel for Koeberg and for admonishing the French to do likewise, they presented a nuclear export policy with a range of approval somewhat wider than mere "health-related" items. For example, a large hot isostatic press (hip) was not approved for export because of its use in weapons fabrication, but a case-by-case policy was adopted with respect to small hips. Then, in approving the export of helium-3 (an element used to produce a nuclear explosion) and a hydrogen recombiner for Koeberg, they stated that "commerce-licensed items needed for the safe or environmentally sound operation of the Koeberg nuclear power plant" would be approved.[42]

Of course, making the Koeberg plant "safe and environmentally sound" could encompass an expansive variety of exports, depending upon the interpretation. One official sought to link this expanded commerce to nonproliferation policy by artfully suggesting that inasmuch as the administration had set a high priority on restoring the role of the United States as a "reliable supplier of nuclear materials," an added reason for this specific policy was that a modest export program could enable the United States to continue a "dialogue with South Africa regarding nuclear proliferation issues." His opposition to the Rangel measure was, thus, that it would thwart exports and, ultimately, the dialogue on nuclear proliferation objectives. A Dept. of Commerce official at the December 2 hearings, however, was more direct in his view that opposition to the Rangel bill was based on its "negative economic impact."[43] This was being said, it should be noted, as Secretary of State George Shultz was reportedly attempting to arrange "a politically acceptable system" for improving international trade in U.S. nuclear technology abroad.[44]

This permissive atmosphere was also undoubtedly a stimulus to American nuclear technicians going to work at the Koeberg plant. Although it was anticipated that the French consortium would train the necessary personnel for Koeberg, a sharp fall-off in immigration in the late 1970s left the engineering field in South Africa short of qualified personnel.[45] ESCOM first advertised in Britain for nuclear engineers, then in the United States for nuclear plant operators and physicists.[46] By January 1985, forty American technicians were discovered to be working at Koeberg, in violation of a 1983 statute which required authorization from the secretary of energy for U.S. citizens to assist in the direct production of plutonium, either at home or abroad.[47] It was further discovered that these technicians had been lured away from such facilities as the Tennessee Valley Authority, Carolina Power and Light Co., and Southern California Edison's San Onofre nuclear plant with lucrative contracts from a secret "strategic fund" maintained by ESCOM in the United States.[48]

U.S. nuclear export policy was closely geared to the general export policy toward South Africa which, on one occasion, Princeton Lyman (deputy assistant secretary of state for African affairs) said was to maintain "continued access to four strategic nonfuel minerals" for which the United States . . . was dependent upon South Africa,"[49] either because lack of suitable alternatives to South African sources or the attractiveness of lower South African prices. While Lyman drew attention to nonfuel minerals, another situation requiring comment is the extent to which the United States is becoming price dependent upon a fuel mineral—South African uranium— that may provide an additional reason for the policy of "constructive engagement" (the general South Africa policy of the U.S.) in the nuclear field. In terms of the impact of U.S. price dependence upon South African uranium, there appear to be two subjects worthy of discussion, the volume of uranium imports and the effect of price dependency for imports upon the domestic purchasers.

Uranium Imports

As my review of the international uranium market previously indicated, the price of the commodity began to slump badly in the late 1970s, after enjoying marked increases in the early part of the decade. A direct reaction to this was the sharp deterioration of the U.S. uranium production industry when "producers discovered that they could purchase the material at prices below their production costs."[50] By the early 1980s, the situation had become so dismal that industry spokespersons such as Eugene Lang (senior vice president for operations of Rocky Mountain Energy Co.) were saying, "I am convinced that we are positioned at a time in history to witness not only the death of the uranium industry in the United States but most of the base metals industry as well."[51] The twin factors of high production costs

Table 6-1
South African Share of Foreign Uranium Imports to DOE for Enrichment, 1977–83
(thousand pounds raw uranium ore)

	Total Foreign Imports	Imports from South Africa	South African Share
1977	1,406	312	22.29%
1978	1,456	212	14.56
1979	3,182	604	18.98
1980	2,482	78	3.14
1981	2,264	444	19.61
1982	5,988	1,784	29.79
1983	4,414	2,038	46.17[a]
Total	21,192	5,472	average 22.06

Source: Survey of United States Uranium Marketing Activity, 1983 (Washington, D.C.: Energy Information Administration, U.S. Dept. of Energy, August 8, 1984), p. 29, Table 17, "Countries of Origin of Foreign Uranium Delivered to DOE Enrichment Plants for Domestic End Use."

[a]South Africa, 46.1 percent; Canada, 28.5 percent, France (including Niger and Gabon), 15.4 percent; Australia, 9.9 percent.

in the United States combined with a low international market price caused by overproduction in the mid-1970s contributed to supply shortages in the United States, especially at certain prices, and an increased penetration of the U.S. market by foreign suppliers.[52] At the same time, imports of foreign source uranium for domestic consumption began to grow as a share of the domestic market (as shown in table 6-1). In fact, it was suggested that by the 1990s, foreign suppliers' penetration of the U.S. market could reach 50 percent of total uranium consumption.[53]

The facts support Lang's assumption, as uranium imports from South Africa to the United States grew by 350 percent from 1981 to 1983 to the point that they constitute 20 percent of South African exports. Indeed, uranium is now the fourth largest import from South Africa overall. The impact of this has been devastating upon U.S. producers as indicated, for between the mid-1970s and mid-1980s, the ranks of producers fell from 362 to only 15. Simultaneously, the work force in the uranium producing industry fell from 9,009 in 1981, to 6,379 in 1982, to 3,723 in 1983, while the South Africans were expanding exports to U.S. utilities.[54] Thus, in 1983, eight of these utilities used over 2,500 tons of South African and Namibian uranium, and projections by NUEXCO (a uranium consulting firm) suggest that by 1995, the United States could be using at least 10 million pounds (or 5,000 tons) of South African uranium.[55] Such a level would be an estimated 10 percent of total U.S. requirements by that time, which would represent a marked level of dependency, but not one that could not be reduced. DOE enrichment contracts would also be impacted, since South

African and Namibian uranium constitutes about 10 percent of total contracts, a doubling of which would bring about a significant government-to-
government relationship in the field of uranium enrichment.

This picture illustrates the point that as foreign source uranium gains
a share of the U.S. market, South Africa's share of uranium imports grows.
In fact, the share of South African uranium has grown faster than the
increased use of imported uranium overall, to the point that by 1984 South
Africa was second only to Canada as a foreign supplier of uranium to the
United States.

The law relating to the importation of foreign uranium has been
extremely permissive, due to the former position of the United States as the
world's leading producer and exporter. For example, in 1974, quotas were
set on the importation of foreign uranium for enrichment (for either
domestic use or export by the owners); the only reference the law made to
potential overdependence is that: "If the extent of domestic use of foreign
uranium should impair or threaten to impair the common defense and
security, the Commission will institute such measures as are deemed necessary."[56] By 1982, however, legislators were considering that such dependence on foreign uranium was calling "into question our future capacity to
obtain uranium for military purpose" as well as for the production of
electricity.[57] Thus, the inevitable concern has led to the consideration of
imposing limits and attempting to restore the productivity of the domestic
uranium industry.

A solution to this problem must take into consideration the question of
limitation of external sources of uranium, but it should also consider the
basis of that limitation beyond the question of mere dependency. For
example, it is highly likely that some of the uranium imported from South
Africa is of Namibian origin, since South African producers participate as
partners in the Rossing uranium mine production in Namibia. In addition, the United States apparently observes no prohibition on the importation of Namibian uranium to domestic utilities. To the contrary, it has
historically been interested in the capacities of Rossing.

The Rossing Mine

In May and June 1976, Congressman Charles Diggs held hearings on the
question of South African nuclear capability and subsequently submitted
questions to ERDA for the record. He specifically requested information
concerning U.S. imports of uranium from the Rossing uranium mine in
Southwest Africa (Namibia).[58] ERDA's public reponse to this question was
that since Rossing had had no production in 1976, there could have been no
uranium imported from there into the United States, but this leaves open

the question of special effort made by ERDA or its predecessor organization, the Atomic Energy Commission (AEC), to check on uranium production in Namibia. Such a question is important because it indicates the degree of U.S. interest in Namibian uranium.

In fact, this interest originated long before Diggs's inquiry. On October 21, 1969, at a meeting between representatives of the AEC and Dept. of State, representatives of the AEC pointed out the importance of its program of obtaining information on activities at the Rio Tinto-Zinc operation at Rossing. They felt that reports from the regional minerals officers of the U.S. Embassy in South Africa were inadequate and that there was a need for AEC confirmation of the Rossing capacity.[59]

By May of 1969, AEC representatives were still convinced of the necessity for an on-site inspection and appeared upset that the Dept. of State had not approved their proposal for a visit to the Rossing site. The view of the Dept. of State was that the political situation made such official contacts in Namibia untenable in view of the dispute over the territory waging in the United Nations, and that under the circumstances, a visit there by U.S. official representatives would give public recognition to South Africa's protectorate status over that territory.[60] Several days after the meeting called for the expression of these sentiments, the matter was taken up at a higher level, as Myron Kratzer (then assistant general manager for international activities of the AEC) said he would "strongly recommend that we be allowed to follow up on the informal contacts already made and attempt to arrange a visit by AEC personnel to the Rossing mine."[61] Representatives of the AEC had met informally in London with members of the South African Atomic Energy Board, and Dr. Roux (president of the board) had written to the AEC extending the invitation for such a visit, thus, adding additional pressure on the Dept. of State to relent.

There are no indications of how many visits were made between 1970 and 1973, but on November 20, 1972, Rafford L. Faulkner, director of the division of raw materials at the AEC, made a visit to the Rossing mine which appears to be the first such visit. This intense manifestation of interest by the AEC in developments at Rossing came about because the potential of the mine was set to be at about 5,000 tons of production per year by 1977, making it the largest open-pit uranium mining operation in the world. Such an operation would automatically make Rossing important in the world market and of immense interest to potential consumers.[62]

Rossing Uranium Limited is jointly owned by the British firm Rio Tinto-Zinc, a multinational corporation and the South African government's Industrial Development Corp., with minor interests owned by General Mining and Finance Corp. Ltd. Rossing, therefore, is essentially a British-South African venture and is undergirded by a long-term contract with British Nuclear Fuels Corp. for the purchase of 7,500 tons of uranium between 1976 and 1982. But the strength of U.S.–South African relations has not depended to any measurable extent upon developments at Rossing, but, rather, on more recent developments in nuclear trade.

Decree no. 1 for the Protection of the Natural Resources of Namibia, of the United Nations Council for Namibia, was enacted in 1974 by the General Assembly, and requires permission of the council for exploration, mining, processing, selling, or exporting any Namibian natural resource. Further, it states that such resources should be utilized for the benefit of the Namibian people.[64] Doubtless, the United States and other importers of raw uranium feed from South Africa are in violation of decree no. 1; thus, imports of South African uranium should be prohibited upon this basis as well.

A second important consequence of U.S. price dependency on uranium was discovered when prices rose in the mid-1970s, causing considerable reverberation among U.S. domestic suppliers such as Westinghouse. The role of U.S. nuclear energy companies as purchasers of foreign source uranium is important in understanding the dynamics of the demand by the way in which the price-sensitive entities react to increases or decreases in the market price. The nuclear energy utilities are also an important part of the domestic uranium industry; it is often at this level of domestic consumption that foreign policy, especially trade policy in any commodity, has its sharpest competitive impact. Thus, it is also interesting to understand whether or not this sector of the industry is at all sensitive to the question of apartheid as a barrier to the utilization of uranium originating in South Africa.

The Westinghouse Case

In September 1974, Westinghouse Corp. officials told their directors that they would be unable to acquire 30 million kg (65 million pounds) of uranium for delivery in the 1978–85 period, for contracts totaling approximately $2 billion. A public announcement followed in August 1975, wherein Westinghouse told domestic client utilities of its inability to deliver the contracted uranium at the old price, citing section 2–615 of the U.S. Uniform Commercial Code, which allowed firms to exempt themselves from contracts due to unforeseen and uncontrollable circumstances.[65]

The price of uranium on the international market had shot up rapidly from about $4 per pound of uranium U_3O_8 to over $40 per pound; producers were attempting to renegotiate old contracts with Westinghouse at $8 per pound in the early 1970s, to the new prices. At the same time, the customers of Westinghouse were demanding that the company stand firm at their old prices and deliver the uranium. Westinghouse was, therefore, caught in the middle, reflecting one of the cartel's prime objectives—to drive Westinghouse, a middleman uranium supplier, out of the market. In one instance, NUFCOR, the South African government-business uranium consortium, received a bid from Westinghouse to purchase an amount of uranium at what was described as 25 percent below "club prices" and they declined to sell to Westinghouse.[66]

Nevertheless, Westinghouse's twenty-seven utility clients sued under breach of contract, since Westinghouse contracts for the supply of nuclear reactors to these firms also contained requirements for the supply of uranium fuel. One case, *Duquesne Light Company, Ohio Edison Company and Pennsylvania Power Company v. Westinghouse,* was tried in Pittsburgh, and resolved in March 1977, when Judge Martin Wekselman agreed to a settlement which involved Westinghouse providing these companies with an undisclosed amount of cash plus certain valuable new equipment, technical services, and engineering.[67]

In Summer 1976, a federal grand jury was empaneled to investigate worldwide uranium pricing to determine whether there had been violations of antitrust laws by Gulf Oil. Then, documents obtained by Friends of the Earth (an environmental group in Australia) from the Mary Kathleen Ltd. mining company which purported to reveal Gulf Oil's involvement in the cartel, together with South Africa, surfaced in California where Congressman John Moss was conducting hearings in November of the same year. Also, on October 15, 1976, Westinghouse sued Gulf and twenty-nine uranium producers in District Court in Chicago, Illinois.[68]

Gulf, meanwhile, countersued Westinghouse on May 9, 1977, alleging that it promised to supply uranium it did not have, while conspiring to monopolize markets in reactor sales and fuel fabrication. Gulf responded to the charges of its involvement by the public defense that its actions were not illegal and that they were taken by its Canadian subsidiary, Gulf Minerals Ltd., in light of "predatory U.S. uranium pricing policies which put a ban on foreign source imports."[69] Here, a *New York Times* "letter to the editor," from William E. Moffett, vice president of Gulf Oil Corp., is instructive:

> When Gulf was forced to surrender certain documents pertaining to the cartel to Congress, we were severely criticized by the Canadian Government. The Canadian Government's sensitivity to this issue is more understandable when it is recognized that one of the reasons it helped form the uranium marketing arrangements was in response to the United States Government's efforts to control the uranium market by banning the use of foreign uranium in U.S. reactors.[70]

The essence of these charges appears to be that the internal U.S. uranium market constituted a closed cartel-like market which could only be competed against through the formation of an external cartel. But, despite the release of some documents, the lack of other pertinent documents produced by Gulf has been sufficient to make allegations against its activities difficult to prove. Accordingly, the grand jury called to investigate its activities finished its work on May 9, 1978, without returning a single indictment.[71]

Another major round of lawsuits involved U.S. uranium producers which had contracted to supply uranium to General Atomic (a Gulf-Royal Dutch Shell joint venture). One of these producers, United Nuclear, Inc., sued General Atomic, seeking to force it to give up $700 million pounds at $6 to 10 per pound. General Atomic was obligated to sell the fuel to the utilities, but the price rose, putting it in a similar position, as a middleman, to Westinghouse. So General Atomic pleaded "commercial impracticability."

If domestic producers had been released from these contracts with utilities, then they would have been free to take advantage of the 300 percent rise in prices, but in the above case, which went to the Supreme Court, the court cleared the way for arbitration of the dispute after a New Mexico court had settled in favor of United Nuclear.[72] In a related case involving Detroit Edison, Duke Power (North Carolina), and Indiana and Michigan Power Company (I and M), the judge ordered General Atomic to deliver the contracted uranium, denying the defense of commercial impracticability.[73]

The New Mexico case involving General Atomic was important because of the finding of Judge Felter that Gulf had shipped documents to Canada, which were impounded by the Canadian government, making "legal discovery" in U.S. courts extremely difficult.[74]

Second, the grand jury might honestly not have had access to sufficient evidence to bring substantial indictments; however, the Dept. of Justice subsequently filed misdemeanor charges against Gulf on May 9, 1978, in the Western District Court of Pennsylvania. The Dept. of Justice alleged that, in effect, Gulf had been involved in a conspiracy to unreasonably restrain trade, "until at least December 21, 1974."[75] This specific date is important, since until then, antitrust violations were only misdemeanors with fines up to $50,000, but after that date, a new law made such charges punishable as felonies with a fine of up to $1 million.[76]

My point, of course, in looking at the way in which the uranium cartel has affected the domestic uranium market is to show the indirect impact of South Africa as a principle uranium supplier and member of the cartel upon U.S. consumption of energy. One effect of the court battles was legal fees running at $300 to 400 million for Gulf altogether and $25 million for Westinghouse in 1977. But while these fees, together with the settlements which could also run into the hundreds of millions, may be written off in taxes as a loss, substantial portions of the costs may be passed on to the consumer in higher energy prices.

Then, there is the direct damage already done in terms of higher energy costs by the operation of the cartel. For example, the documents from the Moss Subcommittee reveal that:

RTZ began an aggressive campaign to tie U.S. prices to world prices in an arrangement which not only tied U.S. prices to world prices (which were rigged), but helped to escalate U.S. prices to world prices so that they could respond in an ever-increasing spiral, providing justification for rising world prices. RTZ was identified as one of the three members of the inner circle which included France's Uranex and South Africa's NUFCOR.[77]

This assertion by the committee staff follows very closely the allegation of the Dept. of Justice, which in its brief of May 9 on the misdemeanor charges against Gulf Oil said in the section on "Effects" that:

(A) United States purchasers of uranium have been deprived of free and open competition among defendant GULF and co-conspirators in the sale of uranium in interstate and foreign trade and commerce;

(B) United States purchasers of uranium have been deprived of the ability to purchase uranium in interstate and foreign trade and commerce except on terms and conditions fixed by defendant GULF and co-conspirators; and

(C) The import and export trade and commerce of United States middlemen have been unreasonably injured and restrained.[78]

By 1981, these legal proceedings, involving perhaps the largest collection of major companies in U.S. history, began to be resolved as Westinghouse and Gulf Oil reached a complex out-of-court settlement in late January. Although details were largely confidential, settlement essentially involved the payment by Gulf Oil of $25 million to Westinghouse and a split of the profits from the sale of the original uranium to be supplied to seven utilities that had contracted to Westinghouse for the supply of uranium.[79] Then, later in the year, Westinghouse settled with 12 more companies active in the cartel. At the same time, the Tennessee Valley Authority's out-of-court settlement was reached with Rio Algom, Gulf Oil, and the five other members of the uranium cartel, which had involved a 1974 contract for 7.7 million kg of uranium.[80] At that point, only 6 of the original 29 defendants had not settled, yet in 1981, other companies such as UNC Nuclear were pursuing suits against the cartel through Gulf Oil Corp. and others.[81]

The Congressional Reaction

The relationship between the United States and South Africa is governed essentially by the perspectives of policymakers on two functional areas— the general state of anti-apartheid politics concerning the two nations and, even more, the politics of nuclear nonproliferation. It is worthwhile to have this firmly in mind because it was the congressional reaction to the deterioration of nonproliferation policy, in the first instance, that prompted a more stringent attitude toward U.S.-South African nuclear relationships. In 1983, for example, one observer suggested that:

> President Reagan is weakening America's ability to slow the spread of nuclear weapons to other countries. He has allowed nuclear exports to go to the most threatening nations without obtaining in return a single open commitment to foreswear nuclear explosives. This encourages an open season in nuclear trade that could unravel the global consensus against nuclear proliferation.[82]

This opinion received substantial support from other close observers of nuclear policy such as John Hamilton and Leonard Spector, who noticed that the new administration, in the process of solidifying the friendship of the nuclear industry and, thus, "stepping up nuclear exports," had attempted to obliterate the nuclear nonproliferation regime constructed by the previous administration.[83] Citing a series of steps beginning with the appointment of James Malone (a friend of the nuclear industry) to the Dept. of State's senior post for nonproliferation, to the approval of controversial sales of nuclear fuel and equipment to Argentina, India, and South Africa (sales circumventing the NNPA), they attempted to establish a pattern of deliberate disregard by President Reagan for the problem the act had intended to help solve.

They also noted in Congress an increasingly important bipartisan reaction to the destruction of the nonproliferation policy. This began with Senate opposition to the president's economic assistance package to Pakistan. The president's effort conflicted with the Symington amendment of 1976, which prohibited aid to any nation accepting imports of special nuclear materials used in nuclear explosives, but the administration's attempt to weaken the amendment was thwarted by Senator John Glenn with strong support from both Democrats and Republicans. As the general struggle to preserve the established nonproliferation policy continued, Congress adopted legislation placing limitations on the U.S.-South African nuclear relationship as well. For instance, in 1983, both the House and Senate passed the Foreign Relations Authorization Act for FY 1984 and 1985, title I, section 1007 of which expressed the sense of the Congress that no nuclear exports should be approved to South Africa, Argentina, or India unless the president determines that certain equipment of nonnuclear materials or technology may be exported to protect health and safety of nuclear operations. This formulation, however, was in practice little more than a confirmation of new policy established by Secretary of Commerce Malcolm Baldrige, as mentioned earlier.

Nevertheless, again in 1984, both the Senate and the House passed measures restricting U.S. exportation of sensitive items of nuclear commerce useful in the fabrication of enriched uranium fuel, unless the specified countries (Israel, India, Pakistan, South Africa, Argentina, and Brazil) agreed to place their nuclear facilities under international safeguards.[84] The measure ultimately failed because of its inclusion in the dissention-racked Export Administration Bill, which had been the main vehicle for anti-apartheid legislation in that year and which failed to be passed out of the Senate/House Conference.

Again, in 1985, both the Senate and the House passed measures restricting nuclear exports to South Africa, as part of the freestanding antiapartheid bills H.R. 1460 and S. 995. The House bill, sponsored by Congressman John Conyers (D-Mich.) was simple in its effect, in that under section 8 said "cooperation of any kind provided for in the Atomic Energy Act of 1954 is hereby prohibited with respect to the Republic of South Africa."[85] While the House bill described in detail the nature of the various prohibitions, the sum of which constituted a ban on all cooperation, the Senate bill was quite similar in such features as prohibiting the issuance of licenses for the export of items used to produce nuclear explosions or equipment to be used in a nuclear production facility of technology, banning the transfer of such materials of technology, and forbidding the involvement of U.S. persons in such activities. The Senate version contained a waiver of the prohibitions to be used by the president if South Africa were to accede to the NPT.

An interesting companion effort to the restrictions on nuclear exports was that by Congressman William Richardson (D-N. Mex.) to similarly restrict the importation of uranium and coal from South Africa and bolster his state's uranium industry. For example, the reported average price of domestic raw uranium in 1983 was $38.21 per pound, while the price of foreign uranium imported into the United States was $26.16, but the price of South African uranium could have been as low as $10 on some 1985 contracts because of the low wage base in the South African mining industry which is inherent in the apartheid system.[86]

In the fall of 1985, the president, faced with the passage of an unpalatable anti-apartheid bill in both houses of Congress and, thus, the obligation to sign a conference version, opted instead to issue an Executive Order containing mild sanctions against South Africa.[87] Section (C) (1) is as follows:

> Issuance of any license for the export to South Africa of goods or technology which are to be used in a nuclear production or utilization facility, or which, in the judgment of the Secretary of State, are likely to be diverted for use in such a facility; any authorization to engage, directly or indirectly,

in the production of any special nuclear material in South Africa; any license for the export to South Africa of component parts or other items or substances especially relevant from the standpoint of export control because of their significance for nuclear explosive purposes; and any approval of retransfers to South Africa of any goods, technology, special nuclear material, components, items, or substances described in this section. The Secretaries of State, Energy, Commerce, and Treasury are hereby authorized to take such actions as may be necessary to carry out this subsection.

This prohibition on U.S. nuclear trade with South Africa would have been an historic break with past policy had it not been for the exceptions the Order went on to enumerate in Section (C) (2):

Nothing in this section shall preclude assistance [to South Africa] for International Atomic Energy Agency safeguards or IAEA programs generally available to its member states, or for technical programs for the purpose of reducing proliferation risks, such as for reducing the use of highly enriched uranium and activities envisaged by section 223 of the Nuclear Waste Policy Act (42 U.S.C. 10203) or for exports which the Secretary of State determines are necessary for humanitarian reasons to protect the public health and safety.

In summary, the Reagan Executive Order, by levying the exceptions in Section (C) (2), merely restores the prohibitions on nuclear trade, thereby confirming the status quo ante. For example, they comport with the existing limitations on trade as observed by the administration pursuant to the NNPA, which had been in place since the Carter administration, and the qualifications on nuclear trade with South Africa announced by Secretary of Commerce Malcolm Baldrige in May of 1982, cited earlier. Although a survey of exports licensed by the Nuclear Regulatory Commission and the Dept. of Commerce revealed no new nuclear exports from the United States to South Africa in the first six months of the new Reagan term, the fact remains that U.S. law still allows such trade, although within the discretionary limits prescribed by the Executive Order.

With respect to the recent attempts to legalize prohibitions on the nuclear relationship between the United States and South Africa, it should be noted that it has taken place as a part of the general political pressures fomented by the American anti-apartheid movement upon the Congress and the executive branch, and not as a result of any objective determination of the danger posed by South African nuclear capability by nonproliferation advocates. Anti-apartheid activists have seized upon the nuclear relationship as one of many aspects of U.S.–South Africa trade, in a comprehensive approach to achieving trade sanctions. Even with such political pressures, however, it is instructive that the administration has continued to hold tenaciously to the nuclear trade relationship with the regime as a manifestation of its "engagement" approach. In the next chapter, we will attempt to understand the implications of this approach where other American regional interests are concerned.

Notes

1. "CBS Evening News with Walter Cronkite," CBS News, New York, March 5, 1981.

2. *The Star* (Johannesburg), February 18, 1981, p. 1.

3. *New York Times,* February 19, 1982, p. 24.

4. *Washington Post,* February 19, 1982, p. A29e.

5. Gary Thatcher, "S. Africa Indicates Weapons Capability," *Christian Science Monitor,* September 30, 1980, p. 9.

6. "New U.S. Policy on South Africa, *TransAfrica News Report,* (special edition) 1, no. 10 (August 1981).

7. Ibid.

8. Ibid.

9. *Nucleonics Week* 22, no. 18 (May 7, 1981), p. 1.

10. *Nucleonics Week* 22, no. 22 (June 4, 1981), p. 1; *Baltimore Sun,* October 4, 1981.

11. *Nucleonics Week,* 22, no. 39 (October 1, 1981), p. 1.

12. *Washington Post,* October 22, 1981, p. A1a; *Baltimore Sun,* October 22, 1981; *Christian Science Monitor,* October 22, 1981; *Nucleonics Week* 22, no. 44 (November 5, 1981), p. 12.

13. See the testimony of William C. Myre, director of nuclear security systems, Sandia National Laboratory, Albuquerque, New Mexico in Hearings, Subcommittee on Energy Research and Production, Committee on Science and Technology, U.S. House of Representatives, Washington, D.C., August 3, 1982.

14. Ibid.

15. *Nucleonics Week* 22, no. 44 (November 5, 1981), p. 12.

16. Paul van Slambronck, "U.S. Dangles Uranium Carrot Before South Africa," *Christian Science Monitor,* October 22, 1981, p. 9.

17. *Washington Post,* November 14, 1981, p. A16b.

18. *Washington Post,* November 19, 1981, p. A25a.

19. *Nucleonics Week* 22, no. 47 (November 26, 1981), p. 1.

20. Reference License Application no. XSNM 1947, Nuclear Regulatory Commission, Washington, D.C.

21. In August 1981, Transnuclear was granted a NRC license to transport 11 kg of irradiated fuel from SAFARI-1 to the Savannah River for reprocessing. South Africa had decided to sell the reprocessed material to West Germany. *Nucleonics Week,* 22, no. 32 (August 13, 1981), p. 1.

22. *Nucleonics Week* 23, no. 7 (February 18, 1982), p. 1.

23. "U.S. Export Policy with Respect to South Africa." Hearings, Subcommittee on Africa and the Subcommittee on International Economic Policy and Trade, Committee on Foreign Affairs, U.S. House of Representatives, December 2, 1982.

24. *Nuclear News* 25, no. 1 (January 1982), p. 60. Also, see the testimony of James L. Malone (assistant secretary of state for oceans and international environmental and scientific affairs) to the Subcommittee on Energy, Nuclear Proliferation and Government Processess, U.S. House of Representatives, November 19, 1981.

25. Letter, John Glenn to Alexander Haig, Jr., January 13, 1982.

26. Public Law 95–242, March 10, 1978.

27. Hearings, Subcommittee on Economic Policy and Trade and International Security and Scientific Affairs, June 24, 1982, U.S. House of Representatives.

28. "Reagan Non-Proliferation Plan Eases Reprocessing Obstacles," *Nuclear Industry* 28, no. 3 (August 1981), pp. 26–28; "President Reagan's Statement of Nuclear Energy Policy," *Nucleonics Week* 22, no. 41 (October 15, 1981), p. 5; *Nuclear Engineering International* 27, no. 317 (May 1982), pp. 22–26.

29. *New York Times*, May 19, 1982, p. 7. See also letter from Secretary of Commerce Malcolm Baldrige to Senator Charles Percy, chairman of the Senate Foreign Relations Committee.

30. *Newsweek*, April 12, 1982, p. 17.

31. *Washington Post*, August 8, 1982, p. A1a.

32. Ibid., p. A11.

33. Ibid.

34. Ford Foundation and Mitre Corporation, *Nuclear Power Issues and Choices* (Cambridge, Mass.: Ballinger, 1977), p. 372.

35. Albert Wohlstetter, "Spreading the Bomb without Quite Breaking the Rules," *Foreign Policy* 25 (Winter 1976–77), pp. 166–67.

36. Joseph Nye, Jr., testimony before the Subcommittee on Arms Control, International Environment and Oceans, Senate Committee on Foreign Relations, May 23, 1977.

37. Ibid.

38. Hearings, June 24, 1982, op. cit. See the testimony of Bo Denysyk (deputy assistant secretary for export administration, U.S. Dept. of Commerce).

39. In fact, The Zanger Committee of the IAEA placed certain mass spectrometers on "trigger list" of items because they serve as auxiliary components in the process of uranium enrichment. *Nuclear Engineering International*, January 1983, p. 9.

40. *Nuclear Engineering International*, January 1983, p. 9.

41. Testimony before the Subcommittee on International Economic Policy and Trade and on Africa, Committee on Foreign Affairs, U.S. House of Representatives, December 2, 1982, Washington D.C.

42. Harry Marshall, Jr., "U.S. Nuclear Policy toward South Africa," *Department of State Bulletin* 83, no. 2074, (May 1983), p. 67.

43. Bo Denysk, testimony, op. cit., p. 14.

44. *The Citizen* (Johannesburg), September 17, 1982.

45. *Engineering and Mining Journal* 90, no. 4151 (June 1979), p. 7.

46. See the advertisement in *Chronicle of Higher Education*, December 1, 1982, p. 36.

47. *Washington Post,* January 20, 1985, p. A1b.

48. *Washington Post,* February 3, 1985, p. 15a.

49. Ibid., p. 26.

50. George White, "Uranium," *Engineering and Mining Journal* (March 1982) p. 114.

51. "Tariffs, Embargoes? Tempting—But There's that Ripple Effect . . .", *Nuclear Industry* 31, no. 11 (November 1984), p. 15.

52. *Nuclear Engineering International* 27, no. 328 (June 1982), p. 14; *Mining Magazine* (August 1977), p. 141.

53. "Uranium Remains in Oversupply," *Nuclear Industry* 29, no. 1 (January 1982), p. 19.

54. *Domestic Uranium Mining and Milling Industry.* U.S. Dept. of Energy, no. S0033, December 1984.

55. Reported by Congressman Bill Richardson(D-N.M.), Congressional Record, July 11, 1985, p. H5501.

56. *Federal Register* 39, no. 208 (October 25, 1974), p. 38016.

57. *Nuclear News* 25, no. 10 (August 1982), p. 62.

58. "Resource Development in South Africa and U.S. Policy," Hearings, Subcommittee on International Resources, Food, and Energy, Committee on International Relations, U.S. House of Representatives, May 25, June 8 and 9, 1976, p. 300.

59. Letter, Walter N. Munster (chief, Market Policy Branch, AEC) to Herman Pollack (director of international scientific and technological affairs, U.S. Dept. of State), Washington, D.C., January 26, 1970.

60. Memorandum to the AEC Files, Walter N. Munster (chief, Market Policy branch), May 22, 1970.

61. Letter, Myron B. Kratzer (assistant general manager for international activities, AEC), to John P. Trevithick (deputy director for programs, Office of Atomic Energy Affairs, U.S. Dept. of State), May 28, 1970.

62. Report on visit to the Rossing uranium deposit, South West Africa, by Rafford L. Faulkner, U.S. Dept. of State, January 26, 1973.

63. *Africa* 51, (November 1975), p. 20.

64. *Report of the United Nations Council for Namibia,* vol. III. General Assembly Official Records, 35th session, supplement no. 24 (1981), p. 5.

65. *Nuclear News* (August, 1975), p. 26.

66. "Draft Minutes of the Eighth Session of the Operating Committee held in London on October 8–9, 1973." Committee on Oversight and Investigations, U.S. House of Representatives. Documents in the possession of the House Committee on Oversight and Investigation indicated that Westinghouse was a specific target of the cartel.

67. *Nuclear News* 20, no. 5 (April 1977), p. 62.

68. *Nuclear News* (November 1976), p. 29.

69. *Nuclear News* 20, no. 9 (August 1977), p. 63.

70. *New York Times,* July 12, 1977, p. 28.

71. *Nuclear News* 21, no. 8 (June 1978), p. 71.

72. *Washington Post,* May 31, 1978.

73. *Nuclear News* 20, no. 3 (February 1977), p. 51.

74. Ibid.

75. Brief, *United States of America* v. *Gulf Oil Corporation*, U.S. District Court for the Western District of Pennsylvania, May 9, 1978.

76. *Nuclear News* (June 1978).

77. William Haddad, "Confidential report to Irwin J. Landes (chairman, Corporations, Authorities and Commissions Committee)," (Office of Legislative Oversight). State of New York, May 20, 1977/revised, p. 14.

78. Brief, op. cit., p. 6.

79. *Nuclear News* 24, no. 3 (March 1981), p. 49.

80. *Nuclear News* 24, no. 1 (April 1981), p. 21.

81. *Nuclear News* 25, no. 9 (July 1982), p. 42.

82. Daniel Poneman, "Risky Nuclear Trade," *New York Times*, November 26, 1983.

83. John Maxwell Hamilton and Leonard S. Spector, "Congress Fights Back," *Society* 20, no. 6 (September/October 1983), pp. 38–47.

84. *Washington Post*, September 27, 1984, p. C6d.

85. See H.R. 1460, section 8, "Nuclear Exports."

86. "Prohibiting Trade and Certain Other Transactions Involving South Africa," Executive Order (8845), Office of the Press Secretary, The White House, September 9, 1985.

87. Price data comes from *Survey of United States Uranium Marketing Activity 1983*. (U.S. Dept. of Energy, August 4, 1983).

7
Global Implications of Western Nuclear Assistance and Commerce

I n any consideration of the impact of South African nuclear proliferation as an international problem, it is important to understand that it is uniquely Western. In this sense, perhaps it may be somewhat overdrawn to regard the regime as totally isolated in world politics, since so many of its fundamental international relations are with Western countries. What has been witnessed in this regard is a fitful relationship, where the Western powers have developed clear patterns of normal relations with South Africa evolving from its historical origin as an extension of Western European civilization. On the other hand, because of the reaction of many countries to the practice of apartheid, there is a reluctance of the West to openly embrace the regime or some of its more odious activities.

A question arises, then, concerning the value of such linkages within the context of international conflict. For example, it might be asked whether or not South Africa has a role in the central strategic balance between the East and West, or whether or not the West would come to the aid of South Africa in any serious regional or continental conflict if its survival were at stake. Of course, a positive answer to either of these questions should immediately make the reader conscious of the disquieting fact that South African nuclear weapons pose an alarming threat, not just to the region of Southern Africa, but to the entire international system. I will argue here that the linkages are, in fact, viable on at least three levels: the participation of Western states in the development of South Africa's nuclear power capability (and, thus, their presumed knowledge of its weapons capabilities), the dependence of Western states on South African fuel minerals such as uranium, and the membership of South Africa in a network of nuclear "pariah states" supported economically, politically, and militarily by the West.

Western Nuclear Support

I begin this brief assessment by noting that since 1959, South Africa has been one of a relatively small number of nuclear supplier states, the Western

Suppliers Group, which at a London meeting in June 1965, agreed to establish an appropriate level of trade in nuclear materials. Beyond this level, safeguards would ostensibly be required. For example, it was agreed that no member would sell over ten tons of raw uranium without IAEA safeguards being applied, and South Africa gave its assurances of abiding by this guideline, as indicated by its statement that:

> The South African Government is in full agreement that the supply of nuclear energy materials and equipment should be accomplished without adding to the proliferation of nuclear weapons capability, and this objective continues to be the basis of South African policy.[1]

Nevertheless, even as the South African government was making this statement, it complained about the new limits and exemptions decided upon at this meeting, expressing serious reservations about acceptance of the proposals of the United States in particular.

Since that time, seven of the nuclear supplier states have continued to attempt to use noncoercive measures with respect to the problem of nuclear proliferation in an effort not to disrupt international nuclear trade, even as the number of states with such capability grows.

However, frustrated by the fact of such growth, these states—Britain, the United States, the Soviet Union, France, West Germany, Japan, and Canada—convened a secret meeting in London in November 1975, in an effort to develop an "international code of conduct" covering "sensitive technologies" such as uranium enrichment, spent fuel reprocessing, and other aspects of the fuel cycle.[2] Although the details of the meeting still remain secret, one report indicated that,

> The seven may also attempt to persuade other suppliers, such as South Africa to adhere to the code, which it was suggested included the pledge not to use nuclear technologies for military purposes.[3]

There has been no indication that South Africa ever made such a pledge and it was significant that it was absent from this gathering in any case.

The United States has been a leader in nuclear trade matters, and although South Africa has been a tacit member of the nuclear club for some time, its present level of development would have been impossible without the valuable assistance given by the United States. The United States provided not only a reactor, but valuable technical assistance to the point that there was even considerable sharing of such information between the atomic energy boards of the two countries.[4]

Even more important, the United States provided funding. Beginning in 1952, the Export-Import Bank provided $10 million to ESCOM to finance uranium production, but a general power crisis in South Africa threatened the mining industry. So, the World Bank came to its assistance with $50 million in loans, while a consortium of eight U.S. banks provided another $10 million, so that by 1960, the power crisis was solved. Nevertheless, the relationship with ESCOM lasted into the mid-1970s as "The World Bank and its leading participant, the United States, recognized the crucial role of ESCOM in the South African political economy, and financed it."[5] This relationship was only stopped by legislation in 1978.[6]

In fact, an amazing tribute to the U.S.–South African nuclear cooperation was paid by A.J.A. Roux, (president of the South African Atomic Energy Board) in October 1976, when he said:

> We can ascribe our degree of advancement today in large measure to the training and assistance so willingly provided by the United States of America during the early years of our nuclear program when several of the Western world's nuclear nations cooperated in initiating our scientists and engineers into nuclear science. . . .
>
> A research reactor at Pelindaba, also in the Pretoria area, is of American design [based on the Oak Ridge research reactor] and that much of the nuclear equipment installed at Pelindaba is of American origin, while even our nuclear philosophy, although unmistakably our own, owes much to the thinking of [American] nuclear scientists.[7]

U.S. support, therefore, has been unmistakably critical to South African nuclear development.

I have also mentioned nuclear agreements between South Africa and the French; collaboration dates from the mid-1960s involving the supply of raw uranium. In 1965, there were unconfirmed reports reaching the U.S. embassy that the South African government was negotiating with the French government for the sale of 25,000 tons of natural uranium over a 25-year period with no safeguards. The only apparent provision was that the French would not resell the material to the Soviet Union or any Soviet bloc country. Obviously, this level of sales amounting to 1,000 tons per year would violate the understanding reached by the Western Suppliers Group on the 10-ton limit without the application of IAEA safeguards—to which the South Africans had objected.[8]

Then, in 1966, after the previous report had been confirmed, officials of the French Atomic Energy Commission, such as Robert Hirsch (administrator general), Dr. Bertrand Goldschmidt (director of external relations and programs), and Jacques Mabile (director of production), visited South Africa and held discussions with South African officials on the "peaceful uses of atomic energy."[9] These French officials also visited gold and uranium mines, and the SASOL and Palabora mining complex in addition to the reactor site at Pelindaba. At the time, there was press speculation that the French were preparing to buy substantial quantities of South African uranium. United States government officials believed that there was also a possibility of an exchange of French military aircraft or atomic weapons for a long-term supply of uranium.[10] Subsequent analysis of this theory by embassy officials in Paris, however, held that the exchange of atomic weapons for uranium was a high price to pay for a commodity in abundance, and that the French Mirage III, the aircraft within the budget of a possible exchange deal, was of limited nuclear capability.[11] It should be noted, however, that twenty-seven French Mirage III aircraft subsequently appeared in the South African military inventory, beginning in 1978.[12]

Then, as is now known, Framatome (a subsidiary of Cruesot-Loire, including Alsthom Atlantique and Spie Batignolles) constructed the nuclear reactor station at Koeberg, and secured an agreement between the two countries for the sale of enriched fuel by South Africa in exchange for nuclear technology provided by the French.[13]

The West Germans, also fierce competitors in this field, have been substantial collaborators with the South Africans in fuel enrichment technology. In this sense, it is more than mere coincidence which led one observer to confirm my suggestion that developments in the two countries were not merely "compatible" in the nuclear enrichment field. A more likely theory than that of a separate and coincidental development of this complex enrichment technology is described in a work on the collaboration between West Germany and South Africa, which details the work of Professor Erwin Willi Becker at the company STEAG in Essen, West Germany (FRG), and the subsequent agreement developed between this company and South Africa in 1968, for the development of the technology.[14]

It is somewhat surprising that at a time when Britain was the major investor and trading partner in South Africa, it could not take advantage of its position to become the major nuclear supplier. In fact, the British technological role was somewhat limited to investments in basic extractive and processing fields, in view of the stiff competition from other Western states. Nevertheless, it is known that British Nuclear Fuels Corp. played a substantial role in reprocessing U.S.-origin spent fuel utilized in South African research reactors, relative to other nuclear facilities in the 1970s.[15]

The international scope of such nuclear contacts by the South African government expanded when tenders for a contract to participate in the construction of its enrichment plant were responded to by a Dutch firm, Rijn-Schelde-Verolme. The company was preparing a formal bid when it came under attack from the Revolutionary Progressive Party in Holland. The party gained support from other groups, reflecting a widely held view that the Dutch government was assisting in providing the South African government the means to produce nuclear weapons. The party then threatened to withdraw from the government coalition unless it took steps to block a bid from the Dutch firm.[16]

This position was expected, but unexpected was the strong opposition to this firm's participation by Dr. de Lange, chairman of the Dutch-run international development financing organization NOVIB. He termed the prospective tender "dangerous and short-sighted," saying that from his experience, "Foreign investment in South Africa had only led to a hardening of the South African position with regard to its internal policies of repression," and that "Holland would lose credibility in the rest of Black Africa by such participation."[17] These unusually strong responses, which threatened to bring down the Den Uyl government and drew the opposition of a credible industrial organization, succeeded in discrediting the initiative by Verolme and caused the South Africans to consider a bid from the other countries on its list.

The Namibian Settlement and Western Nuclear Politics

An important tension for South African nuclear development involves the relationship between its illegal occupation of Namibia, and its role in the development of the uranium holdings at the Rossing deposit with corporate representatives of major Western powers and Japan.

In 1972, for example, the West German government's Science Ministry stated that it had borne 75 percent of the overall contribution to the prospecting costs at Rossing which were conducted through the firm Urangesellschaft GmbH of Frankfurt.[18] Also, in 1973, Total (a subsidiary of the French Compagnie Francaise des Pétroles) negotiated a 10 percent holding in Rossing which was taken over in 1975, by the French company Minatome S.A.[19] But a Canadian firm, Rio Algom, also owns 10 percent of Rossing, while the U.S. firm Engelhard Minerals participates in other mining ventures through its interest in the giant mining conglomerate Anglo-American, which acquired a large mining concession immediately adjacent to the Rossing site.[20]

Given the range of participation in the mineral exploitation of Rossing and adjacent sites by firms from Britain, South Africa, Canada, West Germany, and the United States, it is not coincidental that these governments should also be involved in the attempt to achieve a political settlement in Namibia favorable to their interest. Resolution 366 of the U.N. Security Council, which called for South Africa to dismantle its administration of Namibia, was adopted in 1974, with the support of the United States, but an additional resolution in June 1975, which would have put into effect a mandatory arms embargo against South Africa for its failure to comply with Resolution 366 within six months, was vetoed by the United States, Great Britain, and France. A similar scenario of events occurred in 1976, when the United States supported resolution 385 calling for South Africa to end its illegal occupation of Namibia in six months. The Western powers supported the resolution but vetoed the call for an arms embargo when the six months elapsed on the basis that their own "delicate negotiations" were underway to achieve a settlement without the kind of sanctions envisioned.[21]

These delicate negotiations were initiated by U.S. Secretary of State Henry Kissinger, whose "shuttle diplomacy" in Namibia grew to encompass the five major Western powers with interests there—Britain, the United States, Canada, West Germany, and France. This shuttle diplomacy was continued in the Carter administration under the leadership of U.N. Ambassador Andrew Young, whose deputy, Donald McHenry (in a series of meetings in East Africa, Europe, South Africa, Namibia, and the United States with representatives of the other four European powers, the South West African Peoples Organization, and the South African government), fashioned a settlement which finally won the agreement of the U.N. Security Council.

Although this agreement initiated by the Western Contact Group was subsequently rendered inoperable by a South African-imposed government, it should be noted that the continued control of Namibian uranium by South Africa abrogates decree no. 1 on the protection of the Natural Resources of Namibia by the United Nations Council for Namibia.

Rio Tinto-Zinc (the British multinational giant specializing in mining interests all over the world) manages the mining and export of Namibian uranium, and one of the dominant shareholders is South Africa. South Africa has exported uranium to Britain since the 1952 tripartite agreement, but in 1968, another agreement was made to develop and export 7,500 tons of uranium directly from Namibia, between British and Canadian partners in the Rio family. Occasionally, the British government (depending essentially upon whether it was Labor or Conservative) had wanted to terminate these contracts, and recent indications are that, again, the British government is considering supply arrangements for the future that do not involve the Rossing uranium resources.[22]

Obvious South African-French control of Namibian uranium was discovered by the French General Labor Confederation (CGT) in 1978. Weekly shipments amounting to 120 tons of uranium per week were being flown into French airports for distribution to other places in Europe. These uranium shipments from the Rossing mines were supervised by the French Atomic Energy Commission and were flown in planes operated by the French U.T.A. company and South African Airways.[23] Then, a uranium hexafloride plant, Société pour la Conversion de l'Uranium en Metal et en Hexafloure (COMURHEX), had a contract with Rossing to process its uranium. The French role as distributor and the interests of other European states, have led to the involvement of other firms, including enrichment by URENCO as well as processing by URANIT of the Federal Republic of West Germany and Ultra-Centrifuge Nederland of The Netherlands, and to the use of this uranium by power stations in West Germany.[24] Apparently, the relationship goes beyond mere economic relations, to the maintenance of a private army to protect the security of the Rossing facility by the interested parties, a role that involves them in the policing of apartheid.

It is possible to project comfortably a strong and continuing European interest in the politics of Southern Africa and Europe's need for strategic minerals access because of the shortage of these resources in the rest of the world. In Western Europe, for example, much of the mineral resource, other than fuels, was depleted in the past century, as a result of the great industrial revolution. The impact of this was to turn Western Europe into a region that exported capital and technology and imported raw materials, processing 20 to 30 percent of total world production other than fuels. At the same time, the lack of sufficient fuel supplies has led European countries to make a heavy investment in the development of nuclear power, the original target of 200 megawatts of nuclear capacity by 1985 being reduced to 91 megawatts because of technical difficulties and public opposition to expansion of nuclear facilities. Still, that the continued increase in the demand for uranium fuel is caused by the annual increase in the number of reactors (already under construction) coming into service is an obvious conclusion from any assessment of the European energy situation.[25]

In this context, the active relations between the South African government and the French in the exploitation of Namibian uranium comes as no surprise, since France both has an ambitious nuclear development program for civilian energy and maintains its own program for the development of strategic weapons outside of NATO control. In fact, so tenacious is the determination of the French government in the development of nuclear energy that at the site of its super-breeder reactor Super Phoenix at Crays-Malville, protests by thousands of antinuclear activists in early August 1977 (resulting in one death and the arrests of hundreds) did not appear to dissuade the government in the least.[26]

Next, it has been conceded that a substantial portion of the uranium under the control of South Africa is in Namibia (Southwest Africa). Pressure on South Africa to divest itself of Namibia by the United Nations and by the South West African Peoples Organization may mean that control of these fields of low-grade ore may eventually be lost to South Africa. Nevertheless, countries such as Japan are exploiting this resource through a contract between the Kansai Electric Power Company of Osaka and the South African government to purchase uranium from the Rossing mines beginning in 1977, at a rate of 1,000 tons per year. The contract, which was signed in 1970, and runs until 1986, is meant to fuel a nuclear power station at Oi, Japan, but in the past it has come under severe criticism in Japan from such antinuclear activists as Yoko Kitazawa.[27]

In November 1974, Mrs. Kitazawa's testimony before the U.N. Council for Namibia and the Special Committee against Apartheid revealed the purchases by Kansai from the Rossing mines on the following schedule:

1. 500 tons annually in 1977 and 1978,
2. 600 tons annually in 1979 and 1980,
3. 1,000 tons annually from 1981 to 1986.

She suggested that such imports clearly strengthened the South African regime.[28]

Later, she revealed that Mitsubishi Heavy Industries Group had been one of the major companies to initially bid for the construction of the South African reactors which went to Framatome, and suggested that the pattern of Japanese trade in Namibian uranium violated the U.N. Council for Namibia's decree no. 1 on the protection of natural resources in Namibia. Nonetheless, her conclusion for the future was that Japan, being caught in the same nuclear dilemmas as the United States in the debate over breeders and other kinds of energy systems utilizing nuclear power, would turn to South Africa for supplies of enriched uranium when they were available to supply its twenty-seven nuclear plants scheduled to be commissioned in the 1978–82 period.[29]

The Kitazawa position was that the Kansai contract should be cancelled because it violated the U.N. decree. The Japanese government's position was that the contract was signed before the United Nations had established a position on Namibian resources, and that it would not interfere with a private commercial undertaking. Nevertheless, a coalition of groups, who have lodged mainly environmental complaints, has continued to attack this contract.

It must appear somewhat curious to the casual observer, then, that recently the members of the Western Contact Group have been far less than active in attempting to obtain a solution to the Namibian independence question, except for the United States, which has maintained its individual efforts. It is easily established that the interests of the United States are in helping South Africa to "stabilize" the region on terms favorable to both powers. This fashions a common interest, for example, in attempting to eliminate the Cuban presence from Angola to lessen the perceived "communist threat" on the borders of any newly independent state, a threat conceived to be directed against the interest of the West in securing minerals and its strategic position in Southern Africa. Nevertheless, I have also argued that the United States may maintain more narrow interest in Namibian uranium itself (or in a "uranium option"), as stated in my previous review of the condition of its domestic industry and the price relationship of uranium to the international nuclear industry in the long run.[30]

Taken together, the United States and Western Europe have motives for continued exploitation of uranium from Southern Africa. This fact has traditionally not been lost upon the South Africans in the pursuit of their own foreign policy objectives.

One observer who formulates the oft used doctrine that, indeed, the West is vulnerable to mineral shortages is Dr. W.C.J. van Rensburg (former technical director for the South African Mineral Bureau and currently director of the Institute for Energy Studies and professor of energy economics at the Rand Afrikaans University in Johannesburg). Dr. van Rensburg writes:

> It is not difficult to project the repercussions of a denial of mineral supplies from South Africa to the West. Such a contingency will improve the bargaining positions of other mineral exporters, enhance the tendency toward the establishment of powerful producer cartels, encourage spiraling prices of a variety of minerals and mineral products, and adversely affect the security of supplies of these materials to the West.[31]

While it has admittedly been the practice of South African experts and government officials to encourage such alarmist speculation, it is relatively clear that withholding of mineral reserves by South Africa is one tactic which could be brought to bear in any significant threat of its isolation. Therefore, it should be indicated that most of the measures of isolation proposed as ways of dealing both with the oppressiveness of the South African system in political, economic, and social terms and with its growing military power are intended to be dramatic *short-term* solutions aimed at bringing the sort of pressure to bear upon it that would result in a radical restructuring of that society, beginning with the prospect of black majority rule.

Doubtless, minerals trade would remain a part of the policy of any South African government, but under conditions equitable both to the interest of the majority of people in Southern Africa and to outside interests as well. It is, therefore, in the long-term interest of the West to secure mineral supplies, if indeed current and projected shortages are a major concern, through the pursuit of the kind of foreign policies that will cause any future black majority regime to take seriously the prospect of Western participation in its economy.

Such choices could well be forced upon U.S. policymakers in the short run by the success of the liberation movement. It is worth noting, in this regard, that the assumption of National Security Study Memorandum no. 39 (which posited the ineffectiveness of both the liberation movement and the long-term nature of social change) was not as much an empirical observation as it was a desperate calculation. The current question, then, is whether or not, with respect to the problem of South African nuclear proliferation and the security of fuel mineral supplies from Southern Africa,

U.S. policy is based on actual empirical determinants, or irrational long-term gambling.

Regional Implications of South African Nuclear Proliferation

The Nuclear Pariahs

Previously I discussed the linkage between the Western states and South African nuclear capability as a regional aspect of the global dimension of nuclear proliferation. Such a linkage has also contributed to the development of a set of nuclear relationships among a group of second-level economic and military powers with strong ties to the West through trade and strategic support. These nations (such as Israel, Taiwan, and South Korea) are part of a larger grouping of states considered to manifest some similar regional characteristics in addition to their alliances to the West. While it has been acknowledged that their regional circumstances are not exactly the same, their motivation for the acquisition of nuclear capability, according to Richard Betts, might more closely resemble their role as "pygmies"—states pitted against a superior power in their region; "paranoids"—states cultivating substantial fears for their security in such a region; and "pariahs"—states regarded as international outcasts to the extent that they are isolated from normal relationships both in the region and in the world community.[32]

All the above states are well known to have manifested a combination of such symptoms as described by Betts. More important for purposes here, they all have established trade with South Africa which is widely suspected to include nuclear materials and technology, such that a grouping of highly unstable nuclear powers is developing which, because of their regional characteristics, may constitute an independent and additional danger to the international system.

I have had occasion to point to the suspected nuclear collaboration between South Africa and Israel, based on an evolving trade relationship begun in the early 1970s. For example, when, in 1976, Prime Minister John Vorster visited Israel, press reports indicated his willingness to discuss financing the expansion of Israeli arms production in exchange for Kfir jet fighters and other arms. In fact, such reports suggest, arms from Israel were already on the way to South Africa even before the trip.[33] This trade was extremely significant in view of the highly authoritative guesses that Israel possessed as many as six nuclear weapons at this time.[34] The relationship deepened in the energy field when, in 1979, an agreement was signed for the yearly export of one million tons of steam coal to Israel; the agreement was widely suspected to provide for the supply of uranium to Israel as well.[35]

Israel's proficiency in the development of missiles and its collaboration with South Africa fueled speculation that the two countries were involved in the 1979 suspected nuclear test in the South Atlantic. It will be recalled, at the time, the CIA indicated that the lack of debris from the purported explosion might have been the result of a neutron bomb jointly produced by the two countries. At least one observer, Professor Amos Perlmutter of The American University in Washington, D.C., with two other Israeli authors, published a book, *Two Minutes Over Bagdad*, which alleges that Israel and South Africa were working together to produce neutron shells, and that the two countries, together with Taiwan were "apparently . . . developing a cruise missile that will be able to carry a nuclear warhead 2,400 km."[36] By 1980, amid reports of a secret three-day visit by Israeli Defense Minister Ezer Weitzman to South Africa, authoritative studies were indicating that South Africa had become Israel's largest arms customer.[37]

In Spring 1978, a group of U.S. politicians, after a visit to South Africa, reported to the London-based publication *Arms International* that South Africa was developing a mutual defense agreement with Israel, Iran, and South Korea.[38] In fact, South Africa had become considerably dependent upon Iran for oil and was prepared to provide uranium in exchange, but with the Iranian revolution, this relationship came to a close, while the relationship with Taiwan has prospered. Botha's visit to Taiwan in 1980, which included a trip to a nuclear power plant, presaged wider nuclear cooperation, as an agreement was concluded for the export of 4,000 tons of uranium worth R400 million ($520 million) between 1984 and 1990.[39] Asked about further military cooperation on this occasion, Botha said that if communist countries could cooperate to protect their interest in such matters, he did not understand why "democratic countries" could not do likewise. He added, that should further discussions regarding nuclear matters take place, they will be devoted to the use of such power "for peaceful purposes."[40]

The following year, U.S. intelligence and Dept. of State officials were indicating that Israel, Taiwan, and South Africa were significant actors within a group of countries he described as "politically isolated," whose intentions were "to help each other acquire atomic bombs."[41] In making such charges, it was pointed out that Israel was assisting Taiwan in developing missiles which could deliver warheads; Israeli scientists were working in the South African nuclear energy program; scientists from Taiwan were working on a uranium enrichment project in South Africa; and South Africa, with by far the largest reserves, had become the important supplier of uranium to both countries. Indeed, a study by the Defense Intelligence Agency indicated that a "pariah network" could be emerging which might also include Argentina, Brazil, and Iraq.

Also, a report by the Subcommittee on International Organizations of the U.S. House of Representatives, besides indicating that South Koreans

Table 7–1
Nuclear Power Estimates for Selected States,
1976, 1985, and 1990
(1,000 MW)

	Installed	*Additions*	
	1976	*1985*	*1990*
South Africa	2.0	2.0	2.0
Brazil	11.4	.6	5.6
Taiwan	10.3	4.2	4.9 to 6.7
Korea	9.8	3.6	9.9
Israel	3.9	—	—
Argentina	8.1	.9	1.7
Total	45.5		

Source: 1976 data on installed power come from *Nuclear Proliferation and Safeguards* (Office of Technology Assessment, U.S. Congress, July 1977), p. 246, figure X–9. 1985 and 1990 figures come from OECD, *Nuclear Energy and Its Fuel Cycle: Prospects to 2025* (Paris: OECD, 1982), p. 32.

had successfully tested their own version of the Nike-Hercules missile based on U.S.-supplied technology, also said, "The United States actively cooperated in expanding the ROK [Republic of Korea] nuclear power program and agreed to sell U.S. commercial power reactors in a process which ostensibly has improved both the form and the substance of the energy relationship with the Korean Government."[42]

Moreover, Brazil's acquisition of nuclear facilities has included the installation of uranium enrichment technology by West German firms, similar to that developed by South Africa.[43] But it must also be assumed that this group of states will have access to plutonium, since Argentina and Brazil have plans to develop reprocessing plants, and Israel and South Africa may already have access to the technology and the facilities. Table 7–1 estimates and forecasts six nations' nuclear power from 1976 to 1990.

Thus, with access to both enriched uranium and plutonium (fissionable materials necessary to the development of nuclear weapons), this group of states could have a thriving trade in nuclear materials and even weapons that could eventually be outside the control of the major nuclear materials suppliers of either the Eastern or Western bloc nations. Table 7–2 projects the potential number of 5-kilogram nuclear warhead devices likely to be available to such states by 1990.

My point, again, is that the potential nuclear proliferation of South Africa does not exist in a vacuum, but quite possibly may represent the leading edge of a "radical entente" of states with similar volatile political characteristics. These states collectively could represent a real threat to international peace and security. This thesis supports the reasons why South Africa, as an important member of this group, should be treated as a special case regarding nuclear proliferation.

Table 7–2
Estimate of the Number of Nuclear Warhead
Devices by 1990

Country	Amount
Taiwan	98
Argentina	132
Brazil	216
Israel	200 (to the year 2000)
Republic of Korea	88
South Africa	100
Total	834

Source: U.S. Energy Research and Development Agency, report no. 51, 1974, table V-8, p. 37. Ford Foundation and the Mitre Corp., Nuclear Power Issues and Choices: Report of the Nuclear Energy Policy Study Group, Cambridge, Mass.: Ballinger, 1977, p. 285. Israeli data come from "Middle East Planners Push for Nuclear Energy Development," *Middle East Economic Digest*, 19 (December 21, 1975), pp. 11-12.

Note: All data is based on the ability of the country to fabricate a 5 kilogram plutonium device.

Table 7–3
Total Arms Transfers from the United States and Soviet Union to Selected States, 1967–82
($ millions)

	Donor Country		
	United States		Soviet Union
Recipient	(1967–76)	(1978–82)	(1967–82)
Republic of Korea	2,615	2,100	—
Iran	3,835	—	611
Israel	4,761	4,400	—
Argentina	131	100	—
Brazil	300	70	—
Taiwan	1,781	1,500	—
Total	13,423	8,170	611

Source: *World Military Expenditures and Arms Transfers 1967-1976*, U.S. Arms Control and Disarmament Agency, publication no. 98 (July 1978), pp. 157-8, 160; *World Military Expenditures and Arms Transfers 1972-1982*, U.S. Arms Control and Disarmament Agency, publication no. 117 (April 1984), p. 96.

Accompanying this observation is the fact that these states in the radical entente are supported heavily by the West. This adds considerably to the East–West aspect of the problem, since the pattern of nuclear support will most likely follow the previously existing pattern of military support for these states as expressed in more than a decade of arms transfers, as seen in table 7–3.

The Global Balance of Deterrence

Recall this book's beginning thesis that the internal and external security concerns of South Africa have caused the regime to develop a military role for its nuclear power capability. My case rested primarily on the escalation of the war for liberation as the primary element in the dynamics of regional politics. It is also true that heightened regional political conflicts which escalate to military confrontation increase the proliferation of conventional military weapons, both in the primary area of conflict and in the contiguous regional states, to buttress the power of all combatants.[44]

Heightened tensions and conflict have caused a dramatic change in the position of Southern African issues in the context of world politics. The evidence is abundant in terms of the consistency of major-power political intervention as well as the attachment of Southern African issues to other issues such as the Strategic Arms Limitation Talks in 1976, the role of Cuban troops in Angola, the independence of Namibia, and the internal stability of the regime.

Therefore, the linkages to international politics I have discussed make the development of South African nuclear weapons capability relevant to at least three levels of potential confrontation between the East and West. At the first level, involving the regional politics between the United States and the Soviet Union, South African apartheid is a political problem which has found the major powers on opposite sides of the strategies for achieving political settlements in the region, especially in territories such as Angola, Mozambique, South Africa, Zimbabwe, and Namibia. Second, with reference to the central strategic balance in which NATO confronts the Warsaw Pact, the continuing attempt to extend the range of NATO into the Indian Ocean and the South Atlantic areas legitimizes the role of South Africa as a NATO proxy state and encourages its military development, providing it with an additional reason for acquiring nuclear arms. Third, South Africa is a leading state among a group of second-ranked nuclear powers in the international system, powers allied formally or informally to NATO.

The professed strategic interests of NATO in Southern Africa and the fact that the major powers in NATO are substantially engaged in nuclear commerce with South Africa are factors which have naturally determined NATO strategic planning in the southern Atlantic area.[45] The outgrowth of this "natural" strategic interest by NATO could be that South Africa may already *formally* be a NATO proxy state in the area—an unofficial role that could also be part of an ambiguous strategy.

For example, apart from the quite real aggressive intentions of South Africa with respect to the use of its growing nuclear capability, the development of nuclear power by any other state on the African continent may be pretext enough for the NATO powers to formally invite South Africa to join NATO. But without such a pretext, it would not be out of the question for the South Africans, because of the sheer level of their development, to be asked to join, merely because it might be regarded by NATO as unwise for a major military and potential nuclear weapons power anywhere in the world to be outside the ideological and political alliance structure of competition in the continuing cold war.

For example, South Africa might have an unofficial role in maintaining a protective interest over the southern shipping routes from Western Europe to the Middle East, and in the protection of the Indian Ocean from "communist encroachment." It might also, because of its increasing treaty relations with Israel, have a role in the outcome of the politics of the Middle East from its position as the guardian of the underbelly of the Islamic front.[46]

As early as the period 1951–55, South African government spokesmen were lobbying for a closer relationship with NATO. As Prime Minister Malan said in 1953, "Personally, I would rather be a member of NATO . . . than a member of the United Nations. It is a better safeguard for world peace."[47]

Observers such as Vice Admiral Sir Peter Gretton of the British navy, while suggesting that South Africa should modify its apartheid policy so that it could play a more effective role in the concert of world nations, have felt that NATO had a vital interest in keeping the area stable for the increase of commerce.[48] Gretton further felt that the threat to the 25,000 ships yearly carrying 1.5 million tons of goods around the Cape of Good Hope could come from control of the sea lanes by an unfriendly power. Therefore, he urged that the navies of Western countries should be poised to intervene in the Cape region to protect these strategic interests should they become threatened either by subversion from within the region or by aggression from an external source.[49] Since this proposal of intervention included the Indian Ocean region, it has relevance to South Africa as well. The British delegation to a NATO meeting in 1969 was quick to pick up this sentiment, noting the "power-vacuum" in the Indian Ocean caused by the departure of the British and pointing to the capability of the South African navy to enter into joint operations for the "protection" of Western interests there.[50] Such joint exercises with the British did occur and the South Africans also provided NATO shipping with weather information and intelligence about Soviet naval movements from the Youngfield radio station at Cape Town. But Raymond V.B. Blackman, editor of the journal *Jane's Fighting Ships*, suggested that a new role for South Africa in the South Atlantic should be as a part of a greater Atlantic alliance structure. He asked, "But why a separate SATO [South Atlantic Treaty Organization] and NATO? Why not a combined SATO and NATO in the shape of a GATO or Greater Atlantic Treaty Organization?"[51]

The concept of a South Atlantic Treaty Organization, much discussed during the 1960s and 1970s also, was fed by an exchange of naval visits and other diplomatic contacts among South Africa, Argentina, and Brazil, though as yet, these countries have not publicly created such a military alliance. The dominant rationale for such proposals conforms to the view that the major threat to Western shipping and goods comes from the Soviet Union through its ability to interdict naval traffic and commerce by the buildup of its naval powers in such regions as the Indian Ocean, by the acquisition of client states with adequate port facilities, or by a direct threat to South Africa itself (probably in the guise of supporting the liberation movements).[52] One observer (Charles Latour, of the South African Institute of International Affairs) who views the threat in this manner has even suggested that for its service to NATO as the guardian of its southern-most flank, U.S. troops should be stationed on South African soil as they are in other NATO countries, and,

> since the future enemy is likely to be using modern Soviet aircraft, a complete computerized chain, such as the NADGE (NATO Air Defense Group Environment) system, is required, together with long range missiles, such as the Nike-Hercules and the improved Hawk, and modern fighter/interceptor aircraft.[53]

With the economic and technical assistance of NATO nations, South Africa has acquired the critical strategic facilities called for by Latour on a scale befitting a medium-range power and suitable for its role as a "NATO proxy nation."[54]

In the world balance of forces, then, South Africa's regional role as well as its relation to other regional states heighten the regime's ability to contribute to international conflict, perhaps employing its modest nuclear capability to aid the Western side of the global balance. Thus, the problem of South African nuclear proliferation is related to the problem of world peace to the extent that it potentially destabilizes the central strategic balance.

While the existence of nuclear weapons in South Africa may be regarded as a Western dilemma because of its traditional role as a supportive ally of South Africa in developing its nuclear capability, the Soviet Union is also affected by the existence of any new nuclear nation, both in terms of the unilateral nature of the threat it may pose to the Soviet Union directly and the additions the new force brings to the ability of its main adversary—the United States.

If there exists a military pact among South Africa, Israel, and Taiwan, and the cruise missile they may have developed is capable of being targeted at the Soviet Union in addition to other sites, then, the Soviets obviously have to consider such states to be legitimate targets. Obviously, then, the heightened military threat represented by such states suggests that the danger for the Soviet Union rests in the perception of a deterioration of parity in the stability of the central balance,

> First, by compounding the difficulties faced by the Soviet and American leaders in maintaining a stable central balance, and second, by increasing the chances of nuclear weapons being used in regional contexts, either by aggravating regional security problems themselves or simply by introduc-ing the possibility of nuclear violence into what would otherwise be non-nuclear conflict.[55]

Previously, the problem was conceptualized as existing in largely quantitative terms, as the following statement illustrates: "it is doubtful that any great value would be attached to this [South Africa's nuclear] addition to the West's ample nuclear arsenal."[56] But the problem is infi-nitely more *qualitative*, relating to the degree of the threat posed to the interest of the major nuclear powers in a region where they have invested high stakes in the outcome of a particular conflict. In such a place, the introduction of a nuclear weapons capability, particularly, as I have shown, under conditions of regional political and military instability, could add immeasurably to the instability of the central deterrent situation if there were significant linkages involving the major nuclear weapons powers.

In fact, it has been demonstrated that the United States has a stake in the outcome of the political situation in Southern Africa because of its nuclear connections, but this relationship covers many other bilateral interactions.

For instance, if a nuclear strike against the Soviet Union or one of its close allies were launched by one of the states in the pariah network that is a regional client of the West, the NATO deterrent could be triggered. In such a case, even though South Africa might not be directly involved, its role in furthering the nuclear capability of such a state should also be considered a special danger. Again, this would appear to place special responsibilities on patron states (such as the United States) to greatly mod-erate their nuclear relations with clients.

At the same time, the Soviet Union has invested substantially in the outcome of political struggles in both Angola and Mozambique, as indi-cated by arms sales data. Furthermore, their support of liberation move-ments in Namibia and South Africa has also been important to the ability of Africans to prosecute the war. Yet, it is unlikely that these nonnuclear relationships bear the same quality of threat to international security as would a nuclear relationship.

Nevertheless, such mutual linkages by the United States and the Soviets severely mitigate against the extent to which South African nuclear proliferation may be considered isolated from the problem of maintaining a central strategic balance between these superpowers.

Under the pressures of proliferation, one strategy for the major powers would be to decrease the tendency to exploit a local situation for unilateral advantage and to increase the tendency to intervene to reduce tensions.[57] The other tendency, however, is that precisely because of the danger of triggering regional and extraregional tensions, major powers would be reluctant to intervene in local disputes.[58]

Conclusion

Thus far, however, in the attempt to affect the outcome of political settlements in the region, the self-described objectives of the Western powers have been to reduce tensions. But on a more objective level, the goal of such interventions have been to promulgate the reduction of tensions *on terms favorable to the interests of Western powers*. This objectively equates the activities of the West in Southern Africa to those of the Eastern bloc powers in support of liberation movements which have been the main cause of the tension in their struggle to overthrow the oppressive rule of white minority regimes.

Subjectively, it is far from certain that the combatants in the region see the Soviet Union and the United States allied in a common attempt to bring about the same kind of political solution which might have the effect of reducing the possible uses for South African nuclear weapons. In fact, the joint action referred to above as a "partial" attempt to stabilize the strategic balance has had the other effect of giving an important political advantage to both the Soviet Union and the liberation movement by exposing the linkages in the South African nuclear program to the distinctly Western basis of support.

It is possible to conclude, then, that for such joint action to be effective by the major powers, it must also carry the possibility of *symmetrical dividends*—either positive or negative—as much in fact as in the perception of the regional combatants. At the very least, it means that the West must be perceived to be attempting to counter the disastrous effect of South African nuclear weapons proliferation. I will next pursue the implications of such a responsibility.

Notes

1. Telegram, Dept. of State, October 28, 1965. The members of the Western Suppliers Group were Australia, Belgium, Canada, France, Germany, Japan, South Africa, Britain, and the United States.

2. *The Star* (Johannesburg), November 26, 1975, p. 29.

3. *Financial Times* (London), November 25, 1975, p. 2.

4. "U.S. Policy toward Africa," Hearings before the Subcommittee on African Affairs and the Subcommittee on Arms Control and International Organizations and Security Agreements, Committee on Foreign Relations, U.S. Senate, May 27, 1976, p. 277.

5. Renfrew Christie, op. cit., p. 157.

6. *Banks and Banking*, United States Code 12, 635, p. A,9.

7. *Washington Post*, February 16, 1988, p. A12.

8. Telegram, op. cit.

9. *Johannesburg Sunday Express*, December 11, 1966, p. 1.

10. Telegram, Dept. of State, December 12, 1966.

11. Telegram, Dept. of State, December 16, 1966.

12. *The Military Balance, 1978–1977*, op. cit., p. 49.

13. *The Star* (Johannesburg), August 30, 1974, p. 2.

14. Barbara Rogers and Zdenek Cervenka, *The Nuclear Axis: The Secret Collaboration between West Germany and South Africa* (New York: New York Times Book Co., 1978).

15. *Resource Development in South Africa and U.S. Policy*, op. cit., p. 301.

16. *The Star* (Johannesburg), October 21, 1975, p. 12.

17. Ibid.

18. *Africa* 51 (November 1975), p. 20.

19. Rogers and Cervenka, op. cit., p. 120.

20. Ibid.

21. Gwendolyn Carter and Patrick O'Meara, eds., *South Africa in Crisis* (Bloomington: Indiana University Press, 1977), p. 197.

22. Campaign Against the Namibian Uranium Contracts, *The Rossing File* (Nottingham, England: Russell Press, 1980).

23. *Facts and Reports*, News Clippings on South Africa, Holland Anti-Apartheid Committee, 8, no. 12, (June 16, 1978), item 1193.

24. "Activities of Foreign Economic Interests Operating in Namibia," International Conference in Support of the Struggle of the Namibian People for Independence, Paris, April 25–29, Report of the United Nations Council for Namibia, A/Conf.120/4, A/AC.131/92, March 16, 1983, p. 14.

25. "Uranium: Resources, Production and Demand" (Paris: OECD and IAEA, December 1983), p. 40, table 10.

26. *Le Monde* (Paris), August 2, 1977, p. 1.

27. *The Star* (Johannesburg), November 31, 1975, p. 33.

28. Yoko Kitazawa, *Japan's Nuclear Deals with South Africa*, (Tokyo, Japan: Pacific-Asia Resources Center, August, 1977), p. 1.

29. Nuclear Study Group, "The Politics of Japan's Uranium Purchase," *Japan-Asia Quarterly Review* 8, no. 1 (March 1976), pp. 34–35.

30. Ronald Walters, "The United States and the South Africa-Namibia Uranium Option," *Africa Today* 30, nos. 1 and 2.

31. W.C.J. van Rensburg, "African and Western Lifelines," *Strategic Review* 6, no. 2 (Spring 1978), p. 42.

32. Richard Betts, "Paranoids, Pygmies, Pariahs, and Nonproliferation," *Foreign Policy* 26 (Spring 1977), pp. 165–67. See also Ernest LeFever, *Nuclear Arms in*

the Third World: U.S. Policy Dilemma (Washington, D.C.: Brookings Institution, 1979); and Leonard Sector, *Nuclear Proliferation Today,* op. cit.

33. *New York Times,* April 10, 1976, p. 5.

34. Steve Rosen, "Nuclearization and Stability in the Middle East," in Onkar Marwah and Ann Schulz, eds., op. cit., p. 177.

35. Patrick J. Garrity, "South African Strategy," *Naval War College War Review* 32 (September-October 1980), p. 27.

36. Malise Ruthven, "Fundamentalisms," *London Review of Books,* 4, no. 12, London, July 1, 1982, p. 6.

37. "CBS Evening News with Walter Cronkite," CBS News, New York, 6, no 79, March 19, 1980, p. 9.

38. Cited in *Africa* 81 (May 1978), p. 85.

39. *South African Digest,* July 25, 1980, p. 20.

40. *Washington Post,* October 25, 1980, p. A15.

41. *New York Times,* June 28, 1981, p. 15.

42. *Investigation of Korean-American Relations,* Report of the Subcommittee on International Organizations, Committee on International Relations, U.S. House of Representatives, October 31, 1978, pp. 79-80.

43. U.S. Energy Research and Development Agency, Office of International Security Affairs, March 15, 1977.

44. Frank Barnaby and Ronald Huisken, *Arms Uncontrolled* (Cambridge, Mass.: Harvard University Press, 1975), pp. 40-41.

45. Christopher Cohen, "The Western Alliance and Africa, 1949-1981," *African Affairs* 81, no. 324 (July 1982), p. 322.

46. Ibid., p. 323.

47. *New York Times,* January 18, 1953, p. 1.

48. *NATO and South Africa* (Johannesburg: South African Institute of International Affairs, 1969).

49. Ibid.

50. *The Star* (Johannesburg), October 21, 1969, p. 3.

51. *Jane's Fighting Ships,* London, September 30, 1969, p. 37.

52. See Lary Bowman, "The Strategic Importance of South Africa to the United States: An Appraisal and Policy Analysis," *African Affairs* 81, no. 323 (April 1982), pp. 159-77.

53. Charles Latour, "South Africa: NATO's Unwelcome Ally," *Military Review* 57, no. 2 (February 1977), p. 93.

54. Ronald Walters, "The Global Context of U.S. Foreign Policy toward Southern Africa, *Africa Today* 19, no. 3 (Summer 1972), pp. 13-30.

55. David Gompert et al., op. cit., p. 224.

56. Edouard Bustin, "South Africa's Foreign Policy Alternatives and Deterrence Needs," in Marwah and Schulz, op. cit., p. 224.

57. Ted Greenwood et al., op. cit., p. 46.

58. Gompert et al., op. cit., p. 228.

8
Conclusion: Responsibility and Deterrence

My beginning chapter suggested that perhaps analysts should stop thinking about South African nuclear weapons proliferation as a *potential* fact since the evidence would indicate that it, indeed, has already occurred, although the question remains, to what degree. Thus, the balance of this book was devoted to sketching the outlines of that evidence and to examining the policy responses of the United States in particular, and of other states to a lesser extent. Following this approach to its logical conclusion, it is reasonable to deduce that the solutions proffered to the prevention of South African nuclear proliferation have failed—a failure that in this case means that the international nonproliferation regime and its policy-makers and theorists have failed.

This especially constitutes a failure for Western policy, inasmuch as the Western states constitute the leading nuclear alliance in the international system, the leading patrons of the South African nuclear program, and, at the same time, the foremost proponents of the nonproliferation regime. Below, I will summarize the elements of that failure of the nonproliferation regime, propose a change in the frame of reference for dealing with South Africa as a *new nuclear state*, and address a new set of solutions to what I view as the more realistic assessment of security affairs in Southern Africa at this time.

The Failure of Responsibility

An essay written back in 1968 by Sir John Cockcroft, Nobel Prize-winning director of British nuclear research, closes with a profound but obvious truth: "The 'nuclear powers' have a great responsibility to curtail and to reverse the proliferation of their own weapons."[1] Yet, neither the Soviet

Union nor the United States has led by example in reducing the development of ever more sophisticated nuclear weapons, some of which are finding their way to second-level powers and are being modified to their own regional security situations. Furthermore, not even satisfied with the lack of restraint upon their own nuclear programs, the Western nuclear powers have directly traded nuclear materials and technology utilizing the discredited concept that if they only became "reliable suppliers" of such materials, they might take away the incentive of these states to manufacture their own, thus, gaining access to weapons capability. Apparently, the security situation in each of the recipient states played little role in restraining nuclear trade, and the commercial motive has been pursued on the basis of promises by the recipient states that they would use the capability "for peaceful purposes."

Indeed, trade was not restrained to South Africa by the United States, for example, until the NNPA negotiations in 1978, but the nuclear test of September 22, 1979, made it clear that, by that time, restraint was probably too late. Nevertheless, France continued to construct the South African nuclear power station, and other European countries further weakened the nonproliferation regime by increasing nuclear services and exports, damaging the impact of the United Nations Arms Embargo of 1977. The Reagan administration was even more vigorous in helping to supply enriched uranium to the regime, and in adopting a foreign policy of "constructive engagement" which essentially meant that it had firmly taken the South African side in the security problems of the region.

The relationships I have reviewed in this book suggest that many nuclear powers have not made nonproliferation a high priority in their dealings with South Africa, especially in comparison with their commercial interests. This dichotomy of policy priority has not gone unnoticed:

> An active policy, however, designed to reduce the odds of proliferation by further reducing the apparent gains, would require subordinating other policy interests. If nonproliferation is worth that price, the choice is between using more carrots or more sticks. If other interests take precedence or U.S. policy makers are against taking the risk that carrots or sticks might have the wrong effect, then rhetoric on the nuclear issue should de-escalate to a level commensurate with a passive policy.[2]

Apparently, the West has made its decision that other interests have a higher priority than nonproliferation, which explains why their nuclear relationship with South Africa had until the 1985-86 period "stabilized" at a permissive level. In Betts's terms, the ambiguous proliferation of South Africa has been matched by the "calculated ambiguity" of Western policy, which more recently has placed modest restrictions on nuclear exports to South Africa in response to growing domestic anti-apartheid sentiments.

Elevating the commercial interest in dealing with South African nuclear activities, the major nuclear powers have attempted to shift the burden for nonproliferation to the international nonproliferation regime. I have suggested, however, that South Africa has utilized its connections with international nuclear agencies as an additional source of technical assistance for its program (rather than let them be an impediment to its development) and has carefully shunned the Nonproliferation Treaty which would bring its activities under at least minimal scrutiny. This caused IAEA Director General Dr. Hans Blix to question the efficacy of Reagan's policy of "assigning major responsibility for stopping nuclear arms proliferation to the [IAEA]." Dr. Blix, citing South Africa as one of the countries of most immediate concern, went on to rather bluntly state his view of the impossibility of stopping proliferation by safeguards.[3] One year later in Johannesburg, another IAEA official, Dr. W.C. Alston, also manifesting concern about Pretoria, supported Blix's statements, suggesting that safeguard inspections might limit the misuse of nuclear power, except for the interference of politics. Alston too admitted that safeguards could not prevent proliferation, withdrawal from safeguards agreements, or guarantees about the future nuclear conduct of states.[4]

These officials appear to be saying that the nonproliferation regime is only as functional as the political and economic aspects of state foreign policy make it, a point supported by American expert Benjamin Schiff concerning technical aspects of nonproliferation.

> The vision [universal nonproliferation] is disrupted in practice by the reluctance of states to fully give over to international machinery the control of nuclear technology transfer policies, to allocate nuclear technological assistance to developing countries in significant amounts, and to intrude into areas of international nuclear commerce that appear to hold the promise of significant commercial gain.[5]

These tendencies cast great doubt on the long-term viability of restrictions in trade with South Africa in response to the anti-apartheid presence of the moment.

I have illustrated not only that the international trade in nuclear materials, equipment, and facilities among the major powers is highly competitive, but that it is growing as the market declines. The problem is exacerbated by the ironic situation that the recipient states are, themselves, becoming nuclear suppliers, thus, entering an already crowded market and further stimulating proliferation. The alliance of such states in areas where security fears are high has led to a network of second-level "nuclear pariahs." This would not, in the aftermath, appear to have been the most responsible condition to create, since these regions have volatile, competing actors who, at any moment, could initiate conflicts that might easily involve nuclear weapons.

The Quest for Responsibility

Just as I have posited that the major powers have failed their responsibility to devise measures that might have led away from nuclear proliferation by South Africa, their assumption of responsibility as a response to new nuclear powers entering the system is even more urgent. As John Francis and Paul Abrecht have stated, "they alone can reduce the risk of nuclear aggression."[6] But of course, this raises the question of responsibility for what? I have asserted that the new situation is marked by the fact that South Africa has achieved the status of becoming "militarily significant," which Ernest Lefever says is determined by whether or not a government has a "deliverable nuclear force."[7] Although Lefever fails to mention South Africa in this regard, I have, nevertheless, considered "ambiguous proliferation" to be factual proliferation since is is tantamount to a state of possessing *objective nuclear weapons capability*, together with strong evidence that South Africa has gone beyond the capability threshold to actually manufacture nuclear explosions and the means to deliver weapons.

If one accepts even the strong probability that South Africa has, indeed, stepped over the line of mere capability, especially in light of what one analyst has called the "strategic deterioration" of its security in the region, then there is every reason to view the question of regional deterrence as the most urgent consideration. The question of deterrence implies the horrible reality that perhaps South African nuclear weapons are now ready to be used in one of the scenarios discussed in this book, which implies terrible destructive consequences.

Undoubtedly, it is this prospect which impels the major powers to "think about the unthinkable." Indeed, some have concluded that the problem is so intractable they have yielded to the temptation to ignore the reality and employ permissive stabilization of the nuclear relationship to cover up the danger and ultimately their own culpability for the consequences of the use of nuclear weapons by South Africa. In this case, the stability that is achieved is illusory, since it may quickly destabilize in response to increases in the threats to South African security by forces largely beyond the external powers' control. Although Spence suggests that such dramatic changes might cause South Africa to "declare" that it has nuclear weapons, my position, considered less credible by such analysts, is that dramatic changes could, in fact, cause the use of a nuclear weapon as well.[8] The rational objective here is to move toward a situation of real stability based on deterrence, since, considering the linkages involved, this goal is presumed to bear upon international security in a manner that should give it priority over narrow foreign policy interests of any one state.

The situation, however, warrants choices. The first choice to be made is whether or not, since the concern for deterrence requires a qualitatively different role for major powers, they understand that a shift in posture should occur. *Rather than protecting the security of South Africa as inducement to cause it not to secure nuclear weapons, they should protect the targets of South Africa's nuclear weapons.* This choice is basically whether to play a responsible role of honest broker in stabilizing the military situation or to contribute to South African nuclear hegemony by abdicating that role.

If the decision is made to accept responsiblity for achieving real stability based on deterrence, then, a second choice must be made concerning the level at which it should be achieved. Obviously, for example, the United States has the choice of saying to a regional client that the client is responsible for its own defense, but that the United States will also support the client in achieving the military capability to defend itself, or that its defense will become the direct multilateral responsibility of NATO. One observer has said, however, that in areas such as Southern Africa,

> the choice would be either to try to stabilize regional nuclear situations by supplementing the embryonic deterrents of local powers with nuclear commitments by the super-powers or to attempt to insulate the central balance from the chaotic forces of regional nuclear instability and insecurity set loose by proliferation.[9]

The task of Western nationals assuming the responsibility for stabilizing the balance of deterrence in the Southern African region appears benign, since there is no nuclear power equivalent to South Africa. In this case, the major powers might be tempted to let the status quo exist, since there is no danger that nuclear war of regional powers will occur. However, the situation might be extremely urgent, since, for the very reason that there is no matching nuclear force, the regional states may feel constrained to make security agreements with outside powers in the attempt to prevent a nuclear strike by South Africa. The existence of Soviet nuclear submarines in the Indian Ocean and South Atlantic make such a possibility conceivable.

In the futuristic scenario, the West might develop, through trade and technical assistance, the nuclear capability of the front-line states, or at least one state that has proven friendly to its interest.[10] The model for this is the role of the West in the provision of nuclear assistance to Egypt and Israel, to Pakistan and India, and to Taiwan and very recently China.[11] Since all of these states had reasonably well developed technological capabilities to provide a base for nuclear development, such a strategy in Southern Africa would have to evolve over time because of the obvious fact that the economic, industrial, and military infrastructure of the states in the region could not support the development of nuclear power projects in the foreseeable future.

Nevertheless, there is a growing history of regional economic collaboration though the Southern African Development Coordinating Council (SADCC), wherein Angola has assumed regional responsibility for the development of energy resources. However, the existing civil war in Angola makes this an awesome task at the moment. Still, Italian industrialists are reported to have won a contract for the development of a power station for Bophuthatswana.[12] Eventually, the economies of scale might make a nuclear power station an attractive project for a regional energy system. Nevertheless, any movement toward the development of a potentially competitive nuclear power capability in the region would be watched by South Africa, and if it is true that even the specter of joint military maneuvers by the front-line states would make the regime nervous, then, it is certain that South Africa would oppose any other state in the region possessing the slightest functional nuclear power capability.[13] The result might be a repetition of the scenario where Iraq's Osiris nuclear reactor was bombed by Israel.

In any case, it would be tantalizing to discover what leverage might be gained in achieving symmetry, even by the diplomacy of preparing to balance the nuclear equation. Would this step be considered "provocative" by South Africa, causing it to take a number of preemptive actions that would heighten the tension, or would the pressures created introduce a realistic timetable into the process of achieving political settlements in Namibia and in South Africa itself, by placing an upper limit on the use of military force?

If it is unlikely that the West would seek to "stabilize" the regional nuclear balance over time through developing a local nuclear counteractor to South Africa, it is perhaps somewhat less unlikely that it would assist in the development of a continental African nuclear state. This second prospect does not appear to rest solely upon the action of the West, but upon the existence of African states with the requisite financial resources, the availability of alternate suppliers, and the ability to overcome the limitations of adapting the technology. Francis and Abrecht have indicated some factors that limit such adaptability. First, there is the lack of electrical grids which would permit the construction of a nuclear power plant smaller than the normal size and, thus, economically justifiable. Second, there is the high initial capital investment for such systems, whatever the size. Third, there is the lack of trained technical personnel and backup industries.[14]

However, despite these formidable impediments, the authors make the optimistic prediction that "nuclear energy has promise in Africa in the longer run, i.e., there is ample scope for the introduction of nuclear plants into a number of African countries' power systems."[15] They go on to suggest that, in effect, their fourth limiting factor—industrial growth of a number of countries—will in time overcome the impediments cited above. Also, technological breakthroughs in the nuclear industry producing smaller units may make them more affordable, and international organizations and agencies may reach the conclusion that the development of multinational regional energy systems might benefit from assistance to centralized nuclear power generating stations. At the moment, the only Lome III in Africa involves new and renewable sources such as solar, wind, sea thermal, hydropower, geothermal, and biomass.[16]

It is recognized that the bold suggestion that the West treat Africans vulnerable to nuclear strike from South Africa in the same manner they have treated regional allies in other parts of the world might be considered unacceptable to analysts who believe that it could never come about and those who, in principle, are opposed to the expansion of nuclear weapons capability. It is also noted that while Africans might not proceed directly to fabricate nuclear weapons, they would have available the same option of ambiguous proliferation that other states with such capability are able to employ in international diplomacy. Without such capability, of course, they are unable to even entertain this level of diplomacy at all. Thus, such a suggestion would fly in the face of those in the United Nations General Assembly who have supported resolutions seeking nonnuclear solutions such as an arms embargo or the "denuclearization of Africa." It is interesting that neither South Africa nor the United States has been able to support such resolutions for "denuclearizing" Africa, since those resolutions simultaneously have required support for the cessation of nuclear relations with South Africa. Despite the fact that new initiatives might be made in this regard, the attitude of such African leaders is clearly moving in the direction of deterrence. These ideas have come from African leaders such as the distinguished University of Michigan political scientist, Dr. Ali Mazrui, who argued with Nigerian leaders in 1979, that Nigeria had a role in correcting the nuclear strategic balance with South Africa.[17] Apparently, his advice was persuasive, since Chuba Okadigbo (senior advisor to then Nigerian leader Shehu Shagari) said that Nigeria would build a nuclear bomb if it would provide leverage with which to negotiate with South Africa.[18] Also in June of 1983, at the 19th OAU Summit Conference of Heads of African States in Addis Ababa, Ethiopia, Edem Kodjo, secretary general, said that talk of denuclearizing Africa should be held in abeyance as long as South Africa was manufacturing its atomic bomb to use against African states.[19] This, of course, is a very substantial charge, but in practice little has occurred to make it become a reality, since both the ideas of the African defense force and the nuclear issues are frought with political, economic and technological difficulties.

Table 8-1
African Countries with Nuclear Technology and Materials

	Signed NPT	Research Reactors	Commercial Reactors	Uranium and Tons if Known
Egypt	yes	1 operating	8 planned	—
Algeria	no	1 planned	—	26,000
Libya	yes[a]	1 operating	2 planned	yes
Morocco	yes	1 under construction	1 planned	yes, phosphates
South Africa	no	2 operating	2 operating	531,000

Source: Thijs de la Court, Deborah Pick, and Daniel Nordquist, *The Nuclear Fix* (Amsterdam: World Information Service on Energy, 1982), pp. 54, 86.

[a]Signed and ratified NPT but failed to conclude safeguards with the IAEA in accordance with Article III.4.

Table 8-2
African Countries with Nuclear Materials or Prospecting

	Signed NPT	Uranium and Tonnes if Known
Cameroon	yes[a]	yes, prospecting stage
Central African Republic	yes[a]	18,000, 1 mine open soon
Chad	yes[a]	yes, prospecting stage
Gabon	yes	30,900, 6 mines
Ghana	yes	yes, prospecting stage
Guinea	no	yes, prospecting stage
Ivory Coast	yes[a]	yes, prospecting stage
Kenya	yes[a]	
Liberia	yes[a]	thorium
Madagascar	yes	yes, prospecting stage
Morocco	yes	phosphates
Namibia	—	213,000, 3 mines
Niger	no	213,000, 4 mines
Nigeria	yes[a]	
Senegal	yes	yes, prospecting stage
Somalia	yes[a]	yes, prospecting stage
Sudan	yes	copper
Tanzania	no	yes, prospecting stage
Tunisia	yes[a]	phosphates
Zambia	no	yes, prospecting stage
Zimbabwe	no	yes, prospecting stage

Source: Thijs de la Court, Deborah Pick, and Daniel Nordquist, *The Nuclear Fix* p. 55. (Amsterdam: World Information Service on Energy, 1982)

[a]Signed and ratified NPT but failed to conclude safeguards with the IAEA in accordance with article III.4.

In addition, only a few of the fifty-one African countries have initiated nuclear programs of any consequence, as tables 8-1 and 8-2 show.

As is clearly evident, the only countries that have significant nuclear facilities planned besides South Africa are Libya, Morocco, and Egypt, and only Libya (with Morocco and Algeria to follow) has uranium and is currently utilizing enriched uranium in research reactors. Of these three countries, however, probably only Libya and Egypt (with eight commercial reactors planned) have the necessary motivation to construct nuclear power programs that have weapons implications. Libya, for example, is known to have sought to acquire a nuclear weapons capability for some time through various methods.[20] Then, Egypt has discussed with Westinghouse and other suppliers the feasibility of nuclear power development for electricity to serve its teeming urban population, but it would not be surprising if it also wanted to appear to counter the nuclear capability of Israel as a "stabilizing" element in the Middle East problem. In fact, scenarios have been developed that assume such an eventuality, even though an Egyptian nuclear military capability is far into the future.[21] Another future scenario would find either a Libyan or Egyptian nuclear weapon delivery capability developed to the point that they would threaten South Africa with a nuclear strike. Only with missiles approaching a 4,000-mile range, would a threat be considered credible to the South Africans, however, who may already be approaching this range.

Next, in evaluating the potential of international agencies to play a role in stabilizing the balance, I have dismissed the effectiveness of both the nuclear agency responsible for safeguards as well as a body such as the United Nations as a sponsor of concepts such as "denuclearizing zones." In addition, other passive pledges that the South Africans could make (for example, to accede to the NPT or to declare a "no-first-use" policy) are not considered credible in light of its security problems. It has been observed, assuming that South Africa has created a nuclear force to deter an attack from the north, that it would not give up such a deterrent by making a no-first-use pledge, and African countries are sensitive to the fact that any insistence from the international community that they make such a pledge not to initiate the use of nuclear weapons gives South Africa the tactical advantage it wanted with the development of the weapons in the first place.[22]

It appears, then, that the stalemate cannot be broken by international agencies because they lack coercive power and the ability to control enough of the political dynamics to manage solutions, as indicated by the wreckage of the U.N. plan on the independence of Namibia. The same may be said for attempts to construct international arms control agreements such as the U.N. Arms Embargo of 1977, which I will now briefly review.

The Arms Embargo: International Responsibility

In fall 1977, there were two important actions by the government of South Africa: first, the killing of black leader Steve Biko on September 12, and second, the crackdown on the aroused black consciousness movement on October 18, by massive jailings of individuals, banning of eighteen civil rights groups, and closing of the major black newspaper. These events served as the catalyst for the U.N. Security Council resolution for a mandatory arms embargo against South Africa on November 4. Resolution 418 of the Security Council, operative paragraph no. 4 stated: "all states shall refrain from any cooperation with South Africa in the manufacture and development of nuclear weapons."

The problem with operative paragraph no. 4, however, is its wording and consequent effect (developed through a compromise with the Western powers) that prohibits an action that no state would openly acknowledge and that would be protected by the ambiguity between "peaceful" and "hostile" development of nuclear capability. As Abdul Minty, an expert on the South African military buildup, described the flaw,

> No state will admit that it is, in fact co-operating with South Africa to manufacture and develop nuclear weapons. Hence, the decision of the Security Council is meaningless in so far as it applies to the development of South Africa's nuclear capability.[23]

The point here is that since few countries would acknowledge trading nuclear weapons or direct assistance in their fabrication, more attention needs to be given to the *exchange of materials, equipment,* and *technology* as a focus for such resolutions and counteractions.

Clearly, from the standpoint of an effective solution, more emphasis should be placed on the prohibition of ready access to the raw materials and technology with which to develop weapons. Even here, there is some indication that South Africa probably has advanced to the point where it is even impervious to an accurately targeted sanctions program. Ted Greenwood, Harold Feiveson, and Theodore Taylor have written:

> More important, refusing to sell sensitive technology does not deny access to it. Any government capable of managing a commercial nuclear industry could build its own facilities to produce enough plutonium for a modest weapons program. Most of those for which market dissuasion will not succeed can now or would within a decade be able to build their own pilot-scale commercial reprocessing or enrichment plants.

The authors go on to say that states such as South Africa are "not particularly susceptible to such leverage" where the United States is able to exercise influence over a nuclear program due to its control over the export of nuclear technology or materials. In fact, they suggest that South Africa may be fast approaching the end of the "twilight" where decisions regarding energy and weapons will merge.[24]

In recognition of this problem, the international community began to mobilize in the mid-1970s. The Special Committee against Apartheid of the United Nations and the Subcommittee on Racism, Racial Discrimination, Apartheid and Decolonization of the Geneva Special NGO Committee on Human Rights sponsored an International Non-Governmental Organization Conference for Action against Apartheid in Geneva, Switzerland, August 28–31, 1978. This meeting attracted eighty-six nongovernmental organizations (NGOs) as well as liberation movements from Southern Africa; its four working commissions, included Commission II on South Africa's Military and Nuclear Build-up and the United Nations Arms Embargo violations.

Among the many conclusions of Commission II was the dominant theme that the South African nuclear capability was developed and supported by the major Western powers and some lesser states. The commission "therefore, advocated the intensification of international mobilization of public opinion on the action against collaboration with South Africa." Specifically, the commission urged "complete prohibition of all cooperation with South Africa in the nuclear field—including the supply of nuclear installations, materials, technology and training, development of uranium resources, and purchase of uranium."[25] In addition, the final resolution of the conference, approved unanimously by the conferees, proposed an international mobilization of governments and peoples against apartheid, aiming to end "all nuclear and military collaboration with South Africa."[26]

In most of the resolutions dealing with aspects of the military buildup of South Africa, there was considerable stress on restricting economic relations between South Africa and the rest of the world as a solution, as through economic sanctions and disinvestment. This prefaces a growing understanding that the key to the transfer of nuclear materials resides in lucrative economic transactions between South Africa and developed countries for supplies of nuclear technology, nuclear materials, and trading relationships in a range of nuclear materials which South Africa will eventually be able to supply.

The persuasive logic of emphasizing the trade in nuclear materials and equipment brought the General Assembly of the United Nations to clarify the 1977 arms embargo by passing resolution 35/206B on December 16, 1980, which called for a prohibition on trade in nuclear technology, equipment, scientific experts, and material utilized to fabricate nuclear explosions. This step was based on its alarm "at the enormous threat posed to the peace and security of Africa and the world by the development of an *apartheid* nuclear bomb."[27]

Thus, it was ironic that on the very day the General Assembly had sought to tighten the potential of proliferation by South Africa, reports indicated that another "mysterious flash" had occurred in the South

Atlantic, similar to an earlier one of September 1979, which was widely suspected to have been a nuclear test. In the long run, however, the General Assembly was attempting to effect a cessation or at least a slowdown in the rate of progress of the South African nuclear program in terms of the enrichment plant being built (which could manufacture enriched uranium) and the Koeberg nuclear power plant coming on line (which could manufacture plutonium).

Nevertheless, this approach was also contained in a unilateral action taken by France as a result of the state of emergency declared by the South African government in July 1985.[28] If both the United States and France are successful in prohibiting nuclear exports to South Africa, then an important source of its future growth will be limited, although its current capability will remain unaffected, except for possible difficulties in obtaining enriched uranium fuel for Koeberg. If its own enrichment plant is unable to make up this difference, then perhaps assistance may be available from Israel or even China, since these two countries also maintain a nuclear cooperation agreement signed in May 1979.[29]

The Superpowers

In any event, it is clear that even if international agencies did possess sufficient political and military power to enforce an arms embargo, it would ultimately involve the enforcement capability of the superpowers. Secondly, direct participation in the process of stabilizing this balance helps, as Gompert et al. have said, to "insulate the central balance" against the prospect of two-sided regional conflict which escalates into a two-sided global conflict, possibly involving nuclear weapons.[30] The value of some level of coordination among major powers is illustrated by the complexities that might be created if one of the Western nuclear powers, for example, supported South Africa in an escalating regional conflict, and political pressures grew in other Western states to oppose South Africa.

A current political example of such intra-alliance conflict, one to which I have already made reference, finds France at odds with the United States and Britain over South African sanctions policy at the moment, France having tabled a resolution in the Security Council and invoked unilateral sanctions to which both the United States and Britain have taken objection. In this instance, it would seem that the central balance could not be insulated if the process did not begin with the coordination of alliance policy among major Western and Eastern states.

The rationale for coordination of alliance policy within the two blocs may appear obvious, but it is equally obvious that it is more urgent that coordination takes place *between* alliances in order that an escalating conflict cannot utilize potential linkages to major nuclear powers to stimulate tensions at that level. One model of such cooperation is the joint action between the Soviet Union and the United States in discovering the nuclear test site in the Kalahari Desert in September 1977, and in demanding that it be dismantled. Although there was some speculation on the reasons for such joint collaboration at the time, it was reasonably effective in that South Africa was unable to exploit East–West tension by refuting claims by the Soviets to have discovered a test site, while maintaining and utilizing the site at some later time. In this regard, one possibility is that the United States and the Soviet Union enter into discussion regarding the modus vivendi for dealing with potentially dangerous scenarios in Southern Africa involving South African nuclear weapons which could threaten to bring them into conflict.[31]

These steps might adequately cancel out any advantage South Africa might have gained from being able to exploit the lack of coordination and even help to insulate the central strategic balance. However, it does little to *deter* South Africa from actually launching a first strike at some target in the region, on the continent, or beyond the continent. Considering the likelihood that South Africa would be launching such a strike at African states unarmed with nuclear weapons, the major powers could go further and agree to provide these states with security guarantees involving some effective form of retaliation. Indeed, a declaration against a nuclear attack by South Africa against nonnuclear African states may be an important deterrent in itself. Appropriate retaliation for such an attack would, of course, have to be "modeled out" and, perhaps, even agreed to in principle alone, since predictions of the exact situation in which weapons would be used are likely to be imprecise. A joint pledge of retaliation involving both alliances would be important inasmuch as a pledge by only one nation within an alliance would create the complexities previously commented upon. In any case, in view of the potential serious result from South Africa's use of a nuclear weapon in the foreseeable future, some measures beyond dependence upon a regional or continental African power, or the United Nations, to stabilize the strategic balance in Southern Africa is required at this time, in my opinion.

Conclusion

Finally, estimating the various conditions that provide the context for the military use of nuclear weapons in Southern Africa entails calculating the degree of probable change in the political landscape. It should be understood that the basic political goal of any regime will always be to maintain power, and in so doing, to use its capabilities to lessen the threat to its survival caused by forces arrayed against it from whatever source. The difficulty with South Africa adhering to that concept is that the changing character the threat could provoke a response from South Africa based on miscalculations of political and/or military moves by any of the actors. Nonetheless, there are some primary elements in the security situation that, if handled resolutely by the major powers, might prevent the use of nuclear weapons against virtually unarmed populations in Southern Africa through the mindless drift and escalation of the conflict.

One of these elements is the independence of Namibia; a second is the cessation of the destabilization campaign; and the last is the abolition of apartheid. However, the South Africans have perceived each of these aspects to further jeopardize their security; thus, their methodology for dealing with these problems has involved the application of greater and greater levels of military force in response to the growing counterresistance of the people both within and without the country. If there were a force that could aggressively intervene to influence a political settlement between states in Southern Africa to preempt the pattern of local escalation, then the military situation might dissolve as a consequence. Since apartheid and the colonial control of Namibia are at the root of these problems, a concerted policy of political, economic, and military sanctions by the Western nations that have supported South Africa is the key to the avoidance of the escalating spiral of violence. South Africa is not immediately vulnerable to the Africans in any diplomatic, political, military, or economic sense, but it is vulnerable to the combined influence of major Western powers.

The leadership required, however, in reducing regional tension cannot be exercised without fundamental changes in policy, beginning with an abolition of the failed policy of constructive engagement and its corollary of cooperation with South Africa by other Western nations of the world, including Japan. Such a deep and fundamental change in policy requires reconceptualizing the nature of the threat South Africa poses to Southern Africa, to the continent of Africa, and perhaps to world peace, as well as a resolve to take seriously the question of deterrence to its nuclear weapons capability by determining to stabilize the balance.

It should be clear from this discourse that reconceptualizing the threat requires moving beyond concepts of ambiguous proliferation to consider the real danger; moving beyond the difficulties of the failed nuclear non-proliferation regime, its technology, and its theorists; and, to an urgent degree, moving beyond the failed and dangerous doctrine of "reliable supply" and other rationalizations for nuclear commerce which only strengthen the regime.

When the threat is reconceptualized, then the strategies of the responsible states, African and non-African alike, must logically be reconceived as well. For, as noted by André Beaufre (the French general after whose ideas the South Africans have patterned their defensive strategy), the utilization of increasingly powerful weapons against guerillas comes to look like war against the population. He favors more subtle political methods but, "Failing that, counterguerilla warfare is simply an extremely costly means of postponing political solutions, which will impose themselves sooner or later."[32] This is an appropriate reference to the attempt by the white South African regime to maintain its power through the use of an "ultimate deterrent" to change.

Nevertheless, one should not forget that the most urgent aspect of the possession of nuclear weapons by South Africa is that it constitutes the ultimate "war against the population." In this respect, since this war has already begun, only the responsible assumption of deterrence to the use of these weapons will prevent a terrifying result. With each stage in the escalation of conflict in Southern Africa, all of the people of Africa are increasingly at serious risk that these weapons will be used. This basic reality constitutes the most urgent case for the assumption of responsibility by those with the power to do so.

Notes

1. Sir John Cockcroft, "The Perils of Nuclear Proliferation," in Nigel Calder, ed., *Unless Peace Comes* (New York: Viking, 1968), p. 42.

2. Richard Betts and Joseph Yager, eds., *Nonproliferation and U.S. Foreign Policy* (Washington, D.C.: Brookings Institution, 1980), p. 406.

3. *New York Times*, February 18, 1982, p. 4.

4. David Copel, "Nuclear Era Has Positive Side," *Rand Daily Mail*, January 27, 1983, p. 10.

5. Benjamin Schiff, *International Nuclear Technology Transfer* (Totowa, N.J.: Rowman and Allenheld, 1984), p. 30.

6. John Francis and Paul Abrecht, eds., *Facing up to Nuclear Power* (Edinburgh, Scotland: Saint Andrew, 1976), p. 106.

7. Ernest Lefever, *Nuclear Arms in the Third World*, (Washington, D.C.: Brookings Institution, 1979), p. 11.

8. John Spence, "The Nuclear Option," *African Affairs* 80, no. 321 (October 1981), p. 451.

9. David Gompert, "Strategic Deterioration: Prospects, Dimensions and Responses in a Fourth Nuclear Regime," David Gompert, Michael Mandelbaum, Richard L. Garwin, John H. Barton, eds., *Nuclear Weapons and World Politics* (New York: McGraw-Hill, 1977), p. 228.

10. Lewis A. Dunn, *Controlling The Bomb* (New Haven: Yale University Press, 1982), p. 154.

11. Lefever, op. cit., p. 145.

12. *Rand Daily Mail*, March 25, 1983, p. 13. It was unclear whether it would be a nuclear power generating plant. Simon Willson, "We'd Prefer a Nuclear Submarine."

13. Robert Jaster, "A Regional Security Role for Africa's Front-Line States: Experience and Prospects," *Adelphi Papers* no. 180 (London: International Institute for Strategic Studies, 1983).

14. Francis and Abrecht, op. cit., pp. 133–134.

15. Ibid.

16. *Courier* (Brussels) 71, January-February 1982.

17. Ali Mazrui, *The African Condition* (London: Cambridge University Press, 1980), pp. 121–35.

18. Jonathan Kwitny, "Nigeria Considers Nuclear Armament Due to S. Africa," *Wall Street Journal*, October 6, 1980, p. 39. For a useful discussion of Nigerian nuclear status and intentions, see Mohammed-Bassiru Sillah, "The African Response to Nuclear Proliferation: A Case Study of Nigeria," *Présence Africaine*, no. 136, 4th Quarterly, 1985, pp. 10–30.

19. "African Leader Favors Nuke Buildup," *USA Today*, June 10, 1983, p. 1.

20. *The Nuclear Fix*, op. cit., pp. 65–66.

21. Steven Rosen, "Nuclearization and Stability in the Middle East," in Onkar Marwah and Ann Schulz, eds., *Nuclear Proliferation and the New Nuclear Countries* (Cambridge, Mass.: Ballinger, 1975), pp. 157–84. *The Nuclear Fix*, op. cit. pp. 87–88.

22. David Gompert, et al., op. cit., p. 242.

23. Abdul Minty, "South Africa's Military and Nuclear Build-up," International NGO Conference for Action against Apartheid, Geneva, Switzerland, August 28–31, 1978.

24. Greenwood, Feiveson, and Taylor, op. cit., p. 93.

25. International NGO Conference for Action against Apartheid, *Report of Commission II*, p. 3.

26. International NGO Conference for Action against Apartheid, United Nations, Special Committee Against Apartheid, 1980, *Final Resolution*, p. 3.

27. World Campaign against Military and Nuclear Collaboration with South Africa, Seminar on Implementation of the Arms Embargo, London, April 1–3, 1981, Declaration, Center against Apartheid, United Nations.

28. Alain Rollat, "Les Sanctions Francaises Contre L'Afrique du Sud," *Le Monde*, Paris, July 26, 1985, p. 4.

29. *South African Digest*, February 15, 1980, p. 17.

30. David Gompert, "Strategic Deterioration: Prospects, Dimensions, and Responses in a Fourth Nuclear Regime," in Gompert et al., p. 226.

31. Lewis Dunn, op. cit., pp. 162–63.

32. André Beaufre, "Battlefields of the 1980s," in Nigel Calder, op. cit., p. 14.

Appendix

Table A-1

A Partial List of U.S. Nuclear Trade License Applications for South Africa, 1979–84

Company	Product	Date of License Application	U.S. Import or Export
Matheson Gas	36 G pure deuterium	June 27, 1979	export
Edlow International	U-235	June 29, 1979	import
Transnuclear	73,556.5 kg 3.15%-enriched U-235	July 31, 1979	export
W.J. Woolley	personnel air locks	September 21, 1979	export
Pittsburgh-Des Moines Steel	4 personnel access air-locks, 2 bulkheads cylindrical shell barrell sections	October 2, 1979	export
Paul-Monroe Hydraulics	6 snubbers	November 13, 1979	export
Helix Technology	waste gas management treatment	July 16, 1980	export
Par Systems	inservice inspection system	July 17, 1980	export
Mitsubishi International	1,300 tons U-235 converted U hex	December 14, 1981	import
Aldrich Chemical	20 kg heavy water	January 19, 1982	export
Transnuclear	24,252 kg 3.30%-enriched U-235	March 13, 1982	export
Sigma Chemical	5 kg deuterium oxide	June 4, 1982	export
Philbro-Salomon	500,000 kg 5%-enriched U hex	August 4, 1982	import
Amersham International	2 mg CF-252	December 13, 1982 (Edlow International 8303250352/3,18,83)	reexport
Marubeni America		February 28, 1983	export
Safety Light	360,000 CI tritium	July 8, 1983	export
Reuter-Stokes	fission counter detector	December 13, 1983	export
Reuter-Stokes	U-235 as oxide on internal surface of radiation detector	January 19, 1984	export
Union Oil (Calif.)	10 tons graphite	September 18, 1984	export

Source: Document File, Nuclear Regulatory Commission, Washington, D.C.
Note: These are illustrative license applications, many of which are still pending decision.

Bibliography

Books and Reports

Abrecht, Paul, and John Francis, eds., *Facing up to Nuclear Power*. Philadelphia: Westminster Press, 1976.

Adelman, Kenneth, and Albion Knight, *Impact upon U.S. Security of a South African Nuclear Weapons Capability*. Arlington, Va: Strategic Studies Center, 1981.

Africa Research Group, *Race to Power: The Struggle for Southern Africa*. New York: Doubleday/Anchor, 1974.

Arkhurst, Frederick, S., ed., *U.S. Policy toward Africa*. New York: Praeger, 1975.

"Arms Limitation and Disarmament," *Seventeenth Strategy for Peace Conference Report, October 7-10, 1976*. Muscatine, Iowa: Stanley Foundation, 1976.

Barber, James, *South Africa's Foreign Policy: 1945-1970*. London: Oxford University Press, 1973.

Barnaby, Frank, "Nuclear Proliferation and the South African Threat." Geneva, Switzerland: World Council of Churches, 1977 (pamphlet).

Barnaby, Frank, and Ronald Huisken, *Arms Uncontrolled*. Cambridge, Mass.: Harvard University Press, 1975.

Biddle, W.F., *Weapons Technology and Arms Control*. New York: Praeger, 1972.

Calder, Nigel, ed., *Unless Peace Comes: A Scientific Forecast of New Weapons*. New York: Viking, 1968.

Campaign against the Namibian Uranium Contracts, *Rossing File*. Nottingham, England, Russell Press, 1980.

Christie, Renfrew, *Electricity, Industry and Class in South Africa*. Albany: State University of New York Press, 1984.

Cohen, Barry, and Mohamed A. El-Khawas, eds., *The Kissinger Study of Southern Africa: National Security Study Memorandum 39*. Westport, Conn.: Lawrence Hill, 1976.

Court, Thijs de la, Deborah Pick, and Daniel Nordquist, *The Nuclear Fix: A Guide To Nuclear Activities in the Third World*. Amsterdam: World Information Service on Energy, 1982.

Crocker, Chester A., ed., *The International Relations of Southern Africa* (seminar report of the Center for Strategic and International Studies). Washington, D.C.: Georgetown University, 1974.

Dunn, Lewis, *Controlling the Bomb: Nuclear Proliferation in the 1980s.* New Haven: Yale University Press, 1982.

Ford Foundation and the Mitre Corp., *Nuclear Power Issues and Choices: Report of the Nuclear Energy Policy Study Group.* Cambridge, Mass.: Ballinger, 1977.

Gareau, Frederick H., ed., *The Balance of Power and Nuclear Deterrence.* Boston: Houghton Mifflin, 1962.

Gompert, David, Michael Mandelbaum, Richard L. Garwin, and John H. Barton, *Nuclear Weapons and World Politics: Alternatives for the Future.* New York: McGraw-Hill, 1977.

Greenwood, Ted, Harold A. Feiveson, and Theodore B. Taylor, *Nuclear Proliferation: Motivations, Capabilities and Strategies for Control.* New York: McGraw-Hill, 1977.

Greenwood, Ted, George W. Rathjens, and Jack Ruina, "Nuclear Power and Weapons Proliferation," *Adelphi Papers* no. 130. London: International Institute for Strategic Studies, Winter 1976.

Imai, Ryukichi, and Henry Rowen, *Nuclear Energy and Nuclear Proliferation: Japanese and American Views.* Boulder, Colo.: Westview, 1980.

Kemp, Geoffrey, Robert L. Pfaltzgraff, Jr., and Uri Ra'anan, eds., *The Superpowers in a Multinuclear World.* Lexington, Mass.: Lexington Books, 1973.

Kissinger, Henry, *Nuclear Weapons and Foreign Policy.* New York: Doubleday/Anchor, 1958.

Lawrence, Robert M., and Joel Lazarus, eds., *Nuclear Proliferation: Phase II.* Lawrence: University Press of Kansas, 1974.

Lefever, Ernest, *Nuclear Arms in the Third World: U.S. Policy Dilemma.* Washington, D.C.: Brookings Institution, 1979.

Leonard, Richard, *South Africa at War: White Power and the Crisis in Southern Africa.* Westport, Conn.: Lawrence Hill, 1983.

Marwah, Onkar, and Ann Schulz, eds., *Nuclear Proliferation and the Near-Nuclear Countries.* Cambridge, Mass.: Ballinger, 1975.

Potholm, Christian P., and Richard Dale, eds., *Southern Africa in Perspective.* New York: Free Press, 1972.

Pranger, Robert J., and Dale R. Tahtinen, *Nuclear Threat in the Middle East.* Washington, D.C.: American Enterprise Institute for Public Policy Research, Foreign Affairs Study, no. 23. July 1975.

Quester, George, *The Politics of Nuclear Proliferation.* Baltimore: Johns Hopkins University Press, 1973.

Rogers, Barbara, and Zdenek Cervenka, *The Nuclear Axis: The Secret Collaboration between West Germany and South Africa.* New York: New York Times Book Co., 1978.

Schiff, Benjamin, *International Nuclear Technology Transfer, Dilemmas of Dissemination and Control.* Totowa, N.J.: Rowman and Allanheld, 1984.

Spector, Leonard, *Nuclear Proliferation Today: The Spread of Weapons 1984.* New York: Vintage/Random House, 1984.

Spence, John E., *Political and Military Framework*, Upsala, Sweden: African Publications Trust, 1975.

————, *Strategic Significance of Southern Africa*. London: RUSI, 1970.

————, *Republic under Pressure: A Study of South African Foreign Policy*. London: Oxford University Press, 1965.

Stevens, Richard, and Abdelwahab M. Elmessiri, *Israel and South Africa: The Progression of a Relationship*. New York: New World Press, 1976.

The Military Balance. London: International Institute for Strategic Studies, Issues: 1976–1977, 1977–1978, 1978–1979, 1982–1983.

Turner, Gordon B., and Richard D. Challener, eds., *National Securities in the Nuclear Age*. New York: Praeger, 1960.

Western Massachusetts Association of Concerned Africanist Scholars, ed., *U.S. Military Involvement in Southern Africa*. Boston: South End Press, 1978.

Willrich, Mason E., *Civil Nuclear Power and International Security*. New York: Praeger, 1971.

Yager, Joseph, ed., *Nonproliferation and U.S. Foreign Policy*. Washington, D.C.: Brookings Institution, 1979.

Government Reports and Congressional Hearings

Documents on Disarmament. U.S. Arms Control and Disarmament Agency, publication 46, July 1968.

Export Reorganization Act of 1976. Hearings, Committee on Government Operations, U.S. Senate, on S. 1439, January 19, 20, 29, and 30 and March 9, 1976. Washington, D.C.: U.S. GPO, 1976.

Investigation of Korean–American Relations. Report of the Subcommittee on International Organizations, Committee on International Relations, U.S. House of Representatives. Washington, D.C.: U.S. GPO, October 31, 1978.

Legislation on Foreign Relations through 1976, vol. 2. U.S. Senate and U.S. House of Representatives, Committee on Foreign Relations and Committee on International Relations, February 1977.

Nonproliferation of Nuclear Weapons. Hearings, Joint Committee on Atomic Energy, Congress of the United States, on S. Res. 179, February 23 and March 1 and 7, 1966. Washington, D.C.: U.S. GPO, 1966.

Nonproliferation Treaty. Hearings, Committee on Foreign Relations, U.S. Senate, July 10, 11, 12, and 17, 1968. Washington, D.C.: U.S. GPO, 1968.

Nuclear Non-Proliferation Act of 1978, Public Law 95-242, March 10, 1978.

Nuclear Proliferation and Safeguards. Office of Technology Assessment, U.S. Congress, April 1977 (prepublication draft).

Nuclear Proliferation: Future U.S. Foreign Policy Implications. Hearings, Subcommittee on International Security and Scientific Affairs, Committee on International Relations, U.S. House of Representatives, October 21, 23, 28, and 30 and November 4 and 5, 1975. Washington, D.C.: U.S. GPO, 1975.

Resource Development in South Africa and U.S. Policy. Hearings, Subcommittee on International Resources, Food, and Energy, Committee on International Relations, U.S. House of Representatives, May 25 and June 8 and 9, 1976. Washington, D.C.: U.S. GPO, 1976.

Strategy and Science: Toward A National Security Policy for the 1970s. Hearings, Subcommittee on National Security Policy and Scientific Developments, Committee on Foreign Affairs, U.S. House of Representatives, March 11, 13, 18, 19, 24, and 26, 1969. Washington, D.C.: U.S. GPO, 1969.

Survey of United States Uranium Marketing Activity 1983. Washington, D.C.: U.S. Dept. of Energy, Energy Information Administration, August 1984.

U.S. Export Policy with Respect to South Africa. Hearings, Subcommittee on Africa and Subcommittee on International Economic Policy and Trade, Committee on Foreign Affairs, U.S. House of Representatives, December 2, 1982.

U.S. Policy toward Africa. Hearings, Subcommittee on African Affairs, Subcommittee on Arms Control, International Organizations and Security Agreements, Committee on Foreign Relations, U.S. Senate, March 5, 8, 15, 19 and May 12, 13, 21, and 27, 1976. Washington, D.C.: U.S. GPO, 1976.

U.S. Policy toward Southern Africa. Hearings, Subcommittee on African Affairs, Committee on Foreign Relations, U.S. Senate, June 11, 13, and 16 and July 9, 10, 14, 23, 24, and 29, 1975. Washington, D.C.: U.S. GPO, 1975.

United States–South African Relations: Nuclear Cooperation. Hearings, Subcommittee on Africa, Committee on International Relations, U.S. House of Representatives, June 30 and July 12, 1977.

World Military Expenditures and Arms Transfers, 1967–1976. U.S. Arms Control and Disarmament Agency, publication no. 98, July 1978.

World Military Expenditures and Arms Transfers, 1972–1982. U.S. Arms Control and Disarmament Agency, publication no. 117, April 1984.

Index

About the Author

Ronald W. Walters is a professor in the Department of Political Science at Howard University, where he served as chairman from 1971-74. He formerly served on the faculties of Syracuse University and Brandeis University, and he has been a senior foreign affairs staff consultant to members of the House of Representatives and an expert consultant to the Special Committee Against Apartheid of the United Nations Security Council. He is the author of several pioneering articles and special reports on South Africa and South African nuclear capability, and he has lectured and traveled widely in the United States, Europe, and Africa. Dr. Walters is a Ph.D. graduate of The American University School of International Studies.